D1612318

214 916

Water-Resistant Design and Construction

Water-Resistant Design and Construction

An Illustrated Guide to Preventing Water Intrusion, Condensation, and Mold

William L. Walker

Daniel J. Felice, Sr.

NORWICH CITY COLLEGE LIBRARY

Stock No.	214916		
Class	691	WAL	
Cat.	3wk	Proc.	ASN 2

New York   Chicago   San Francisco   Lisbon   London   Madrid   Mexico City
Milan   New Delhi   San Juan   Seoul   Singapore   Sydney   Toronto

The McGraw·Hill Companies

Library of Congress Cataloging-in-Publication Data is on file with the Library of Congress.

Copyright © 2008 by The McGraw-Hill Companies, Inc. All rights reserved. Printed in the United States of America. Except as permitted under the United States Copyright Act of 1976, no part of this publication may be reproduced or distributed in any form or by any means, or stored in a database or retrieval system, without the prior written permission of the publisher.

1 2 3 4 5 6 7 8 9 0   DOC/DOC   0 1 3 2 1 0 9 8 7

ISBN 978-0-07-149276-8
MHID 0-07-149276-3

This book was printed on acid-free paper.

The sponsoring editor was Cary Sullivan, the editing supervisor was Maureen B. Walker, and the production supervisor was Richard C. Ruzycka. It was set in Times by International Typesetting and Compostion. The art director for the cover was Jeff Weeks.

Printed and bound by RR Donnelley.

McGraw-Hill books are available at special quantity discounts to use as premiums and sales promotions, or for use in corporate training programs. For more information, please write to the Director of Special Sales, McGraw-Hill Professional, Two Penn Plaza, New York, NY 10121-2298. Or contact your local bookstore.

Information contained in this work has been obtained by The McGraw-Hill Companies, Inc. ("McGraw-Hill") from sources believed to be reliable. However, neither McGraw-Hill nor its authors guarantee the accuracy or completeness of any information published herein, and neither McGraw-Hill nor its authors shall be responsible for any errors, omissions, or damages arising out of use of this information. This work is published with the understanding that McGraw-Hill and its authors are supplying information but are not attempting to render engineering or other professional services. If such services are required, the assistance of an appropriate professional should be sought.

To my family past, present, and future. To my parents whose sacrifices and love made my life rich in experiences. To my wife and children who bring me such joy with the simplest acts and whose touch fulfills me, whose look says a thousand words.

To our children's children- for whom all decisions should be considered... our actions have such long-lasting consequences.

And to the family of man
Who all need good shelters
Places to live, to worship and to work,
Spaces that are stimulating and safe
Lasting and good.

Knowledge is such a cumulative thing. I am aware of the contributions of my parents, teachers, coworkers, and even my grandfather have made toward what I know today. There are countless millions of people who have learned something before us. Many of them were involved in building practices using countless materials. There are hundreds of thousands of lessons learned in the past that have been communicated to us and are integral today in our design and construction practices. We can only hope that some of the information presented in this book will prove useful to others.

ABOUT THE AUTHORS

William L. Walker was born in Saint Louis and moved to Florida in 1959. He grew up walking through the walls of his grandfather's houses on Saturdays when he was only a few years old. His father was both an aeronautical engineer and a licensed general contractor. This taught the son an analytical approach toward problem solving that hopefully is present in this book. William is a licensed architect, with both a bachelor's degree and a master's degree in architecture. He is a member in good standing of the American Institute of Architects and works in the Orlando area as a senior project manager with CT Hsu and Associates, Architects. He is also an active member of the Construction Specifier's Institute (CSI).

William has worked in many roles in the construction industry. When he was in his twenties, he worked as a design/build general contractor in Florida's east coast. Among his many duties, he was chief designer for custom homes, small commercial buildings, and remodeling jobs. His duties included ordering materials and quality control of construction activities. Since that time, he has worked in architectural and engineering offices and was field engineer on many of central Florida's larger commercial buildings. He has worked as project manger for design and construction for hundreds of millions of dollars worth of buildings. He has had the pleasure of living in two single-family residences of his own design and was head of engineering and operations for 5 years in a 500,000-square-foot laboratory building that he helped to design and build.

William has worked in Brevard, Orange, Leon, and Osceola counties for years overseeing design and construction of government, commercial, and recreational facilities. Some of this time was spent as senior project manager of Osceola County, where his duties included design and construction of Osceola Heritage Park and solving problems in existing county buildings. Many of those problems were the result of water intrusion. Some of them were at grade, whereas others came from roofing, windows, walls, plumbing piping, roof drains, wall paper, caulking, and insulation. He has developed a reputation as an excellent problem solver. His attention to detail and basic understanding of applied physics have enabled him to find cause in some challenging situations. Coupled with his design and construction background, this allows him to develop a good fix. Continued observation after work has been performed has led to a confidence in his process and the products he recommends. He has honed these skills through participation on high-end condominium, government and commercial projects alike.

William is also a pretty good architectural illustrator. He has developed construction details for more than 35 years. He has taught design and graphics at the university level. He has done technical drawings for patents and designed the cover for and contributed a chapter to the *Handbook for Manufacturing*

Engineering. He has chosen to use computer-aided design (CAD) for most of the technical drawings contained in this book. This enables enlarged details to be presented that illustrate some of the subtle but important differences between good and bad detailing. William has been invited to present seminars to both AIA and CSI audiences which teach building envelope principles contained within these pages.

Dan Felice, contributing author, is vice president of Felice and Associates, a specialty waterproofing and roofing consulting firm. Dan has worked for more than 15 years on some of Florida's most challenging projects. His firm focuses on waterproofing and performing preconstruction design review and inspections during the construction process. His clients include some of the largest developers in the industry in Florida and as far away as China. Dan began as a roofing specialist and years ago branched out to include the entire building envelope. Dan and William developed a great working relationship while teaming together as construction administrators for the World's largest entertainment company on commercial projects in the Orlando area.

Contents

Illustrations

Tables

Abbreviations

ABC	Association of Building Contractors
AC	air conditioning
A/E	architect and engineer
AIA	American Institute of Architects
AIB	air infiltration barrier
AFD	architect's field directive
ASHRAE	American Society of Heating, Refrigerating, and Air-Conditioning Engineers
ASI	architect's supplemental instructions
ASTM	American Standards for Testing and Materials
BIM	building information modeling
C	celsius
CAD	computer-aided design
CAM	computer-aided manufacturing
CD	contract or construction document
CDX	exterior glued plywood with C-face and D-face quality
CE	civil engineer
cfm	cubic feet per minute
CM	construction manager
CMU	concrete masonry unit
C of O	certificate of occupancy
CO	change order
COR	change order request
CO_2	carbon dioxide
DB	design-build
DBA	design-build architect
dc	direct current
DCA	design-criteria architect
DCD	design contract document
DCO	directives and change order
DD	design development
DP	differential pressure
DXU	direct expansion unit
EIFS	exterior insulation and finish systems
EPDM	ethylene propylene diene monomer
EPS	expanded polystyrene
F	Fahrenheit
FBC	Florida Building Code
GC	general contractor
GMP	guaranteed maximum price
GS	general superintendent
HVAC	heating, ventilation, and air conditioning
IAQ	indoor air quality

IBC	International Building Code
IEQ	indoor environment quality
LEED	Leadership in Energy and Environmental Design
Mod. Bit.	modified bitumen
MPDS	Material Product Data Sheet
MRB	moisture reduction barrier
MSDS	Material Safety Data Sheet
NRCA	National Roofing Contractors Association
OSA	outside air
OSB	oriented strand board
PM	project manager
psf	pounds per square feet
PT	posttension
RCO	request for change order
RFI	request for information
RFP	request for proposal
RH	relative humidity
ROM	rough order of magnitude
R value	resistance to heat value
SA	supply air
SAM	self-adhesive membrane
SD	schematic design
SEER	seasonal energy efficiency ratio
sf	square feet
SOM	Skidmore, Owings, Merrill
SPF	sprayed-on polyurethane foam
SSBC	Southern Standard Building Code
SYP	southern yellow pine
T&B	test and balance
UL	Underwriter's Laboratory
U value	rate of heat loss (reciprocal of R value)
UV	ultraviolet
VAV	variable air volume
VCT	vinyl composition tile
VE	value engineering
VOC	volatile organic compounds
VWC	vinyl wall covering
XPS	extruded polystyrene

Preface

An Illustrated Guide to Building Envelope Design and Construction was developed after more than 50 years of combined experience in North America and abroad. The authors present successful principles and practices to minimize water intrusion and related problems that they have learned over time and which have been tested in the field. This information is presented with more than 100 drawings, photos, details, and tables to communicate their findings to people from varied backgrounds and experience levels. This book is intended to be a useful reference to those planning, designing, and constructing buildings in any climate and setting. The authors have written it so that most readers can easily follow the sometimes technical contents.

The first chapter begins with historical precedents, describing social and economic forces that continue to shape our societies today. The authors list common problems contributing to building envelope failure and begin methodical explanations on how to avoid them. A systematic approach is used for applications to all building types, with numerous examples (both good and bad) of how to avoid air and water intrusion.

In Chapter 2 the authors discuss the principal concepts of gravity, geometry, and technology for use in a basic recipe for success in making sound decisions throughout the processes of design and construction. A section is included that describes mold, how it can be transported, and how to minimize the potential for mold growth.

Chapter 3 makes the transition into the predesign phase. This is where most of the decisions that have an impact on the ultimate performance of the envelope are made. Predesign activities are discussed, such as building programming and establishing a hierarchical listing of achievable project goals and objectives. Design processes will differ based on client and project delivery processes and have an effect on the building envelope. Examples of many different roles played by designers and builders (building delivery systems) are provided, along with discussion of the pros and cons of each. Among project goals are image and performance expectations and time and budget considerations. The authors stress the importance of developing a blueprint for success, as well as getting buy-in from all stakeholders, before proceeding into the next phase.

Chapter 4 covers the design process, from selecting the right firm to developing schematic plans and completing the building design. Real-world examples are used to discuss value engineering and how to prevent value engineering decisions from resulting in a building envelope that performs poorly. The different ways water moves into our buildings is explained, with a focus on how to prevent intrusion and formation within buildings. This analysis starts with site design, includes foundation and floor systems, and then moves to wall and roof systems. The major performance categories of wall systems are introduced, along with recommendations on which to use in what climate. There are sections on membranes, sealants, and flashing installations. The discourse continues with a review of the many different kinds of roofing systems and addresses the role played by mechanical systems, including heating, ventilating, and air conditioning (HVAC). Of special interest are several award-winning examples of modern buildings in China, Canada, and the United States, all of which use glazing as it has never been used before.

Chapter 5 moves into the preconstruction phase by explaining the need for clearly defined project scope and discusses ways to avoid the root causes of scope creep and a reduction in project quality. Cost-cutting is differentiated from value engineering. Common mistakes are pointed out that might result in lesser-performing systems than were designed, especially when they could result in future moisture intrusion, condensation, and mold problems. Success stories are shared as to the ways value engineering has been approached successfully in past projects.

Chapter 6 looks at construction. The chapter reiterates the holistic approach that has proven to be most successful, relying on a team approach to problem solving in which the synergy of the whole yields the best results. Tips are given on how to handle preconstruction meetings, the process of documenting change, and how to work with contractors to avoid problems that could result from out-of-sequence installations. The discussion proceeds to substantial completion and the importance of a punch list. Postconstruction is also assessed as an important role in envelope performance, as well as relationship building and limiting liability. The emphasis is on open communication with all parties as the best means to avoid future problems.

There is a list of abbreviations, with their expanded meaning. We hope that each of you finds something useful in this illustrated guide to building envelope design and construction, and by using it can avoid problems.

Acknowledgments

The two people who provided encouragement and support for this endeavor did so willingly and expertly. The biggest challenge was in making the adjustments to time allocation for nonbook related personal and family activities. My wonderful wife, Mary Lee Walker has been a huge help in keeping our world in relative balance throughout the process. She alone has aided me in the countless hours of editing and proofing the written text, without complaint. Jack, our young son, has been so understanding that it shows a sensitivity far beyond his years. This book is dedicated to my parents, to my immediate family (yes including you Bekah) and to our future together. I hope that this effort has made me a better communicator, I certainly have learned a great deal in the process.

Water-Resistant
Design and Construction

1

Changes Over Time

1.1 HISTORICAL OVERVIEW

Ever since humans began to evolve, we have been struggling to do more than survive. We want to protect our families from predators, feed and clothe them, and protect them from a sometimes hostile environment. Global warming isn't anything new; researchers tell us that we've been having cycles of hot and cold every hundred thousand years or so. The hot cycles lasted about 20,000 years, followed by another 80,000 years of ice. Our human ancestors learned to adapt to their changing environment.

Early shelters were constructed mainly out of native materials such as cut earth, stone, wood, and animal hides. African fossils have led many historians to the conclusion that the Olduvai Gorge area of Africa must have been the home for the earliest hominid habitat, around two million years ago. We find evidence of changing climate, both temperature and humidity. It had a tropical climate and lush vegetation between 1.2 million and 700,000 years ago, which then changed to a dryer, arid climate. In northern China, prehistoric people used naturally occurring caves and caverns to survive the cold winters as early as 800,000 B.C. In Europe, basalt and granite walls were used as wind breaks as far back as 970,000 B.C. Our ancestors may have seen and used fire earlier, but it seems they learned to control fire about 500,000 years ago. Could you imagine the sense of security that fire must have brought to them back then? Not only did it offer warmth and light their caves, but it also offered protection against many predators. Nomadic hunter-gatherers are believed to have built the first artificial shelters nearly 180,000 years ago (see Fig. 1-1) around the same time they learned to use tools. Humans soon learned to plant food and raise domesticated animals. This changed everything. Soon, civilizations began to form in support of common goals.

Figure 1-1
Early shelters.

The last ice age ended about 35,000 years ago. Since then, the explosion of knowledge and development of specialized tools has led to rapidly advancing cultures across the globe. We have seen tremendous advances in travel, medicine, arts, and sciences. As people satisfied the more basic needs of food and shelter, they began to seek out ways to satisfy higher-level needs, such as knowledge and wealth. In some cultures, this led to war; in others, a search for meaning.

Each culture since that time has been developing an identity of its own in response to climate and social differences. In Asia, civilization was deeply influenced by the ruling class. Different dynasties and conquering invaders tended to shape the built environment. In coastal Chinese areas, average annual rainfall exceeds 80 inches (2 meters) per year. Steeply pitched roof forms and wide overhangs were used to combat the natural forces. Central columns were used to support the roof systems. Buildings became highly ornamental in the Ming and Han dynasties. As intercultural trade expanded, so did the forms of building expression. The Chinese developed a process of apprenticeships for developing construction skills through generations of workers. In Europe, the dominant forms were mostly constructed of masonry, as brought by Greek and Roman conquerors. Stone and wood were used to span between closely spaced stone columns. The Romans forced their skilled masons to travel as part of their army, engineering solutions and building masonry buildings wherever they extended their empire in Europe, Africa, and Asia.

1.2 CHANGES OVER TIME

In North America, native settlers were quite nomadic until the Europeans overwhelmed them some 500 to 700 years ago. These Spanish, English, and French conquerors brought their customs and building forms with them as well. Following the Industrial Revolution, mass transportation and electricity began to change the world at an entirely new pace. With the invention of locomotives and automobiles, there was no limit to where we could go and how we could get there. It was more a question of how fast we could get there and what we would do when we got there.

Starting about 1950, people were now able to live in areas where conditions were previously difficult to bear. We really began to dominate our environment in true European fashion. With the end of World War II and a recovering economy, Americans began moving to the hot, humid areas of the South at a record pace. Rich and poor alike were on the move. Many of those migrating built only modest structures in their new locations, limited by their means and uncertain futures. Lower cost homes commonly were shotgun-style one-story structures, considered perhaps temporary or short-term solutions in case the family didn't like them, or they couldn't stand the bugs. Some people, however, brought their comfortable forms with them from the colder climates, building a Cape Cod–style home out of lap siding in coastal Florida. Well, coastal Florida has a different climate than Cape Cod. In the summertime, such structures needed more roof overhang, and in the winter, they benefited from more thermal mass and insulation.

Recognizing a need to protect the public health and welfare, people began to establish building codes. Engineers, builders, insurers, designers, and businesspeople all worked together to form associations and draft regulations. Since establishment of the codes and regulations, permitting agencies have continued to introduce more rules for building envelope performance. Many jurisdictions adopted energy codes as a means for requiring more efficient consumption and to encourage conservation of energy.

1.3 RECENT TRENDS

Many of the early buildings in the United States were constructed of native materials. Pine and cypress were the most common wall materials used. Some cities where clay was mined locally made bricks. Most building occupants relied on natural ventilation and shade for human comfort (see Fig. 1-2).

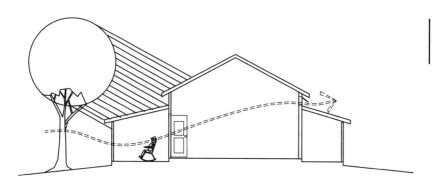

Figure 1-2
Shade and natural ventilation.

Figure 1-3
Simple wall section, plan view.

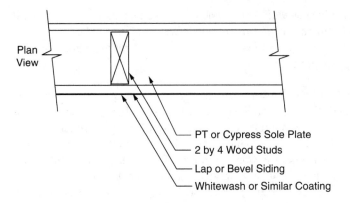

Plan View
- PT or Cypress Sole Plate
- 2 by 4 Wood Studs
- Lap or Bevel Siding
- Whitewash or Similar Coating

After the Industrial Revolution, more and more building materials were widely distributed. Concrete block became as common for walls as frame construction. Since the 1960s, most of our commercial buildings have been designed to be air-conditioned. Even residential buildings typically operate with all the doors and windows closed. Occupants have become more reliant on air-conditioning systems to introduce outside air for breathing and comfort. The building envelope has become much more complicated during the same period of time. Where we used to nail cypress siding right to exterior wood stud framing (see Figures 1-3 and 1-4), we now use layers of sheathing, vapor retarders,

Figure 1-4
Simple wall section, elevation view.

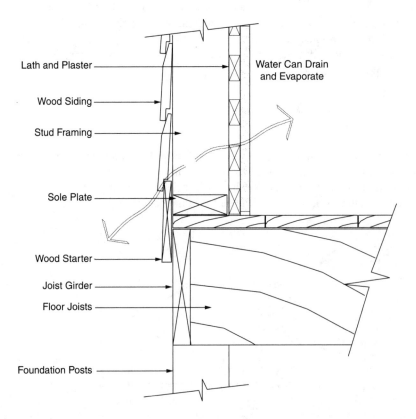

Lath and Plaster
Wood Siding
Stud Framing
Sole Plate
Wood Starter
Joist Girder
Floor Joists
Foundation Posts
Water Can Drain and Evaporate

Figure 1-5
Complex wall section.

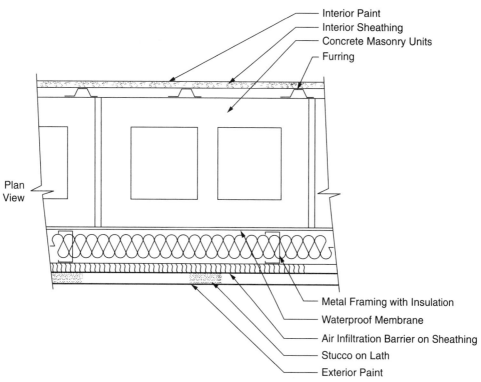

insulation, and a variety of finish materials (see Fig. 1-5). As a result of these and other factors, buildings have become more difficult to design and construct.

With improvements in living conditions, more and more people are moving to coastal regions. They have begun to spend more of their time inside buildings than previous generations. With this has come the increasing challenge of keeping the indoor environment healthy. With increased energy costs, we find our buildings becoming "tighter." By this we mean that we have less air moving through the building envelope. This also means that it is more difficult for water that may get into the building to drain out (see Fig. 1-6).

Another result of the increased population is the drastic need for housing. Homes are being built faster and selling for higher prices than ever before. Many buildings that were built as hotels or apartments have been sold as condominium units. The result of all these factors is that we have seen an increase in the number of claims against developers, builders, and designers (see Fig. 1-7). What can be done?

The answer is both simple and clear. We need to design and build better places. Designers must do a better job of developing plans and specifications that lead to good solutions. Builders must make good decisions and do a better job of

Figure 1-6

Water becomes harder
to drain out.

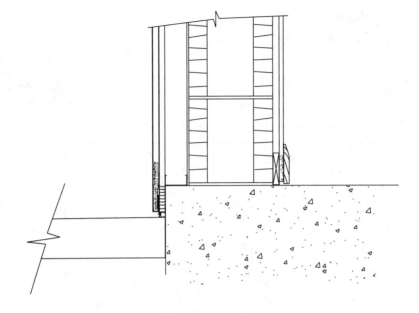

quality control during construction. Developers must enable design and construction teams to come up with long-term, successful solutions. We can't let
poor management decisions lead to lawsuits. As a team, we must resist the
urge to save a few bucks if it can result in problems in the future. This is not
to say that just by spending more money we can prevent problems either. What
is the right answer? How can we design and build better places?

Figure 1-7

Increase in number
of claims.

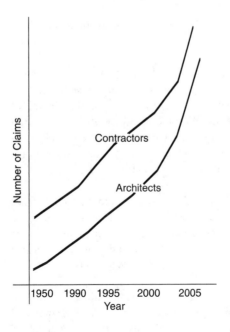

We need to learn from problems of the past. We can look at cause-and-effect relationships. Then we can pay attention to details. We can provide excellent construction details and help to make sure that they get installed right. It takes a cooperative team effort from the office to the field—and back. Lessons learned in the field need to be communicated back to the designers and programmers and should be used to educate owners (see Fig. 1-8).

Figure 1-8
Feedback loop.

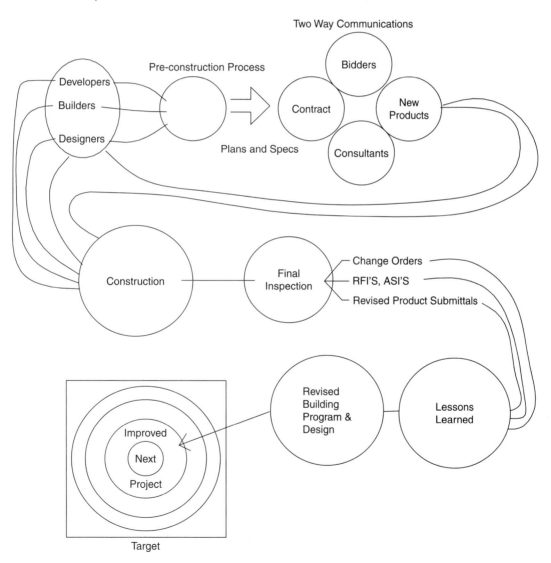

1.4 COMMON CAUSES AND EFFECTS

This section looks at problems that have been identified from the past. It looks at the contributing factors causing problems and explores ways such problems could have been avoided. In Chapters 3 through 6 you will find more detailed information for application through design and construction. This includes typical roof, wall, and floor details for different building types. These details are discussed in relation to the most basic geometric aspects. Materials are called out, and fasteners are shown, as well as flashings and sealants. Our objective is to provide a methodology for preventing the most common problems identified as contributing to building envelope failures and potentially to mold growth. Following is a list that includes 25 of the most common problems:

1. Materials got wet during construction.
2. Dew point is reached in a wall without planning for condensation removal.
3. Insulation is inadequate, misplaced, or on the wrong side of the vapor barrier.
4. Leaks at windows and doors or at other holes in the walls.
5. Roof penetrations.
6. Water comes in at the intersections between walls and floors.
7. Inadequate ventilation.
8. Negative-pressure building.
9. Inadequate air-conditioning.
10. Bad laps of membrane.
11. No vapor barrier.
12. Expansion of materials over time.
13. Bad design.
14. Poor construction.
15. Membranes damaged during construction.
16. Poor joint geometry.
17. Building below finish grade.
18. Hydrostatic pressure.
19. Poor maintenance.
20. Reliance on sealants.
21. Wrong material for the job.
22. Exposure to ultraviolet (UV) radiation during construction.
23. Failed roofing products.
24. Reliance on coatings instead of membranes.
25. A series of bad decisions and/or other forces.

1.4.1 Materials got wet during construction

Very few building materials can be rained on during construction without increasing the potential for future problems. Many builders today strive for just-in-time (JIT) delivery for materials in order to minimize the risk of exposure, theft, damage, etc. With the volatility of the markets and the competition for materials, some materials often get stocked months before they are installed. General contractors struggle to protect stored materials, often renting warehouses for months just to limit their exposure to inflation or shortages. There are times when a contractor may choose to install drywall or other interior materials before the exterior building envelope is complete. Any organic material such as drywall should not be installed in standing water or where it can be rained on. There are more inert materials such as glass-fiber-reinforced sheathing materials that have no paper backing and that can experience incidental water exposure without requiring removal. Block and brick should be stored so as to stay clean and dry until used. Even the best-stored materials can grow mold if spores are present and temperature and humidity are right to support growth. If materials get wet, you must make a decision about their removal. If organic or hygroscopic materials remain wet longer than 12 to 24 hours, they should be removed and replaced. (see Fig. 1-9).

1.4.2 Dew point is reached in a wall without planning for condensation removal

When humid air cools by a few degrees, condensation can occur. Condensation is the formation of small water droplets. These drops are formed when air cools to where it can no longer hold water vapor in the gaseous state.

Figure 1-9
Moldy sheathing.

We call this the *dew point*. Water is needed for mold growth. If we can prevent condensation, we will reduce the potential for mold growth. Careful consideration should be given to modeling the point in the wall section where condensation is likely to occur. Temperature and humidity can be calculated to prevent condensation in normal conditions and to provide drainage pathways for moisture formed in extreme conditions. Condensation can form on a cool surface in a wall, such as metal furring or studs. Good design dictates that each material used in the wall cavity must be selected carefully. Refer to Section 4.4.5 in Chapter 4 for condensation avoidance. If condensation is allowed to build up, structural damage can result.

1.4.3 Insulation is inadequate, misplaced, or on the wrong side of the vapor barrier

Some designs leave inadequate space for proper insulation. Others may use cold-climate wall sections for hot-climate buildings. This problem can be as simple as insulation being installed on the nonconditioned (warm in the summer) side of the vapor retarder in walls. Some builders use foil-backed fiberglass batt insulation in such a way that the fiberglass stays wet and drips liquid water into the wall cavity, increasing the potential for bacterial growth. If the insulation has too low an R value, interior finishes may warm to where the dew point is reached. Wood paneling, ceramic tile, and drywall can provide environs for mold and other undesirable growth.

If the vapor retarder is placed on the cool (interior in the summer) side of the insulation, the increase in the moisture level of the insulation will reduce its effectiveness. This results in wasted energy and potential moisture problems in the wall. Refer to Section 4.6.8 in Chapter 4 for more on insulation.

1.4.4 Leaks at windows and doors or at other holes in the walls

This is a wide-ranging issue and includes openings in wall planes. Window and door frames can be difficult to seal properly against leakage. Other problematic penetrations may include such things as louvers, vents, lights, and beams. As designers, we can carefully select the right kind of product to match the materials and methods of construction. We should skillfully create the plan and section view details to both prevent wind-driven moisture from entering the walls and to allow drainage pathways for water that may pass the outermost protective barriers. This must occur at the head, jamb, and sill and continue to below grade (refer to Section 4.5.2 in Chapter 4 for more on flooring systems).

With the development of better sealants and products such as expanding-foam fillers, builders have become more dependent on them. Whereas we used to rely mostly on positive detailing applied over the flange or water tables at the head, we now have a tendency to leave an intentional gap and use negative detailing. These gaps may vary from $1/4$ inch to more than 3 inches. Both foam fillers and sealants (formerly referred to as *caulk*) have been proven to fail over time (see Fig. 1-10).

Figure 1-10
Sealants fail over time.

1.4.5   Roof penetrations

There are many different problems we see related to roof penetrations and construction. One is the result of water continually ponding or left standing on the roof membrane. As a result of continued contact, the membranes begin to break down. Membranes are not meant to stay wet. Most roof failures occur at penetrations or where different systems come together. Failure to seal and flash intersecting roof planes and vertical parapets causes most common problems. The result is damaged substrates, which can lead to mold and mildew problems over time. When a roof membrane is being removed during renovation, remodeling, or reroofing, you can see where water has been repeatedly defeating the membrane. This typically occurs at hard-to-flash areas, such as skylights, chimneys, and vent stacks on sloped roofs.

Another common problem results from difficulties in fully sealing scupper penetrations and internal gutter or leader construction. Metal gutters in commercial buildings also can fail to hold water for a number of reasons. Most integral gutter failures are related to movement over time, but horizontal and vertical laps also can be problematic (see Fig. 1-11).

1.4.6   Water comes in at the Intersections
between walls and floors

Many one-story buildings use slab-on-grade construction. Multilevel commercial and residential buildings have walkways and balconies. Accessibility codes have made it more challenging to keep positive drainage away from walls. The point where walls connect to floors is one of the most difficult-to-control

Figure 1-11
Integral gutter section.

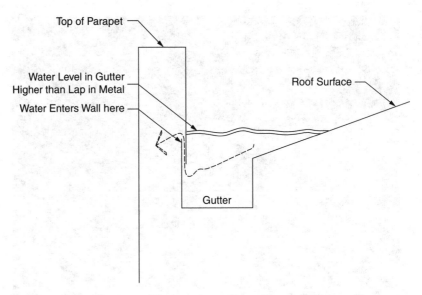

moisture infiltration areas. The best protection against infiltration of large quantities of liquid water is to keep the finish floor more than 6 inches above finish grade (see Fig. 1-12). There are several proven methods for closing the voids between sill plates and floor slabs, but the best prevention is an elevated slab. We recommend use of gravity and geometry as a basis for prevention of water intrusion at the base of walls.

During storms, wind-driven rain can impact our walls at more than 100 miles per hour. Sometimes the droplets come in horizontally or even in an upward direction. Good design and construction can provide barriers that prevent

Figure 1-12
Finish floor above finish grade.

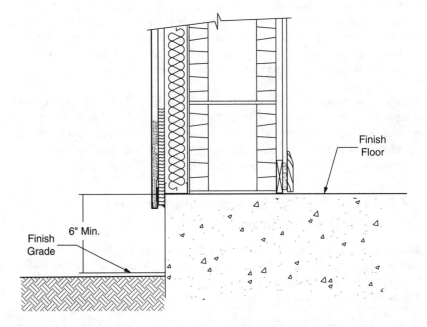

water from natural or human-made sources from defeating the building envelope. It starts with good detailing.

These details must provide planned-in pathways for the moisture to drain out. Some studies in 2003 reported that block walls built on slabs at grade with no insulation, no furring, and no drywall typically have not supported mold growth as much as some of the more complex wall types. It is believed the biggest contributing factor to their resistance is that there is no place to trap water in the wall. After a rain event, the wall can dry out fully.

Multiple wythe walls create an even bigger challenge. Water can get trapped in between the wythes, creating good environments for organic growth. Brick, block, and stone walls built today often have interior components framed into them. Insulation is often installed between the framing members. Designers must pay special attention to details where multiple layers of wall construction are used.

1.4.7   Inadequate ventilation

Ventilation is important for human comfort, as well as to prevent or minimize bacterial growth. Studies have shown that the best way to avoid bacterial growth in walls is to keep the temperature cool and the air dry. This is difficult to do in warm humid climates or if it is cold and damp out. The difference between indoor and outside air temperatures can cause condensation in the walls. The moisture in walls needs to be removed. It should be aided by ventilation. Attic spaces, wall cavities, and crawl spaces must have adequate ventilation to inhibit bacterial growth and to maintain relatively dry materials to prevent rot. Historically, builders strove to maintain less than 50 percent relative humidity (RH) in occupied spaces.

The American Society of Heating, Refrigeration and Air Conditioning Engineers (ASHRAE) is working to develop new guidelines slated for adoption in 2007 that lower design values to new levels (among which is a recommended 40 percent RH in hot humid climates). This should result in two things. First, it will result in larger cooling-coil capacity. Second, it should help to prevent humidity from reaching high levels in the building, even in peak conditions. We should keep air in the wall cavities, especially those inside of vapor barriers, at less than 50 percent RH to minimize the potential for mold growth.

In brick and stone walls, for example, we typically design vents and weeps to minimize trapped water in the cavity (see Fig. 1-13). Vents typically are installed under window sills and at the tops of walls under roof overhangs. This enables water vapor in the cavity to migrate out as it rises up. Weeps are important at the low points of these walls. They should be installed by way of tubes, flashings, or water tables to get liquid water (from infiltration or condensation) out of the wall cavity. Ideally, the point of discharge is below finish grade so that any staining caused by the discharge is not visible. Discharge above grade requires additional treatment, such as change of materials, or acceptance of discoloration. Removal of the liquid and vapor water is important to minimize the possibility of contaminating

Figure 1-13

Brick vents in section.

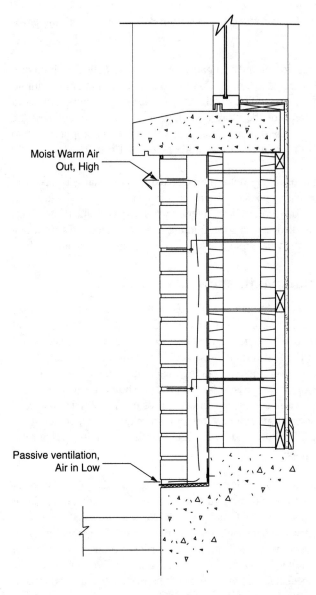

Moist Warm Air
Out, High

Passive ventilation,
Air in Low

the conditioned spaces. Ventilation is the key to removing water in the walls.
Inadequate ventilation also can take many forms. If conditioned air is not circulat-
ing properly, there can be warm dead-air spaces in the rooms. These also can be
places for growth on and in the walls. It is also key to remove warm, moist air from
occupied, closed spaces within buildings. An example of this would be in showers
and laundry areas (see Fig. 1-14). Ventilation is also important for flat roof systems. We like to specify vented deck to promote drying if light- or normal-weight
concrete is applied. This removes moisture from curing concrete faster. Then we
design vented membrane systems to allow hot air to escape above the concrete.
One challenge with vented metal deck is to limit the problems that can result
from dripping and deck draining long after concrete placement.

Figure 1-14
Plan for moisture removal at sources.

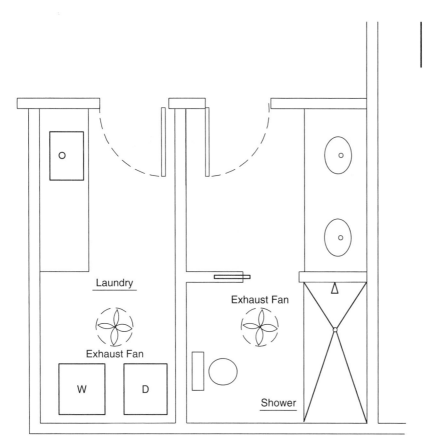

Laundry

Exhaust Fan

Exhaust Fan

W   D

Shower

1.4.8   Negative-pressure building

It is now a building code requirement in many states to have positive pressure in occupied buildings. What this means is that more air is brought into the building than is exhausted. Figure 1-15 shows a section through a representative four-story building. In it you can see a schematic flow of air to and from the outside air conditioner. It also indicates the other components of a building pressurization study—exhaust, vents, and exfiltration. *Exhaust* is the sum of all building fan–induced components, such as bathroom, kitchen hood, or bathroom exhaust. *Vents* are dryer vents, items such as gas appliances, and plumbing vents. The *exfiltration* component is for air exiting the building through windows, doors, and perimeter leakage. The sum of all the negative values must be less than the amount of outside air coming in for the building to stay positive.

In most cases, the outside air is ducted to the suction side of the air-conditioning system and mixed with the return air. Some buildings have sophisticated sensors that measure exhaust air and outside-air makeup and, through a series of variable-speed fans, are able to maintain positive building pressure (see Fig. 1-16). The sensors work together to control fan speed or dampers to keep more air coming in than goes out. An enthalpy wheel is sometimes used to

Figure 1-15

Outside air system diagram.

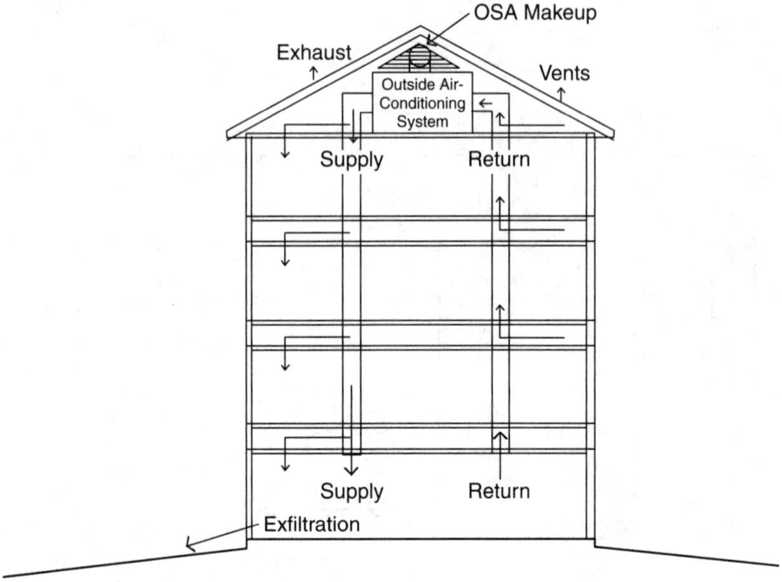

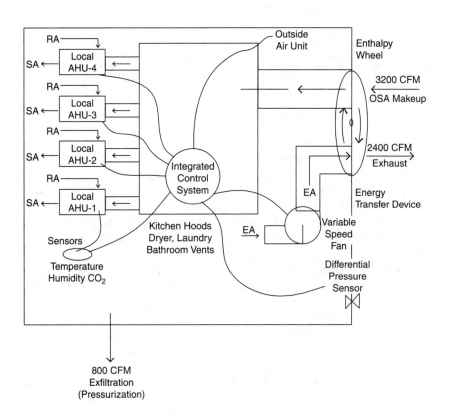

Figure 1-16

Heat wheel.

capture energy from leaving air and transfer it to entering air. Such wheels, often referred to as a "heat wheel", result in lower energy costs as well.

The key component of a well-designed and well-balanced system is the unit air-conditioning system. Figure 1-17 shows ducted return air and a backdraft damper to the outside air duct. This can prevent unwanted loss of return (pre-conditioned) air.

By keeping the building pressure positive, we can minimize relative humidity in our building roof, exterior walls, and their cavities. Negative-pressure build-ings can lead to the continual introduction of warm, moist (in some cases dirty) air. This can lead to the slow buildup of hidden mold that can be toler-ated at low levels for a long period of time. Sometimes a single trigger event, such as a hurricane, can cause the rapid spread of bacterial growth to intoler-able levels within a few days. The hurricane force winds can blow water into the envelope and then afterwards loss of electrical power for days or weeks. If you couple a negative-pressure building with high-humidity conditioned air (such as may be caused by an undersized coil section, high chilled-water tem-peratures, or too high an air velocity), you have created a moist environment where bacteria can flourish. Once mold reaches this level, remediation is quite costly and requires many affected materials and systems to be removed com-pletely and replaced.

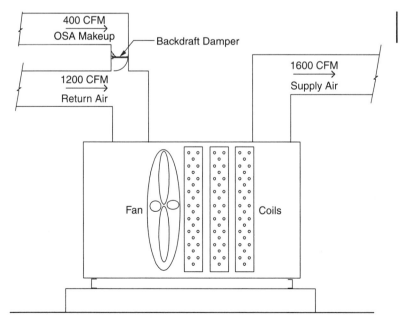

Figure 1-17
Unit air-conditioning system.

1.4.9   Inadequate air-conditioning

There are many ways the air-conditioning system can contribute to indoor environmental problems. There are just as many reasons why a project can end up with inadequate air-conditioning. On some projects, design decisions or assumptions may be flawed. The design team has to make many decisions. Maybe some of those decisions may not have been fully communicated to all team members.

Perhaps design insulation values were miscalculated or otherwise not achieved. Perhaps cost-cutting decisions were made that were not consistent with design values. Maybe the system was designed for 95°F days and fails if temperatures hover around 98°F (see Fig. 1-18). In the figure we see that temperatures stayed above 95°F for a long period of time. If the envelope was not sufficiently insulated (and few are), the transfer of heat through the envelope will exceed the unit's ability to reduce temperature and humidity in the conditioned spaces. This will result in the perfect environment for bacterial and fungal growth. The way around this is to have the design engineers raise the design values. In most cases, about 5°F more in design values will provide enough additional cooling capacity to handle the worst summers. Some systems can keep the air cool enough but fail to dehumidify it adequately. This can result in RH in the space exceeding 65 percent, an undesirable value.

Maybe chilled-water values discussed during planning stages, and supposedly delivered by the local municipal utility company, were never actually provided to the building site. This happens in cities that are experiencing rapid growth. Cities, counties, hospitals, schools, and large commercial projects often provide the design team with expected values for chilled water to be provided by existing supply loops. As more users are brought into the loop, historical values may not be met. This can result in reduced capacity for cooling and dehumidification in the new building, as well as problems in the older ones in the same loop.

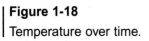

Figure 1-18

Temperature over time.

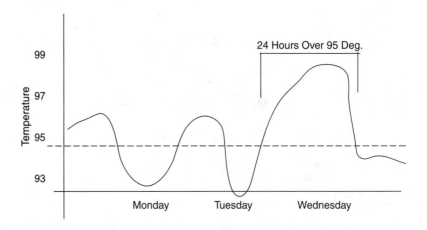

There are many operational reasons why the system can prove inadequate. Perhaps there is insufficient maintenance of the condenser water tubes or poor control of chemical treatment. Both of these can lead to poor heat transfer and less cooling capacity. Sometimes there can be a great system that was installed poorly. Perhaps the ductwork is leaking, crushed, or undersized. Controls failures or bad settings also can lead to poor performance.

The system must be capable of maintaining temperature and humidity control in whatever operating conditions. Most designers will derive guidance from standard practice in the industry. Most owners or developers will not review or participate in the establishment of system design parameters. We often get feedback from owners or contractors about ways to save initial costs on the air-conditioning system. Some projects suffer from poor cost-savings measures. There was one project a major firm worked on where the owner was offered a big savings to switch from a central plant and chilled-water system to direct exchange (DX; i.e., air to air) units. The designers recommended against the change, but ultimately, it was made. The DX units had undersized coils for the amount of outside air and could not provide enough cool, dry air to the spaces. Problems were observed by fall of the first year. Litigation followed against the designers, who had recommended against the change in unit.

There are other ways the system may not perform as well as needed. The system may be well designed and fully capable of doing the job. Sometimes the problem may be the result of controls settings. After owners and operators take over control of a building, things are likely to change. One of the first things to change is set points. In a large building with a central plant, air and water set points can be changed by anybody with a password. In an attempt to lower heating or cooling energy costs, operators can change set points. If the supply air temperature is set 2°F warmer, the operator might save a thousand dollars per week in the summer. This is an easy and obvious decision for someone with budget responsibility, especially if he or she has no training in mechanical engineering.

Other tempting changes include closing off the outside air makeup grill, raising the humidity set point, or turning unit resistance heaters off. All these changes are likely to result in an increased potential for mold and mildew growth. The way to avoid these problems is by keeping focus on the big picture—long-term successful operation of the building. Do not permit decisions to be made only to help the short term if they have long-term negative effects. It is up to the decision makers in each project to balance the input with the project needs and come up with a good, well-balanced set of design and construction values to be met. This should be done in the programming phase, not after design documents are near completion. Good project managers will use their experience to adjust the design values provided by others so that the design and construction teams end up providing a successful building.

1.4.10   Bad laps of membrane

In walls and roofs that use sheet membranes for vapor or air infiltration barrier, the manner in which the membranes are installed is very important. Manufacturers provide clear instructions on recommended procedures and will only warrant properly installed products. Sometimes even the simplest tasks can be performed poorly. The most basic aspect of a properly installed sheet membrane for air infiltration is sealing the seams. The joints between successive layers of sheeting must be sealed by the right product. For example, manufacturers may recommend that applications of XYZ Air Infiltration Barrier are sealed at fastener penetrations, ends, and laps with XYZ brand tape to maximize performance of the product.

After you get past the obvious, each penetration through the wall, such as windows or electrical devices, must be sealed in the same manner. Rather than rely on foam or tape, installers should seal penetrations, lapping each successive sheet of material from the bottom up. All laps above grade typically need to be installed from the bottom up, with each successive layer lapping over the one below. Just as with roof sheathings, membranes on wall surfaces should be installed to direct water down and away from the building. Whether air infiltration barriers or waterproof membranes, laps should be installed using gravity to prevent the introduction of water (see Fig. 1-19).

Figure 1-19
Avoid backwater laps.

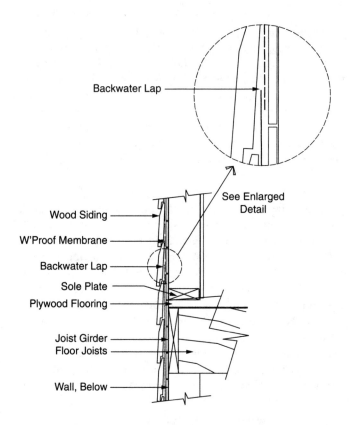

There are proper ways to seal the tape to the membrane as well. Both surfaces should be dry and free from dirt, grease, or foreign materials. Self-adhesive membranes should follow similar procedures. Fully detailed plans will include graphic and written instructions for proper application of membranes. Specifications should match products with applications. Special care must be taken to match sealants with membrane products if they come in contact with each other. For more on air and moisture barriers, refer to Section 4.6 of Chapter 4.

1.4.11   No vapor barrier

Each climatic condition requires a different treatment with regard to air and vapor retardant. Each client and building system has different requirements. Many buildings have problems resulting from not having an effective air infiltration or vapor barrier. Many thousands of buildings have been constructed without any vapor barrier at all (see Fig. 1-20). Others rely on stucco on block to prevent water (in liquid or vapor form) from entering the building envelope. Some use flake board or siding to protect the shell, whereas others rely on a coat of paint to function as air and water protection. Even if this works when new, it relies on proper maintenance, such as additional coats after 5 or at most 10 years. Beyond this, in the flake board or plywood sheathing example we are relying on a system component to do more than it should. If building felts are installed in a wall, can they be an effective air barrier? Perhaps, if the joints are sealed tight with a roofing cement product, but this is not what it is designed for. Some types of sheathing, when joints are sealed with proper materials, such as a fiber reinforced mesh and mastic system can be used as an air infiltration barrier. The biggest issue here is matching the wall type with the climate, especially amounts of rainfall and temperature ranges.

1.4.12   Expansion of materials over time

Some building envelopes may work well when constructed, only to fail later. This can be the result of material movement over time. Forces such as deflection resulting from wind, expansion and contraction due to temperature changes, or

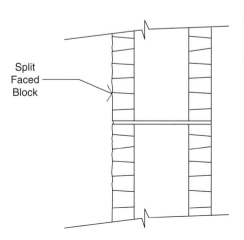

Split Faced Block

Figure 1-20
Wall section without vapor barrier.

Figure 1-21

Slots to permit movement.

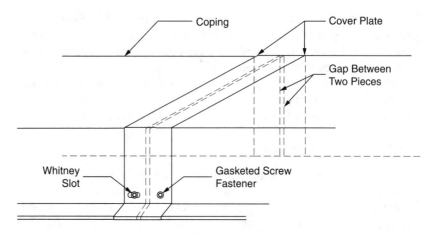

uneven foundation settling can lead to leaks. In some cases, leaks are caused by cracking of structural and/or finish materials. In others, leaks can be the result of failed sealants at joints. If initial installation of roofing membranes does not provide for adequate movement, resulting forces can rip the materials. All materials tend to expand and contract as they change temperature over the course of a season or even a 24-hour period. Temperatures on a roof coping can vary more than 80°F in one day. Therefore, long lengths of any envelope component must be designed and constructed to permit movement without loss of protection. In metal, we often rely on elongated fastening slots, such as Whitney slots, to allow for tight fit and expansion, or contraction without compromising the performance of the joint (see Fig. 1-21). Similarly, joint covers are designed to be pinned on one end and slide on the other. Refer to Section 4.6.7.3 in Chapter 4 for more on roof flashings.

1.4.13 Bad design

It may be that the design documents show a bad detail or neglected to address an important force. In an attempt to create a certain aesthetic, some designers can end up with a bad detail. This could occur at any location in the building but most likely would be at the floor or windows and doors. Another possibility would be at the roof edge, such as drip, parapet, or fascia. Figure 1-22 shows plan and section locations that must be designed and detailed in even the simplest buildings to control water intrusion.

Poor design can result in water intruding into or forming in a wall cavity or building interior. Good design typically will locate roof planes above door openings to reduce wind-driven rain energy. Some designers feel the need for new expression. They develop new ways to solve timeless problems. A different explanation for a bad detail might be the lack of experience on the part of some member of the design team. For less-experienced designers, using time-tested details will reduce the possibility of bad details. Many project teams use waterproofing and roofing consultants to review plans and specifications during the design process. This reduces the likelihood of bad details. Some consultants will develop your details for the project and share in the liability.

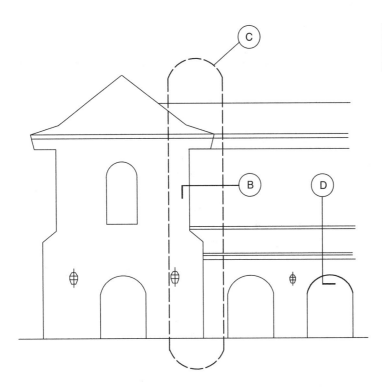

Figure 1-22
Building section where details need to be drawn.

There are other ways designs may not illustrate the best solution for construction. If, for example, we have long spans that may deflect over time or with changing live loads, the right design response might include deflection tracks or expansion joints to accommodate the movement without leaking over time. Another example of bad design could be the location of a chimney flue or mechanical vent in a valley condition. Still another would be failure to slope the exterior grades away from all four sides of the building. These and other flawed design decisions can be caught in peer review before release of drawings, by building contractors, by plans examiners, or by other design professionals during their review. Only by all of us working together as a team can we consistently produce the best product. A significant portion of this book (all of Chapter 4) focuses on design. We felt that this was necessary because so many decisions are made in the design process that affect envelope performance.

1.4.14 Poor construction

Alternatively, the design decisions all could have been sound. The submittals all could have been equivalent to the basis of design. A poorly performing building can be the sole result of poor construction practices. It can be the result of a poor application of materials designed to prevent liquid water intrusion. If the air-conditioning system dries the indoor supply air adequately, water vapor is much less likely to be the cause of bacterial growth or material damage. It is most often the result of condensation or liquid water intrusion. Even small quantities of liquid water, if frequent, can lead to big problems.

As you can imagine, the roof can be the most frequent location for a source of water intrusion. Low slope or flat roofs, if installed improperly, can trap water where it can find its way into buildings (see Fig. 1-23). If the installers do not install flashings and membranes properly, the building will likely have problems. Frequently, leaks can occur at corners and where horizontal surfaces meet vertical surfaces.

As the materials expand and contract with changes in temperature, rips and tears can occur in the membrane. Laps and seams are less frequently the cause of leaks, yet leaks still can occur there. Proper application and protection would be more important in the use of a single-ply roofing system than with the case of a three-ply membrane system. On sloped roof surfaces, there can be many causes of leaks as well. Commonly, the dry-in membrane is installed months before the metal or shingles go on. Most manufacturers will not warrant performance of their products if they are exposed to UV radiation for more than 30 days. If the membrane is not nailed properly or fully adhered, rips can occur. If it is not stretched properly or installed when the rolls are cold, it can develop big bulges or humps in it when the material warms. Some roofers have been known to cut the membrane with knives to get the bumps out prior to installing the shingles. This practice basically voids the integrity of the membrane.

Shingles are not intended to serve as the membrane; they are intended to keep the sun off the membrane beneath. Additionally, flashings along sides of sloped roof surfaces need to be installed in such a way as to prevent water intrusion. Laps in metal or sheet membranes must be made the right way. Penetrations such as vent pipes or equipment supports must be sealed properly and should extend a minimum of about 12 inches above the roof (see Fig. 1-24).

Figure 1-23

Water can enter a building when trapped on the roof.

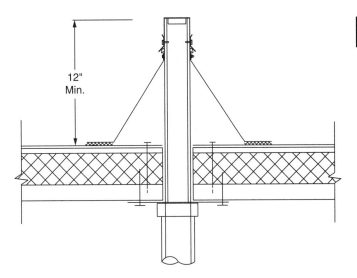

12"
Min.

Figure 1-24
Plumbing vent detail.

All too often, walls and roofs are penetrated after the air infiltration barrier or waterproof membranes have been applied. Proper installation of penetration protection relies on timely or sequenced installation requiring coordination among many trades. Many of our projects today are built entirely by subcontractors specializing in one trade only. It has become more difficult to manage the sequencing and coordination of trades. The roofer usually installs flashings and membranes at the roof, it is a good idea to have the responsibility for roofing membranes and flashings to reside with one contractor.

A building could have some concrete, some block, and some metal stud (usually including drywall and exterior gyp sheathing) subcontractors. The electrician, plumber, air-conditioning, and miscellaneous metal subcontractors often penetrate the other contractors' completed work. One way to seal the late penetration is to remove finish materials back far enough to access the membrane. Then slit the membrane above the new penetration and slip a piece in behind the original sheet. Tape it, and fit the new piece around the penetration. Then replace finishes.

In some contractual arrangements, the sealing of the penetrations falls to the person penetrating the other subcontractor's work, whereas in others it goes back to the original installer. Some projects may have a caulking and sealant subcontractor. It gets very challenging to get them all to work together with the time constraints of the other interdependent subcontractors. It only takes one of the many trades not being cooperative to cause problems for all the others.

Figure 1-25 presents an enlarged detail for a portion of the envelope, calling out materials requiring coordination. It also lists some of the many trades that all need to go in the right sequence. Prior planning and two-way communications are the best preventive measures. It used to be that sleeving wall and slab penetrations was the norm. The space between the sleeve and the penetrating

Figure 1-25
Enlarged plan detail.

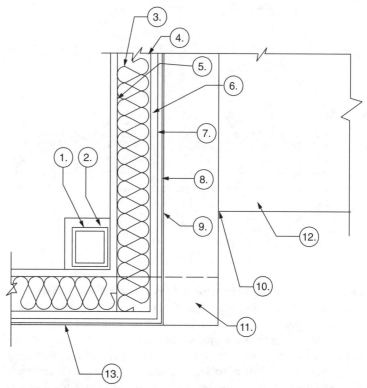

1. Structural Steel
2. Fireproofing
3. Light Gage Metal Framing
4. Insulation
5. Drywall
6. Densglass
7. Air Infiltration Barrier
8. Paper-Backed Lath
9. Stucco
10. Roof Flashing
11. Miscellaneous Metals
12. Roofing Membranes
13. Painter

pipes or conduits would be filled later. Now, the norm has changed. It is more common to see the penetration core drilled through a floor slab or busted through a wall. In many cases, the membranes are already complete and finishes installed. Any penetration at this late stage cannot be sealed properly at the air infiltration barrier level without backing up (as opposed to moving forward). If the air barrier is not sealed to the penetrating object, the integrity of the building envelope's continuous air barrier is at risk for failure.

Windows and doors are the next likely source of leaks. We have seen many projects where concrete walkways around the exterior walls were constructed at an elevation slightly higher than the finish floor elevation. Let us assume that they were not designed as such, but are the result of inconsistencies in placing concrete at slab-edge forms, thus the walks got placed too high. You can see this condition in Figure 1-26. This can lead to frequent introduction of water under perimeter walls.

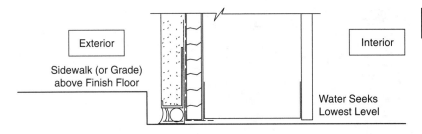

Figure 1-26
Poor geometry at floor.

When this occurs at entry doors, water can find its way in easily. The addition of sill pans at doors can help prevent intrusion at doors. At windows (and louvers), flashing is also extremely important. Many installers tend to rely on sealant (often by others) to prevent water from coming in at their penetrations. Holes are often cut the wrong size, air infiltration barriers (AIBs) are installed before blocking, flashing is omitted, or worse. One contractor tried to fill in the void along a slab edge at grade that resulted from bad layout of the slab and walls with additional pieces of filler material (see Fig. 1-27 for the detail

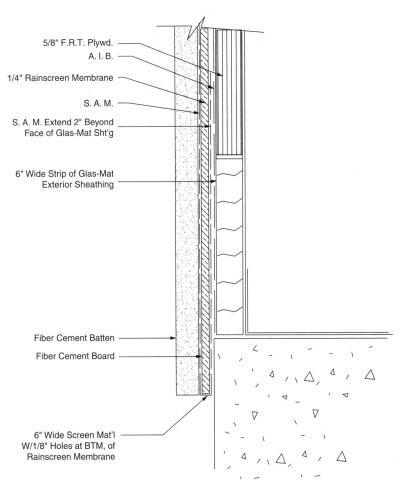

Figure 1-27
Detail as intended.

Figure 1-28

Photo as detail was constructed.

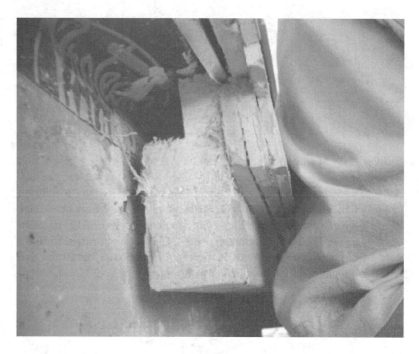

as intended and Fig. 1-28 for a photo of the filler and surrounding voids.). This required corrective concrete work (backing up) and properly adhering cementitious filler to the slab edge.

We would like to take this opportunity to discuss an opinion that we formed over the past several years working on large commercial and government projects. Our detailed drawings need to be done to a different level of detail than in past decades. We seem to have a less-skilled workforce available. Many of our workers do not speak or even understand the language in which the plans are provided. For these reasons, our plans, sections, and details need to be more graphic and easily understood than in recent history. It used to be that a section at $^1/_8$ inch per foot scale and some general notes would suffice for defining a wall-to-roof intersection. We can no longer just note "Install as per manufacturers' recommendations."

Now we have to almost provide a recipe for construction. We have to show every part of the system, call each component out, and indicate where it goes. We can't even expect our workers to understand abbreviations anymore. We have begun providing enlarged details at 3 inches = 1 foot, or even full size. This is the best way that we have found to guarantee proper estimating and construction. This places a huge burden on our design teams, requiring more time and effort to be spent on details than ever before. The people designing our buildings, and especially those drafting the designs, must know what each and every line stands for. Figure 1-29 provides a good example of a detail that required extra large illustrations for workers to fully understand the proper

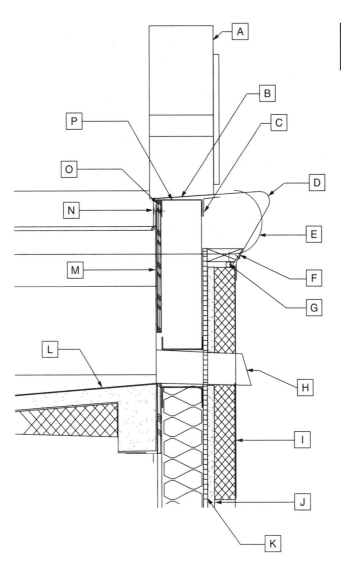

Figure 1-29
Enlarged detail at roof edge.

sequencing of materials. Without enlarging the detail and pointing out the various materials and methods of construction, we were certain that the people looking at our drawings could not understand, comprehend, and build the building the right way. We learned a lot about our workforce that week. We learned that we have to provide a lot of enlarged details to get complex walls built right.

Poor construction can take many forms. For every job that is done, there can be many wrong ways that it can be done. Backwater laps in waterproof membranes can lead to water intrusion. Laps in flashings and membranes should be made from the bottom up so that falling rain can drain over the previous layer at the laps and not behind the previous layer. The enlargement helps us to understand the importance of all these lines and words.

Corners can be lapped wrong, metal can be fastened wrong or cut wrong, and there can be countless other errors. The best means for prevention of improperly installed materials is to hire experienced, well-trained installers. Those installers need the right materials, at the right time, and in the right sizes. Then there should be a quality-control process, such as frequent walks by experienced observers such as general superintendents and trained inspectors. Many owners or developers hire specialists to observe projects during construction for good waterproofing practices. If the architect has a contract for full time, on-site construction administration, that should help with the quality review and observation process. Section 6.13 in Chapter 6 focuses on quality control during construction.

1.4.15 Membranes damaged during construction

Roof and wall membranes can be damaged during construction. They often get installed long before all the work around them is complete. Other workers may be less than careful working on or around a membrane. Roof membranes probably take the worst abuse (see Fig. 1-30). People may leave nails lying around, and others may walk on them. Nail or screw heads can easily punch holes in a membrane.

Sometimes we have welding that occurs above a membrane. There may be a torched-on cap sheet, during which AIBs can be damaged or melted if nearby (see Fig. 1-31). Scaffolding may be assembled and rolled around on the membrane. Some of these scaffolds have sharp corners that may puncture sidewall

Figure 1-30

Photo of punctured sidewall roofing membrane.

Figure 1-31
Melted wall membrane
from torch applied roofing.

flashings or membranes. Other workers may fasten their work to or through a membrane. Some of these membranes may be difficult to patch, whereas others, such as a good self-adhesive membrane (SAM) or ethylene propylene diene monomer (EPDM), are relatively easy to patch properly.

Contractors and designers need to work together to specify the right roof membrane for the sequence of construction. If they know that the dry-in or base sheet likely will be damaged by workers performing a series of applications on scaffolding, for example, they should make sure that future plies are going to go on. This is a benefit of three- and four-ply membranes. No matter what the intentions are, it can be difficult to protect a membrane if masonry is installed above it, say, on a side wall, for example. A roof membrane with a bunch of patches is not as reliable as a roof membrane that no one punctured while working above it.

1.4.16   Poor joint geometry

Joint geometry is a term we use to describe the physical shape of the path rainwater would have to take to get into a wall. Poor joint geometry allows water to get behind flanges, sidings, or any finish material more easily. Membranes can be installed improperly, flashings omitted, trim installed at the wrong depth in the wall, etc. There are many ways that the manner in which the details are installed can permit easy entrance of water (see Fig. 1-32). Joint geometry is important to keep out normal water. By this, we mean the way the joint is constructed physically. In the macro sense, this can be divided into positive and negative detailing. Negative details are developed with the fewest number of pieces and often rely on sealants to close off the joint to the weather (see Fig. 1-33).

Figure 1-32
Poor joint geometry at wall.

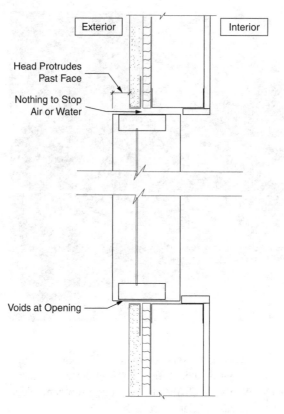

Exterior

Interior

Head Protrudes
Past Face

Nothing to Stop
Air or Water

Voids at Opening

Figure 1-33
Negative detail relies upon
sealant.

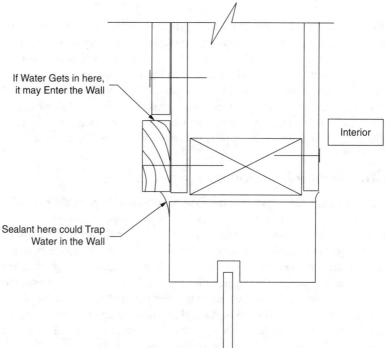

If Water Gets in here,
it may Enter the Wall

Interior

Sealant here could Trap
Water in the Wall

Negative details often expose all the fasteners and structural members to view. Post and beam framing is an example of negative detailing. Positive details, in contrast, typically do not expose connections to view and use more applied pieces of trim (see Fig. 1-34). There are pros and cons of the two different methodologies. Negative detailing typically has a lower initial cost and relies on sealants to keep out the weather. This often leads to higher maintenance and upkeep costs. Positive detailing typically has a higher initial cost and lower maintenance costs. While both methods can work, we observe that positive details tend to keep out wind-driven rain better than negative-detail joints. The down side is that if not detailed, installed, and maintained properly, positive-detail joints can create places where water can be trapped and find its way into the building over time.

Positive and negative detailing both have their places in keeping with the style and expression of the architectural concept. Traditional architectural styles such as shingle style, colonial style, and Mediterranean style typically have used positive detailing. Pieces of stone, stucco, wood, or metal frequently cover the voids between materials and planar surfaces.

We believe that well-conceived positive detailing can be the most effective at keeping water out of our buildings located in wet or humid regions over the long term. Details that place a piece of material over potential voids along a window jamb and head have the best success in preventing wind-driven rain from entering the building envelope. Similarly, we should use positive detailing

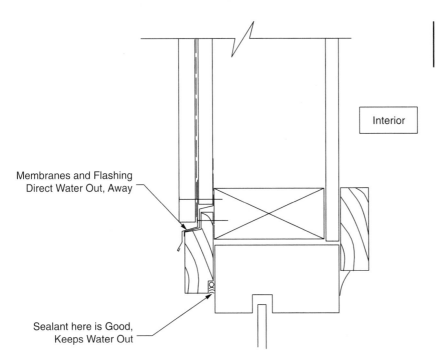

Interior

Membranes and Flashing
Direct Water Out, Away

Sealant here is Good,
Keeps Water Out

Figure 1-34
Positive detail keeps out wind-driven rain.

at the bases of walls. Trim shapes for a window or door sill should slope away from the building facade—first down, then out. Similarly, positive detailing can be used at other types of joints as well. Positive detailing at the slab edge or top of a wall, for example, can take on many forms. In each, the objective is the same: Make it harder for water to get behind the membrane(s).

Our idea of good detailing is to make wind-driven water lose energy by making it oppose gravity, change direction, or both. At the very least, we want to slow it down and make it change direction. Except in the most extreme conditions, water will not enter a detail horizontally, turn vertical, and then travel more than a few inches upward. This is the basis of most good positive detailing. Block the easy way in. Make the water lose energy, change direction, and go uphill (see Fig. 1-35). Then, by having a vertical leg that is taller than the water will climb, we effectively keep it out of the building. Along the coastal areas, that vertical leg on flashing is preferred to be a minimum of 12 inches; in lower-wind-speed zones, 8 inches may suffice. For window sill pan flashings 2 inch minimum is preferred on the interior vertical leg.

Beyond this overview, there is the microgeometry, that is, the detail level. Depending on the system chosen, this can take on many different forms but will have features in common. The idea is to keep water from getting behind the waterproof membrane. Whether it is the paint on the face of stucco or wood siding or a sheet membrane several layers in the wall, the big idea is the same. The challenge is to keep (predominantly) liquid water outside the membrane. Metal and sheet membranes can be used in concert to keep water from getting behind windows, door, and louvers in walls. Sealants can be used to augment the whole, reducing voids between and beneath flashings or behind and around trim. If such measures are installed right, the water will have pathways to drain

Figure 1-35

Geometry to reduce energy of rain.

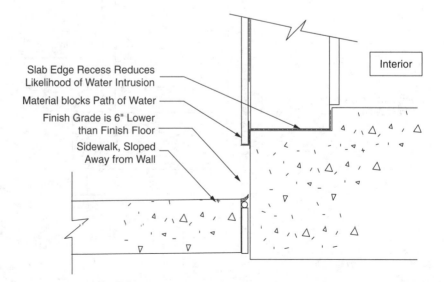

Slab Edge Recess Reduces Likelihood of Water Intrusion

Material blocks Path of Water

Finish Grade is 6" Lower than Finish Floor

Sidewalk, Sloped Away from Wall

Interior

at the low point in the cavity/detail condition. Refer to Chapters 2 and 4 for more on geometry.

1.4.17 Building below finish grade

Despite many building codes requiring the finish floor be more than 6 inches above finish grade, we find many buildings do not meet this requirement. This should only result from conscious decisions of expression and not from a lack of coordination between site and building designers. Architects must instruct civil engineers as to desired spot elevations around the building perimeter. There is one building type where finish grade is intended to be elevated above finish floor (not including basements, etc.). This is when buildings are intended to be earth sheltered. This decision should have resulted in special design details that would include special insulation and waterproof membrane details (see Figs. 1-36 and 1-37). In addition, many designers add a designed-in pathway for the water to drain out, such as a socked perforated drain in a rock exfiltration bed.

The only way these earth-sheltered buildings can avoid problems from condensation, vapor, or water intrusion is to keep temperatures and humidity in

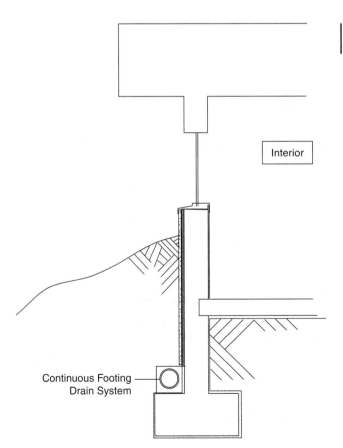

Figure 1-36
Design for earth shelter.

Figure 1-37

Enlarged detail at sill.

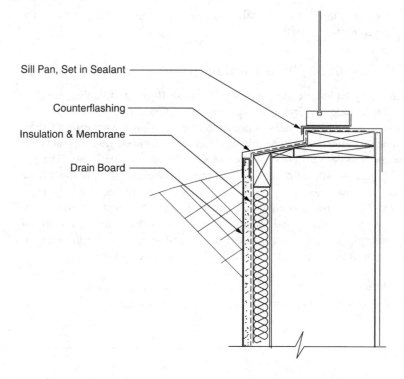

Sill Pan, Set in Sealant

Counterflashing

Insulation & Membrane

Drain Board

the wall under control. These measures often include an applied sheet membrane on the exterior face of the wall and closed-cell foam insulation.

If the finish floor is constructed below finish grade, gravity can make it easier for water to cause problems in the wall. To make matters worse, subterranean insects can erode the building protection system. Good design will only result in finished floors less than 6 inches above finish grade only when absolutely necessary. At accessible doorways, for example, walks should be designed at about $3/8$ inch below floor elevation. Exterior walks begin to gently slope away from that required elevation when beyond the door area so as to maintain the 6-inch code-required offset.

1.4.18 Hydrostatic pressure

Additional measures must be taken to prevent hydrostatic pressure from introducing water into occupied spaces. In many coastal regions, there are areas that typically are well above the groundwater table. As a result of seasonal conditions, the water table may rise temporarily. Some soils create perched water tables, artificially keeping water locally higher than the average water table in the surrounding area. When the ground has more water than can be absorbed, it seeks relief. Often the rise can exceed 2 feet in elevation. This water will seek relief through even the smallest microscopic voids in concrete floors and walls.

There are several methods for preventing migration through walls and into a conditioned space, but the best protection is to keep the water from getting past the outside face of the wall. Two of the most common means for preventing water from getting into a wall are bentonite mats and plastic- or rubber-based impermeable sheet membranes. Some builders prefer the bentonite where the moisture levels are somewhat constant. Others rely only on the impermeable sheet membrane.

One of the inherent challenges is to prevent any punctures of the membrane. Pipes, conduit, and other required penetrations will need to be sealed properly according to manufacturers' recommendations. Whichever system is chosen, if water does find a way in, there is likely to be a void in the system. That void must be dealt with. One proven method is to inject grout into holes that were drilled in the wall or floor slab near the apparent source of the leak. Another method involves the application of crystalline coatings that change the chemistry of the interior concrete to reduce water transmission.

Even well-intentioned maintenance procedures can result in hydrostatic introduction of water at the slab edge. Some maintenance practices include frequent pressure washing of walls and walks. The proper angle for the wand would be close to the wall so that deflected water moves away from the wall. In most cases, the pressure wand is located so as to spray toward the wall, potentially degrading sealants and reflecting water into the wall cavity (see Figs. 1-38 and 1-39).

If maintenance plans are known in advance, the design team can develop a detail that will effectively prevent introduction of spray into the wall cavity. Again, go back to good geometry first. There must be a way to reduce pressure and velocity of the pressurized water spray.

Figure 1-38
Pressure washing.

Figure 1-39
Failing sealant.

1.4.19   Poor maintenance

No system or product lasts forever. Whatever the products used, there exists the need for maintenance, repair, or replacement. Some system components need more maintenance than others. Decisions made in material selections, methods of application, frequency of maintenance, and environmental forces all can affect the length of service of a waterproofing system. If we rely solely on the elastomeric coatings on our exterior stucco for water resistance, the wall surface will need recoating as the original paint loses its effectiveness.

Sealants used will need to be removed and replaced over time. Even terra-cotta roofing tile applied over a three-ply modified system will last only about 50 or maybe 100 years before it may begin to have problems. These problems typi- cally manifest as failures at valleys, copings, or where movement, water, or sunlight may have affected the membrane. If the tile is nailed, the nails can come loose over time. If copper or lead flashing is used, it may rot as a result of deposits from animals or plant materials. Operation and maintenance manuals or manufacturers' recommendations should be followed in order to keep the system components working to their fullest capacities.

Poor maintenance can manifest itself in many different ways. If one area of a building is maintained poorly, it can result in other problems. If the air-conditioning filters are not changed often enough, it can lead to condensate pan overflow or failure to cool or remove humidity from the conditioned spaces. This alone can cause bacterial growth.

If organic material is allowed to maintain contact with metal flashings (especially copper and aluminum flashing), the metals can degrade quickly. If the lawn sprinkler system is not well maintained, it can spray water into the building over time or cause hydrostatic pressure by creating an artificially perched water table. If vent fans aren't lubricated properly, extra moisture can build up in kitchen and bath areas. Poor maintenance in one area also tends to reflect on maintenance as a whole. When a building is new, everything usually works well without any care. It is typically after the first five years that things which have been ignored begin to fail. If the building heating, ventilation, and air-conditioning (HVAC) controls are not functioning properly, the air-conditioning system may not function as designed.

Maintenance that may have good intentions can have bad results too. Untrained applicators may apply sealant where water is intended to drain, effectively damming water behind the sealant. Perhaps they used the wrong paint, applying an epoxy paint to the inside face of exterior walls, which can lead to condensation at that point in the wall. They may change HVAC system settings to try to save energy, resulting in high humidity in the building. We have seen countless mechanical equipment rooms with filters that have not been changed as recommended (even with a supply of filters lying up against the wall). This can lead to reduction in air volume and reduced dehumidification. Omitted filters or filter bypass can cause cooling coils to get dirty and reduce heat transfer, raising supply air temperatures. Perhaps the exterior wall was designed as a drainage mass wall to allow moisture in and out through the face at a controlled rate. Maybe the contractor used white stucco on the face with a 4.0 perm rating block sealer on the concrete masonry unit (CMU) wall below. After 10 years, the wall may have been discolored, or the owner may have gotten tired of pressure washing it. Maybe the painter used an elastomeric paint, effectively trapping water behind the coating and prohibiting drying to the outside. We have seen outside air grills closed off, heaters turned off, bypass valves closed off, foam sprayed on leaking roof membranes, and all kinds of other well-intentioned but short-sighted maintenance actions affecting envelope performance.

1.4.20   Reliance upon sealants

This is an area where we have seen a lot of localized water intrusion problems. Since the science behind our industry has advanced so greatly in the past 40 years, the materials we have available today are far superior to any in history. Sealants have better adhesion and elongation properties and wider temperature ranges. We have begun to rely on technology more than in times past, to the point where sealants are being relied on to stop water. We see 30-story condo towers with 2-inch sealant joints as the only means of protection against water intrusion at window and door jambs. When coupled with the changes in design philosophy (more negative detailing) and increased labor costs, we can begin to understand the move toward reliance on sealants to solve design issues. "Beat to fit and caulk to match" has become a common attitude among builders.

With the better, more specialized chemistry in the makeup of sealants today comes an increased need for understanding. It has become more difficult to match the specialized sealants with each condition in a building. Designers must take care to specify the proper sealant product for the job, not just in color and number of years in the warranty period. Some of these sealants cannot be used if they are to be in contact with certain other materials. Some react with copper, some with paint, and many of them with waterproof membranes. Active ingredients may include solvents that react with paints.

The area and surfaces of the materials being sealed are important too. Many manufacturers will limit the gap being filled to $^3/_4$ inch, whereas others can be used to fill a 3-inch gap. There are three forms of sealant joints, and the geometry of the joint is critical to the success of each. Sealants should be shaped like an hourglass in section to best maximize adhesion to end surfaces and to reduce transmission of forces in the bonds (see Fig. 1-40). Properties of sealants vary greatly, and the selection should be matched to the operating conditions and stresses. Chapter 4 provides an overview of sealant design. Some sealants can be driven over with a fork lift without compressing. Others will elongate more than 400 percent. Birds and insects will pick out some types of sealants. If the designer or builder relies only on sealants to close the void in a joint, he or she has to consider providing access to the location for future replacement. Sealants fail. Consider the maintenance crew, schedule, and skill set before you decide to rely on sealants. Flashings should be designed to protect sealant joints and to reduce exposure to UV light, wind, and the force of rain. Then, when the sealant fails, less water will get into the wall or parapet cavity.

Figure 1-40
Sealant shape.

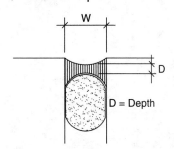

1.4.21 Wrong material for the job

Too often the wrong material is used. Recently we heard of a contractor proposing a substitution request to use an air infiltration barrier in lieu of the specified waterproof membrane under asphalt shingles on a 3-in-12 pitched roof. Proper match of material for each job is very important. Some subcontractors want to use 15-pound felt as an air infiltration barrier. In some conditions, designers rely on details which allow water vapor exfiltration, whereas others do not. The design may call for vented sidewall roofing membrane, soffit vents, ridge vents, AIBs, or a series of materials used in concert. Some contractors accidentally omit the vents or use the wrong roofing membrane. Some may try to rush the job and forget to order a long-lead item far enough in advance. This can lead to the use of substitutions that are not equivalent to originally specified materials, or worse—omission of a key component.

We have heard of subcontractors installing foil-faced fiberglass insulation where unfaced insulation was called for. Others have used galvanized furring strips where pressure-treated wood was shown on the plans. In both cases, condensation occurred at the cool face, and bacterial growth began. The right material is important for every job, whether we are talking about major components such as the air conditioner or roof system or small items such as the right kind of tape or screws. Builders need to be detail-oriented. Designers have to know a lot about materials and methods. Both have great responsibility and, today, great liability. The two teams need to work together to have the best chance for success.

Contractors need to ask questions, especially if they see something that looks out of the ordinary. The way the question is worded will have an impact on the way the designer receives the question and ultimately answers it. Try not to make it sound like finger pointing or ridicule. It often helps if alternate solutions are provided, along with an explanation of what is perceived to be deficient in the original detail.

Architects often rely on guidance from specialists on many topics. Due to the complexity of the projects these days, building systems are getting pretty specialized as well. The complexity of the building envelope can cause even well-intentioned installers problems. For example, let us imagine the design for a concrete block wall with stucco over lath on 15-pound felt. Assume that the wall was designed to allow moisture to penetrate the stucco and block, where the CMU was to absorb a limited amount of water and dry back to the outside after a rain event. Maybe it was designed as a mass wall with no insulation. Specified paint was to be latex inside and out. Now let us imagine further that the builder wanted to improve the design. Maybe he or she changed the paint to enamel on the outside and epoxy on the inside (both vapor barriers). This would tend to increase the potential for condensation in winter or summer and could trap moisture in the wall. Not good!

1.4.22   Exposure to ultraviolet (UV) radiation during construction

Several products we use in construction are negatively affected by exposure to weather. Many roof underlayments and air and vapor retarders should be limited to less than 30 days of exposure to UV rays. The warranty may be voided, and the membrane could crack and fail sooner than usual. Manufacturers' recommendations typically state the duration and types of exposure that are acceptable without significant impact on the product's performance. Most roof underlayments rely on the final surface product to keep damaging UV rays from degrading them. If a membrane's exposure exceeds manufacturer's recommendations, you should remove and replace it. Putting a second layer on could lead to problems you haven't considered. Pay attention to flashings in relation to membrane placement. An exception might be a fiberglass roof dry-in membrane for shingles or a tile roof. We will typically use a 30-pound felt instead of the minimal 15-pound felt if we know that it is likely to be left exposed for longer than 30 days. Then, right before the finish material is applied, a new overlay of membrane (perhaps 15-pound at this point) would suffice. You may need to remove and reattach the flashings after the new membrane is applied. The concern is that you are deviating from the original permeability of the system as designed. Perhaps that permeability is critical to drying of the ceiling cavity. Ask the designer before changing the permeability of any components or adding additional layers.

1.4.23 Failed roofing products

This may be one of the most expected problems. Whether it is the ridge vent that came loose from high winds and tree branches or cracked, broken, or missing roof tiles (see Fig. 1-41), a roof needs to be considered a holistic system. If one or more components of the system are not working properly, the system is at risk for failure. For a big commercial project, there could be 20 or more components interacting that can affect the outcome. It can begin with uneven settling at the foundation. Perhaps the spans were too great for the roof beams or joists, causing too much deflection. There can be problems with the lightweight concrete cracking. If batched or applied wrong or if not engineered to limit problems caused by thermal expansion, the concrete may crack, causing a chain of events above it.

Figure 1-41
Cracked or missing roof tile.

The tapered insulation may have been applied too thick for the fasteners. Insulation boards may not have been applied properly. Perhaps it was raining or the slurry was sitting in the drum too long. Maybe the bag mix got rained on previously. Maybe there was a loss of power, and materials were not placed in a timely manner. The project may have been designed for 90 mile an hour winds and seen 125 mile an hour wind-driven rains. Perhaps the base sheet was applied too early, trapping excessive moisture under the membrane. Maybe the wrong type of decking was used. The basis of design may have been vented metal decking, and it may not have been installed as such. Perhaps the crew installing the flashings went to lunch, and another crew came in to finish without sufficient knowledge of the product. Maybe it started raining during the mopping-in of the roof plies.

There are countless reasons why the system can fail later. Perhaps a bad batch of product was manufactured that month. Some of the rolls of material could have been stored improperly, causing flat spots in roll goods that prevented full flat adhesion. Perhaps the vents were not installed properly. Maybe there were skylights that showed up late and got installed out of sequence. This can lead to membrane lap issues, patching, and potential problems. Maybe the roof curbs were installed $1/2$ inch too low. Perhaps sill pans were damaged during installation (see Fig. 1-42) or holes were drilled in them that went unnoticed.

Figure 1-42
Sill Pan damaged during construction.

There can be inadequate ventilation in the roof cavity; maybe the birds picked out all the sealant at the precast copings. The masons may have punctured the membrane with rolling scaffolding. Maybe everything was done according to the manufacturer's recommendations, and it still failed. Perhaps the primer used to seal the seams had been stored in too much heat. The best way to prevent roof leaks is by paying attention to details and executing the installation to the best of everyone's abilities.

1.4.24   Reliance on coatings instead of membranes

During the late 1980s, we saw an increase in energy costs that led to an increase in the use of insulated roof coatings on low-slope roofs. You can find them on many schools and commercial buildings, often applied directly over tar and gravel systems. The old tar and gravel roof may have been leaking. There could have been localized patches. The application of foamed-on roof coatings had two common immediate results. It lowered short-term operational costs as a result of the added insulating value. This was achieved by lowered cooling and heating bills. It also temporarily reduced roof leaks.

The down side of this was often not discovered for a few years. Many of these roof coatings used a two-part foam that formed a skin where exposed to the air at the surface. Unfortunately, some of these foams were not fully mixed during application. This resulted in a continuous expansion of portions of the foam. The off-gassing of the curing also created bubbles above the roof. These bubbles eventually exceeded the material's elastic properties and popped. Some of these foam products are not really a closed-cell foam, meaning that there were small pathways for water to migrate through the foam. The water would find its way down to the original roof. If there were voids or failed patches in the original roof, this water would find its way into the ceiling cavity. It would be impossible to tell from below where the membrane was leaking.

Many building owners were forced to keep patching the foam topping by cutting out a portion of the affected area of foam and reapplying the same product. As a result of the physical nature of the system, other patching products have a difficult time adhering to the silicon skin. If the roof membrane were leak-tight prior to application of the foam, the building would not be experiencing these problems.

There are countless other examples where a coating is used in lieu of a membrane. Generally, membranes perform better than coatings. A few examples are below-grade exterior wall membranes and flat-roof systems. In exposed, accessible flat-surface applications, sheet membrane system applications place less importance on the performance of the installer than liquid applied coatings. For hard-to-reach places or horizontal areas with a lot of corners, liquid applied coatings depend less on the skill of the applicator, and are therefore utilized.

For sealing roof penetrations, the traditional solution was to use pitch pans filled with liquid roofing products such as hot tar or modified asphalt. New liquid products have much better long-term performance, such as the hybrid silicon and elastomer compounds. Many waterproofing experts still prefer metal flashing applications over liquid-filled pans (see Fig. 1-43). Figure 1-44 shows a poor example of a pitch pan used to seal a roof penetration. Sealants were added to the liquid applied roofing product as leaks were observed over time. Details like this are why owners prefer a properly installed penetration with sheet membranes.

1.4.25 A series of bad decisions and/or other forces

Sometimes failures can be the result of bad decisions. We may specify the wrong product or apply the wrong detail to a condition. There have been designs that

Figure 1-43
Pipe penetration detail using a pitch pan and collar flashing.

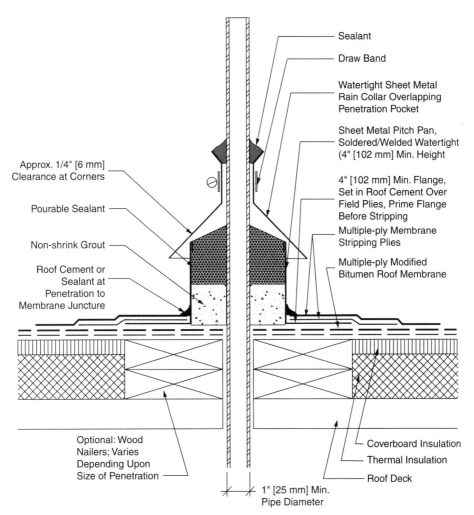

Figure 1-44
Photo of pitch pan as
installed.

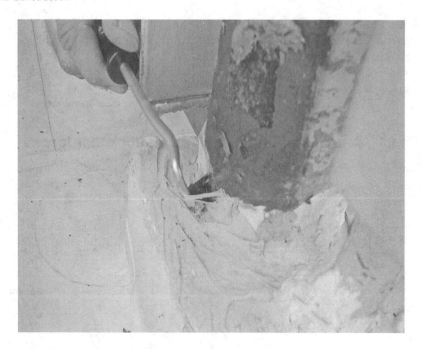

worked in one location that get imported into a project located in a different climate. If this happens in the early stages of the design process, there should be a system of checks and balances in place to prevent the poor decision from being built. Other examples could include finish grade above finish floor (without proper detailing), omission of crickets on roofing against vertical surfaces (such as chimneys), improper flashing design, lack of protection above windows and doors or louvers, inadequate ventilation, undersized air-conditioning equipment leading to a negative-pressure building, bad value engineering, etc.

There can be hundreds of reasons for a poorly performing building. It usually requires a combination of bad decisions and poor construction to create an indoor air-quality problem over time. Let's make up an example of decisions made in the process of design that could lead to a problem building. In our make-believe project, let's imagine a $40 million mixed-use building. Let us imagine that it is to be built on the Atlantic Coast. During schematic design, it is detailed using a primary structural steel post and beam system with $3^5/_8$-inch light-gauge stud exterior infill walls. It is assumed to have $3^1/_2$ inches of insulation in the walls, exterior fiberglass sheathing, vapor barrier, air infiltration barrier, and rough stucco over lath.

It was designed to use long overhangs on a hip roof to shade the east and south glass sliding doors and walls. The mechanical design was done assuming insulated tinted glass, R30 minimum roof insulation, and existing vegetation to block late-afternoon sun from west walls. The developer wanted to have gas water heaters with solar cells.

Let us imagine that the cost of construction went up 15 percent during the next four-month period of design. The developer already pre-sold the units based on schematic estimates with a 4 percent escalation estimate built in. Does this sound possible or maybe even familiar up to this point? Our pretend developer made the decision to try to cut 10 percent of the initial cost to make up a big chunk of the escalation. It seems that the price of steel went up the most, so the project changed to load-bearing concrete block exterior walls. This only saved 6 percent, so the team next had to save on something else. The next decision affected the roof. Instead of three-ply modified bitumen, the contractor changed to single-ply EPDM roofing and saved another 2 percent of project cost. One more value-engineering offer accepted was to change from rough three-coat to a new one-coat stucco system. The developer decided to pay the last 2 percent out of his 5 percent contingency budget (this is what contingency lines are for, isn't it)?

At the end of design development, the team had the bidders go through the pricing check again. It seems that the more completed scope shown on the design development documents cost another $1,350,000. Now what can the team do? More value-engineering (cost cutting) decisions were made. The first one cut back the roof overhangs, and the second deleted the furring, vapor, and air infiltration barriers on the exterior walls, placing the one-coat stucco right on the block walls. The trade-off is to rely on a high-quality elastomeric paint to limit moisture in the building.

Guess what! These changes were not made known to the mechanical designer, who instead was asked to try to cut a few hundred thousand dollars from the air-conditioning system costs. Since he had oversized the coils, the designer agreed to reduce the tonnage by a half ton per unit. Insulation on ducting was reduced from 2 to 1 inch on supply ducts. Insulation was reduced to R20 average in the roof. Do you see a pattern developing here? The project reaches the 100 percent contract documents phase and goes into construction just 3 percent over budget. The developer decides to proceed knowing that he might have to pay the overage but commits the $300,000 out of his contingency budget, leaving him just about $50,000 in contingency remaining.

During the subcontract award phase, the contractor realizes that he didn't cover all the underground piping scope on the civil and plumbing drawings. So the contractor's contingency budget is almost gone too. The mechanical contractor offers his own value engineering (VE), offering a savings of more than $350,000 to go to a lower-cost, lower-seasonal-energy-efficient-ratio (SEER) system instead of the designed system. Things are looking better to the contractor, who was worried about his rising costs affecting his profit margin. What else can go wrong?

Now it seems that the roofing contractor cannot bond the job. The second-low bidder was $400,000 higher than the apparent low bidder. It seems that the roofer was selling his business and used the job to sweeten his selling price to the ultimate buyer. Things were starting to back up on the job site, and finally, the contractor and owner were forced to take a hit and award the roofing to the second-low bidder. The drywall contractor is pushing the schedule, needing to maintain the original schedule to meet other commitments. The window subcontractor was late getting his submittals together. As often happens, a huge summer storm is approaching. The roof sheathing is almost done, and the roofer hasn't even gotten his contract signed yet. The general contractor decides to proceed with the roof sheathing and dries it in with his own staff of framing carpenters.

In order to maintain the schedule, the general contractor authorizes the drywall subcontractor to begin hanging drywall. The special-order insulated windows are still eight weeks out. The contractor submits a substitute window that he can get in two weeks. The stucco contractor starts applying stucco to the exterior block.

The storm hits, and it rains for four days. Only a little of the drywall gets soaked when a portion of the dry-in membrane comes loose and blows off. In another corner, the window openings allowed wind-blown rain to soak the drywall stacked on the floor. Are the warning flags going up yet? Before now, every experienced project leader should have already become concerned. An entire series of decisions is combining with natural forces to create potential future problems.

Rather than continue to follow every step of the way, let's jump to the conclusion. The first year there were no big problems reported. A few windows leaked, and one roof leak occurred during a tropical storm. The builder takes care of them because the building is still under warranty. A little caulk and some roofing cement later, things seem to be going well. Then the trees died. It seems the roots were cut during site utility work. The trees were replaced by 4-inch caliper oaks and 20-foot palms. Obviously, they don't provide much shade. The next summer was a hot, humid summer. The temperature stayed over 98°F for three straight days, and the humidity was 100 percent. Then the rainy season started. Did we mention that the cheaper windows used were not insulated?

To make things worse, the stucco installed on the parapets damaged the single-ply membrane. The flashings were not put in in the right sequence of construction, so when the rain came in sideways, it overflowed the flashing and soaked the roof insulation. The mold started growing in the walls and around the windows on the exterior wall surfaces. When power was lost for three days, the bacterial growth was accelerated. When the owners got power back, the undersized air-conditioning system could not get the moisture out fast enough. Guess what happened next? The building owners sued the developer, builder, and architect. You can see where a series of decisions made during the heat of the construction process can lead to future problems. This is where a system of checks and balances can help to prevent catastrophic failure. In many projects, the inclusion of a water-proofing consulting firm to the processes of design and construction can reduce or even avoid such disastrous results. At a minimum, have a peer review of your planned details reviewed by someone with years of proven experience in the building type and climate. The relatively small investment in review services prior to construction begins may prevent time and money lost later.

2 Water Intrusion and Mold

2.1 A PICTURE IS WORTH A MILLION DOLLARS

A picture used to be worth a 1,000 words. With the recent increase in litigation related to mold and mildew, we believe that a good picture (illustration) may be worth millions. A lawsuit on a commercial building can exceed $10 million for remedial work alone. If the architect can show that he or she provided good design and proven details that have successfully prevented water intrusion and mold in similar projects, then the courts may choose not to find fault with the architect. Imagine that the contractor has documented evidence that the building was well built, with better-than-industry-standard water test results for the roof, window, and wall systems, as well as the building air-conditioning system. Might the courts have a hard time proving either of them at fault and perhaps find someone else to pay the price? What could be better than that? How about avoiding the problems and lawsuits altogether. Well-conceived design and clearly communicated architectural detailing can lead to fewer problems in building construction, operation, and maintenance.

Today, more developers and builders are willing to make the commitment of time and money required to prevent indoor environmental quality problems, such as mold and mildew, through proper application of materials in the proper sequences. At the same time, labor and materials costs are escalating. In some areas, such as China and the southern United States, buildings are going up at a record pace. This increased demand is causing an infusion of workers with little or no training in the building trades in these areas. To make matters more challenging, many workers don't speak the same language as their supervisors or the language in which the drawings were done. This places a large burden on leadership in design, construction, and development firms. In a business where thousands of decisions are made for a single building and where one missed membrane or improper lap can lead to millions of dollars worth of problems years later, what can we all do?

Throughout this illustrated guide, we will discuss the importance of teamwork and cooperation among all the participants in the building process. We have found that the best recipe for success is a series of sound decisions made throughout the processes of design and construction that keep in mind the basic principles contained in this book using gravity, geometry, and technology (in that order of importance, please).

Regardless of the style of the building, the budget, or even the location, there are common ways that we all design a building envelope. Gravity always will be acting in the same general direction. We all must use the force of gravity to help our building envelopes perform as intended. Whether we are talking about resisting live and dead loads, stack effect, temperature and pressure of gases or raindrops falling on a roof, gravity is the single most constant physical force that acts on all buildings. Gravity, therefore, is the first thing to consider as we design our buildings. This applies at all levels from the location of the building on the site to the way the ground slopes away from the front door and walls (see Fig. 2-1). Gravity affects the slope of the roof, the direction and lapping of materials, and much more.

Other physical forces are less consistent than gravity, such as sun and wind, making it more difficult to fully consider them through design and construction. Throughout this book, we talk about the benefits of using geometry and applied technologies to combat the forces of the natural environment. We explain the relationship between the geometry of flashings and their ability to keep water out of joints or penetrations (see Fig. 2-2). We discuss ways and means to take advantage of gravity and geometry to reduce the force of wind-driven water and ultimately to prevent liquid water from defeating the building

Figure 2-1

Slope grades away from the building.

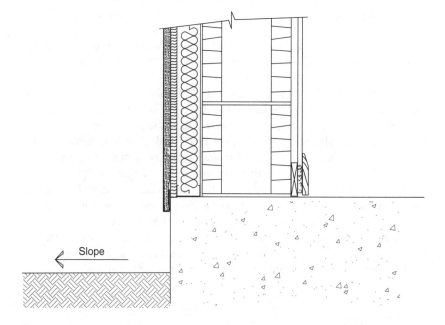

Slope

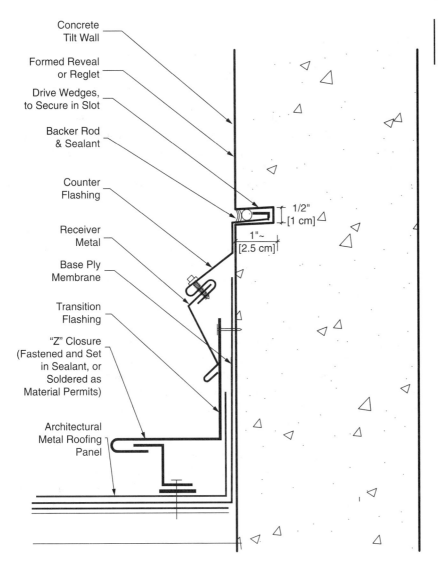

Concrete Tilt Wall

Formed Reveal or Reglet

Drive Wedges, to Secure in Slot

Backer Rod & Sealant

Counter Flashing

Receiver Metal

Base Ply Membrane

Transition Flashing

"Z" Closure (Fastened and Set in Sealant, or Soldered as Material Permits)

Architectural Metal Roofing Panel

1/2" [1 cm]

1"~ [2.5 cm]

Figure 2-2
Flashing geometry to prevent water intrusion.

envelope. Gravity and geometry are the primary forces to be considered for the slope of the roof and selection of roofing materials such as modified bitumen or shingles. In addition, these forces are instrumental in determining the lengths of laps in applied waterproof membranes such as fiberglass or felt underlayment, as well as heights of skylight flashings and door thresholds.

We introduce the premise of relying on available technologies as a final line of defense against water intrusion, vapor migration, and condensation. By technology, we mean powered systems, such as ventilation or air-conditioning, and chemically engineered systems, such as self-adhesive membranes, backer rod, and sealants. It is our belief that technology needs to play a significant but tertiary role in building envelope performance as it relies upon variables such as the reliance on electricity, maintenance, repair and replacement, or proper operation for it to perform its intended function. We recommend strongly that sealants are not relied on as the only line of defense against water intrusion!

We are calling this manuscript an illustrated guide for many reasons. Without pictures, it would take too many words. With pictures, it crosses the language barrier. With clear pictures, there is reduced possibility for misinterpretation by the person in the field. One can see the location of each of the critical components in a successful cavity wall system. We have seen the benefit of large-scale details in practice and of holistic coordination of trades in the field. Our clients have benefited from reduced numbers of change orders during construction and in significant reductions in operation and maintenance costs over time.

We believe that by following our guide, you will be able to apply a systematic approach to any family of building-type decisions as they apply to building envelope performance. Included in the guide, you will find numerous examples of plan and section details that have been time tested to provide good levels of water and vapor protection against the elements.

We also provide some examples of good and bad details for the same condition so that you can all see the difference a small change can make. While no one in the world is perfect, we have found that if all the people in the chain do their best to apply sound practices, the end result will have few significant failures. By working together with the developer, designer, contractor, and installer, all working toward the same stated goal (and at the same time learning from each other), we can all continue to build better and better buildings for centuries to come.

The decisions made in relation to the building envelope will determine how well the systems perform over time even more than how the building will appear when finished. As designers and builders, we must make informed decisions that lead to the creation of a built environment that will stand the test of time and lead to long-lasting relationships with developers and clients of all kinds. Our most important clients are the public who live in and around our buildings.

2.2 MOLD AND HOW TO STOP MOLD GROWTH

We need to design and construct buildings to prevent the intrusion of water. Now we know that this sounds like a very simple statement, one we presume that at least most of you will agree with. But all too often water has created problems in the past. As you get farther into this book, we will discuss just what those problems are and what caused them. By studying causes of past problems, we should be able to better prevent them in the future.

As most of you know, water is made from two of our most common elements, hydrogen and oxygen. Water is sometimes referred to as the *universal solvent* due to the wide variety of materials that can be dissolved in water. As it relates

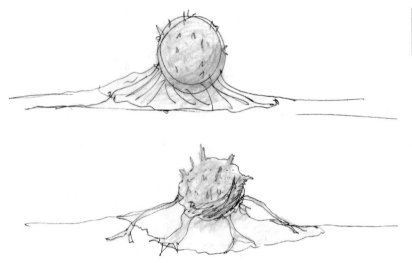

Figure 2-3
Mold is a single-celled organism.

Figure 2-4
Mold spores extend hyphae.

to the topic of this book, water is also necessary for survival and growth of nearly every life form on earth. This certainly holds true for mold.

What is mold? Mold is a single-celled organism that comes from spores (see Fig. 2-3). Mold spores are very small and light. Their two most common means of movement are by hitchhiking or by becoming airborne. The spores can land on surfaces during construction or may be carried in by wind, on animal hair or human clothing. They can lie dormant for a long period of time, waiting for an opportunity to grow. They thrive in the same general temperature range as humans, from about 40 to 100°F. Only in the presence of oxygen, nutrients, and moisture can most reproduce.

Spores rely on moisture to dissolve food to fuel their growth and reproduction. If the surfaces they come to rest on do not provide food, then they cannot grow. Spores can lie dormant for a long time. In the presence of food and water, the spores will germinate, producing filaments called *hyphae* (see Fig. 2-4). If the hyphae have a sustained source of food and moisture (typically for more than 48 hours), they will continue to grow and change appearance. As hyphae grow, they extend their filaments in all directions to form a protective layer (see Fig. 2-5).

A portion of the hyphae root into the surface on which the spore came to rest, whereas others form a protective shield around them. This works to keep the roots moist, even if the air around them dries out. In the final stage, the mold grows a kind of bloom, called *conidia* (see Fig. 2-6). When the conidia reach a certain point, they generate and release spores into the surrounding air.

We cannot live in an environment without water or oxygen. What we can do is try to limit the concentration of spores, limit the amount of nutrients in and on surfaces where spores may come to rest, and limit the moisture in contact with those surfaces.

Figure 2-5

As hyphae grow, they form a protective layer.

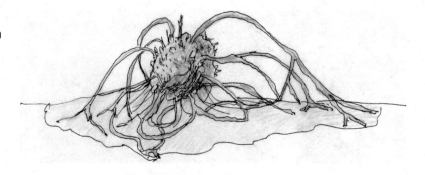

Figure 2-6

Final stage of growth, release of new spores.

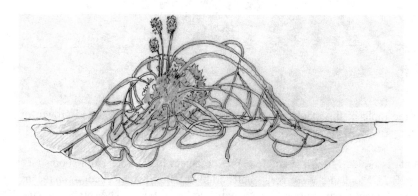

2.2.1   Limiting the spores

Spores come into our built environments during and after construction. The best way to limit spores during construction is to keep things under protective cover until they are installed and the building air-conditioning system is on. Stored materials, especially those containing organic materials such as cement, wood, and paper products, should be kept clean and dry. In addition, we can wipe exposed materials often and vacuum floors and other horizontal surfaces. Before hanging drywall, we can wipe all exposed surfaces with a dilute solution of chlorinated water and let them dry fully. Before assembling ductwork sections, we can clean the surfaces, especially those that will be in the airstream.

After the building is dried in, we can continue to try to minimize the admittance of spores. Keep doors and windows closed. Use the leeward doors to enter the building. Use garages or warehouses to store materials. Wipe materials before bringing them in. Use walk mats. Try to keep pets and other animals from the building. Clear away brush from the building proximity. Use construction filters on return and outside air makeup. Change these filters often. Make a conscious effort to keep the building clean during construction. At least once a week (Friday is a great time for this activity), clean the entire project using a vacuum rather than sweeping. Brooms raise the dust, letting air currents move the spores to new surfaces. If you must sweep, use the specially formulated sweeping compounds that minimize airborne dust and pollutants.

2.2.2 Limiting nutrients

This begins with specifying the right materials. Designers may have to spend more time researching and writing new materials into our specifications, but the results are worth it. A good rule of thumb is that if it ever grew, it probably still contains nutrients. If it is open-celled, it can absorb nutrients from the surroundings, such as dirt and dust, and it may fuel growth. Products that contain cotton, jute, paper, or wood provide nutrients. Many synthetic materials, such as nylon, fiberglass, as well as glass, and metal, do not provide fuel for growth. Some wood is less conducive to mold growth than others. If wood is used, we must consider how to protect it, such as using paint or other coatings that effectively prevent spores from being fueled. Manufacturers provide material safety data sheets (MSDSs) and material product data sheets to inform users of the contents of materials (see Fig. 2-7). Something that is high in volatile organic compounds (VOCs) would be something to avoid. Most organic compounds are acceptable forms of nutrients for mold growth. Keep food and drinks out of the building envelope. Never permit waste products to remain in wall framing.

During construction, workers can help to minimize nutrients introduced into the building by keeping materials covered when stored, uncovering them when inside, and covering work. Covering work in place can keep dust and dirt from settling on it. Sometimes work from other trades cause small particles to be carried by the air moving inside the building, bringing sawdust, drywall compound, or paint with it. Sawdust, spray fireproofing, and most paints make great food for spores.

2.2.3 Limiting moisture

Moisture must be limited at every phase of construction. How many times have you seen building materials delivered long before they are needed? And how many times have you seen stacks of lumber or cubes of masonry products left uncovered during a rainstorm? Until recently, we never could put our finger on exactly why it bothered us so. Not only does uncovered material have a good chance of getting dirty (see above), but in most climates it is probably going to get wet. Yes, masonry should not be "dry" when set, but neither should it get wet a week or a month before it is used.

Block that gets wet by the rain or, worse, sits in a big pond in the yard after a rainstorm has a potential for growing spores into mold before you even put the roof on. We recommend that you try hard to keep the masonry as dry as possible until an hour or two before it gets laid and then wet it with clean water that you know has no dirt or spores in it. The same goes for exterior plywood or treated-wood products. They should never be allowed to get wet, and if they do, they should be dried thoroughly. We don't mean that it has to be stored in a dehumidified warehouse, although a warehouse is a great idea. Many clients will pay for materials up front in order to limit inflation and reduce the risk of potential shortages. If it rains on the slab, sweep and shop vacuum it off before placing wood or concrete walls. Limit the moisture content. Protect work from

Figure 2-7
MSDSs and product data.

Product Information
Silicone
Sealants

DOW CORNING

Dow Corning® 795
Silicone Building Sealant

FEATURES

- Suitable for most new construction and remedial sealing applications
- Versatile – high performance structural glazing and weathersealing from a single product
- Available in 11 standard colors; custom colors also available

BENEFITS

- Excellent weatherability – virtually unaffected by sunlight, rain, snow, ozone, and temperature extremes of -40°F (-40°C) to 300°F (149°C)
- Excellent unprimed adhesion to a wide variety of construction materials and building components, including anodized, alodined, most coated, and many *Kynar*®[1]-painted aluminums[2]
- Ease of application – ready to use as supplied
- Ease of use – all-temperature gunnability, easy tooling and low-odor cure byproduct
- Meets global standards (Americas, Asia, and Europe)

COMPOSITION

- One-part, neutral-cure, RTV silicone sealant

Neutral, one-part silicone sealant

APPLICATIONS

- Structural and nonstructural glazing
- Structural attachment of many panel systems
- Panel stiffener applications
- Weathersealing of most common construction materials including glass, aluminum, steel, painted metal, EIFS, granite and other stone, concrete, brick, and plastics

TYPICAL PROPERTIES

Specification Writers: Please contact your local Dow Corning Sales Application Engineer or Dow Corning Customer Service before writing specifications on this product.

Method	Test	Unit	Result
As Supplied			
ASTM C 679	Tack-Free Time, 50% RH	hours	3
	Curing Time at 25°C (77°F) and 50% RH	days	7–14
	Full Adhesion	days	14–21
ASTM C 639	Flow, Sag, or Slump	inches (mm)	0.1 (2.54)
	Working Time	minutes	20–30
	VOC Content[1]	g/L	28
As Cured–After 21 days at 25°C (77°F) and 50% RH			
ASTM D 2240	Durometer Hardness, Shore A	points	35
ASTM C 794	Peel Strength	lb/in (kg/cm)	32 (5.7)
ASTM C 1135	Tensile Adhesion Strength		
	at 25% extension	psi (MPa)	45 (0.310)
	at 50% extension	psi (MPa)	60 (0.414)
ASTM C 719	Joint Movement Capability	percent	±50
ASTM C 1248	Staining (granite, marble, lime-stone, brick, and concrete)		None
As Cured – After 21 days at 25°C (77°F) and 50% RH followed by 10,000 hours in a QUV weatherometer, ASTM G 53			
ASTM C 1135	Tensile Adhesion Strength		
	at 25% extension	psi (MPa)	35 (0.241)
	at 50% extension	psi (MPa)	50 (0.345)

[1]Based on South Coast Air Quality Management District of California. Maximum VOC is listed both inclusive and exclusive of water and exempt compounds. For a VOC data sheet for a specific sealant color, please send your request to product.inquiry@dowcorning.com.

DESCRIPTION

Dow Corning® 795 Silicone Building Sealant is a one-part, neutral-cure, architectural-grade sealant that easily extrudes in any weather and cures quickly at room temperature.

This cold-applied, non-sagging silicone material cures to a medium-modulus silicone rubber upon exposure to atmospheric moisture. The cured sealant is durable and flexible enough to accommodate ±50 percent movement of original joint dimension when installed

in a properly designed weatherseal joint. In a properly designed structurally glazed joint, the sealant is strong enough to support glass and other panel materials under high windload.

APPROVALS/SPECIFICATIONS

Dow Corning 795 Silicone Building Sealant meets the requirements of:

- Federal Specification TT-S-001543A (COM-NBS) Class A for silicone building sealants
- Federal Specification TT-S-00230C

[1]*Kynar* is a trademark of Atofina Chemicals Inc.
[2]Contact your local Dow Corning Sales Application Engineer for specifics.

- (COM-NBS) Class A for one-component building sealants
- ASTM Specification C 920 Type S, Grade NS, Class 50, Use NT, G, A, and O
- ASTM Specification C 1184 for structural silicone sealants
- Canadian Specification CAN2-19.13-M82

COLORS

Dow Corning 795 Silicone Building Sealant is available in 11 colors: black, white, gray, limestone, bronze, sandstone, adobe tan, dusty rose, rustic brick, blue spruce, and charcoal. Custom colors may be ordered to match virtually any substrate.

HOW TO USE

Please consult the *Dow Corning Americas Technical Manual*, Form No. 62-1112, for detailed information on state-of-the-art application methods and joint design. Please contact your local Dow Corning Sales Application Engineer for specific advice.

Preparation

Clean all joints, removing all foreign matter and contaminants such as grease, oil, dust, water, frost, surface dirt, old sealants or glazing compounds, and protective coatings.

Application Method

Install backing material or joint filler, setting blocks, spacer shims and tapes. Mask areas adjacent to joints to ensure neat sealant lines. Primer is generally not required on non-porous surfaces, but may be necessary for optimal sealing of certain porous surfaces. A test placement is always recommended. Apply *Dow Corning* 795 Silicone Building Sealant in a continuous operation using positive pressure. (The sealant can be applied using many types of air-operated guns and most types of bulk dispensing equipment.) Before a skin forms (typically within 15 minutes), tool the sealant with light pressure to spread the sealant against the backing material and

joint surfaces. Remove masking tape as soon as the bead is tooled.

HANDLING PRECAUTIONS

PRODUCT SAFETY INFORMATION REQUIRED FOR SAFE USE IS NOT INCLUDED IN THIS DOCUMENT. BEFORE HANDLING, READ PRODUCT AND MATERIAL SAFETY DATA SHEETS AND CONTAINER LABELS FOR SAFE USE, PHYSICAL AND HEALTH HAZARD INFORMATION. THE MATERIAL SAFETY DATA SHEET IS AVAILABLE ON THE DOW CORNING WEBSITE AT WWW.DOWCORNING.COM, OR FROM YOUR DOW CORNING SALES APPLICATION ENGINEER, OR DISTRIBUTOR, OR BY CALLING DOW CORNING CUSTOMER SERVICE.

USABLE LIFE AND STORAGE

When stored at or below 27°C (80°F), *Dow Corning* 795 Silicone Building Sealant has a shelf life of 12 months from the date of manufacture. Refer to product packaging for "Use By Date."

PACKAGING

Dow Corning 795 Silicone Building Sealant is supplied in 10.3-fl oz (305-mL) disposable plastic cartridges that fit ordinary caulking guns, 20-fl oz (590-mL) sausages and 2- and 4.5-gal (7.5- and 17-L) bulk containers.

LIMITATIONS

Dow Corning 795 Silicone Building Sealant should not be used:
- In structural applications without prior review and approval by your local Dow Corning Sales Application Engineer
- In below-grade applications
- When surface temperatures exceed 50°C (122°F) during installation
- On surfaces that are continuously immersed in water
- On building materials that bleed oils, plasticizers or solvents that may affect adhesion
- On frost-laden or wet surfaces
- In totally confined joints (the sealant requires atmospheric moisture for cure)
- If the sealant is intended to be painted (paints do not typically adhere to most silicone sealants)
- To surfaces in direct contact with food or other food-grade applications

This product is neither tested nor represented as suitable for medical or pharmaceutical uses.

HEALTH AND ENVIRONMENTAL INFORMATION

To support customers in their product safety needs, Dow Corning has an extensive Product Stewardship organization and a team of Product Safety and Regulatory Compliance (PS&RC) specialists available in each area.

For further information, please see our website, www.dowcorning.com, or consult your local Dow Corning Sales Application Engineer.

LIMITED WARRANTY INFORMATION – PLEASE READ CAREFULLY

The information contained herein is offered in good faith and is believed to be accurate. However, because conditions and methods of use of our products are beyond our control, this information should not be used in substitution for customer's tests to ensure that Dow Corning's products are safe, effective, and fully satisfactory for the intended end use. Suggestions of use shall not be taken as inducements to infringe any patent.

Dow Corning's sole warranty is that the product will meet the Dow Corning sales specifications in effect at the time of shipment.

Your exclusive remedy for breach of such warranty is limited to refund of purchase price or replacement of any product shown to be other than as warranted.

DOW CORNING SPECIFICALLY DISCLAIMS ANY OTHER EXPRESS OR IMPLIED WARRANTY OF FITNESS FOR A PARTICULAR PURPOSE OR MERCHANTABILITY.

DOW CORNING DISCLAIMS LIABILITY FOR ANY INCIDENTAL OR CONSEQUENTIAL DAMAGES.

A 20-year Weatherseal Limited Warranty is available. Some testing may be required. Consult your Dow Corning Sales Application Engineer for details.

Printed in USA
Form No. 61-885L-01   AGP6877

Dow Corning is a registered trademark of Dow Corning Corporation.
©2000-2004 Dow Corning Corporation. All rights reserved.

getting wet after installation. Design and construct buildings so as to limit rain's impact on completed portions of the work. If stored materials do get wet, dry them as soon as practical (preferably less than 24 hours).

There are three different ways water moves in walls: gravity, pressure, and capillary action. Gravity is a constant force, one that we can count on when we design details that use it to our advantage in preventing water intrusion. By pressure, we mean forces other than gravity, such as wind. Wind-driven water can strike the exterior walls and reflect at any angle. Another force is momentum, the tendency for any mass in motion to remain in motion until acted on by another force. The third way water moves in walls is by capillary action, by wicking through porous materials. This occurs as a result of differences in saturation, temperature, or pressure.

Where does the water come from? Most water comes from rain, but it can result from condensation on cool surfaces, from leaks in pipes, from surface drainage, from subterranean infiltration or from use of water in everyday activities. Showers, cooking, mopping hard surfaces, carpet cleaning, and pressure washing are the most common activities with water leakage potential. Condensation is caused by vapor (water molecules in gaseous air) changing temperature and/or pressure to a point where it changes phase from vapor into liquid water. The temperature is called the *dew point*, the point at which gaseous water changes to liquid water. Most of us know that warm air holds more water molecules than cool air for the same volume of air. I'm sure we all understand the dynamic temperature ranges that exist in an annual cycle of seasons. But I'm not sure how many of us are aware of the many different temperatures that exist in the cross sections of a typical wall or in different areas of the same room.

By use of thermography, we can find surfaces ranging from about 45°F at supply grilles to more than 90°F on glass. Why is this important? Because often the temperatures in the exterior wall are within a few degrees of the dew point. The location and R value of the insulation in the wall can be as important to the prevention of problematic condensation in our walls as is the quality or size of the air-conditioning system. When condensation takes place within the wall cavity, it can lead to mold growth, as discussed previously. By carefully considering inside and outside temperatures, as well as proper placement of insulation (see Section 4.6.8 in Chapter 4) and vapor barriers in the wall systems, we can minimize the potential problems. As discussed earlier, some materials are better sources of nourishment for spores than others. We need to plan the location where condensation takes place in the wall to be on a surface where there is no food to sustain growth. Then we need to create a way for accumulated condensation to drain out of the walls without causing damage or promoting fungal growth.

2.3 PUTTING IT ALL TOGETHER

A good first step is to grade the site so that water sheet flows away from the building pad. If an area is designated for future stored materials, build it up and slope adjacent earth away. Put enough money in the bid for labor and material to cover this work more than once. Assign a senior staff person the responsibility of keeping materials dry. Work to dry in the building as soon as practical. Whether you are working on a small residence or a 20-story commercial building, it is wise to dry-in the shell as soon as possible (certainly prior to installing paper-backed drywall or kraft-backed insulation). Many builders have switched to paperless glass-mat gypsum drywall for use as a wall sheathing for installation before air is on for just these reasons. These materials do not contain fuel for growth. If plywood is installed, it needs to be protected before the first dew or rain. Get the building dried in and air conditioning on before installing products containing organic materials, whenever possible.

For designers and builders to reduce the number of mold and mildew cases each year, we need to limit the number of spores in or on our construction projects. We must limit fuel and moisture that enable spores to mature. By limiting organics inside the membrane, we will reduce fuel for mold growth. This can be accomplished by material specification and protection. By then reducing water, vapor, and condensation, we can limit future problems.

We could foresee a heating, ventilation, and air-conditioning (HVAC) system in the future with a series of integrated temperature, humidity, CO_2, and differential pressure sensors all networked into a central processor. This is within the capabilities of today's building automation systems. The software would manage a series of variable air volume supply and exhaust systems. In this way, we could sense local differential pressure conditions at multiple points around the perimeter and balance the entire building's outside air and exhaust systems to maintain a desired differential pressure at the skin in the most cost-effective way. The differential pressure sensor function would assure us that all the pressure-driven water vapors are always moving from the inside out. If we have stopped wind-driven and differential pressure-driven vapor transmission, we will in most cases have successfully limited indoor mold growth resulting from vapors. The humidistats placed in wall and roof cavities could sense when moisture is building up in an area of the building envelope. This could serve as an early-warning system that could let maintenance personnel know of changing conditions. If this level of feedback were available, maintenance staff might learn of a wall that needs repainting, sealant that is failing, or a roof membrane that has developed a leak long before the problem spreads.

So now that we have discussed the growth cycle, you can see the importance of moisture (water) to the process. Later we will discuss how to minimize spores in the built environment. More important, let us now focus on how to keep the water out of the building. How does the water get into the building? The different ways can be broken down into four main categories: (1) bulk water (in the liquid state), (2) air-transported moisture (typically water vapor), (3) vapor transmission (through materials that are permeable), and (4) condensation formation. Of the four, the most important to stop is liquid water. A small void in the building envelope can let in more water than leaving out half the vapor barrier. So how do we best stop water?

We have to take into account winter and summer thermoclines. We recently learned of an architect being sued for condensation that was forming on the interior face of exterior walls during winter months in south central Florida. The project was designed and built as low-income housing. Stucco exterior concrete masonry unit (CMU) walls had metal furring with $^3/_4$ inch of insulation and drywall. Kitchens, laundry, and bathroom walls had been painted with enamel. With the increase in energy costs, occupants had reduced heating set points or turned off systems to save money.

You can imagine a number of scenarios in which the occupants contributed to the conditions that led to mold growth. Perhaps there was a cold night, with temperatures in the thirties or lower. The heat was turned off, and lots of blankets were used to sleep. Due to the thermal mass of the block, temperatures never got below 50°F in the house. Around 9 A.M., the occupants arose and took a long, hot shower to warm up. Imagine that the area vent fans were not used; perhaps they were too noisy. The room air temperature could get up to the 85°F and 100 percent relative humidity (RH). Moisture would then form on every cool surface in the room, potentially saturating the paper facing on the drywall.

2.4 SELECTING THE RIGHT CLASS OF CONSTRUCTION

In areas such as Florida, where there is a high probability of high winds and rain exposure, it is recommended that we use a rain screen wall referred to as a cavity wall system. In this way, we have a dedicated drainage plane for water to drain down and out, as well as a pathway for removal of warm air vapors up and out at the top. Another advantage is that the break between the two parts of the wall serves as a thermal break for conductive materials and reduces the potential migration of moisture by capillary action or vapor diffusion. The big challenge in design and construction of a cavity drainage scheme is in preventing pathways for moisture to flank, penetrate, or bypass the drainage cavity membrane.

Depending on project budgets, preferred materials, and available skilled labor, there are many ways to achieve a good wall system. Every well-designed wall will take advantage of the inherent physical properties of the materials used. As designers, we have to balance performance with budget, client's preferences, and in some cases prejudice based on ignorance. It is our duty to do our best to ensure that an acceptable level of performance can be achieved. A cavity wall can use many layers of defense against bulk water intrusion, starting with the outside face of the wall. The outermost material is the one exposed to sun, wind, and rain, as well as dirt and ultra violet rays. For these reasons, vinyl siding, stucco, and exterior insulation and finish systems (EIFSs) are very popular. Each of them has different initial, operating, and maintenance costs associated with their use. Each is resistant to ultraviolet (UV) radiation and is durable. Each also has inherent limitations, and we must take care to design and specify all the right component parts to enable the finished wall systems to keep out moisture and limit condensation.

Amt. of Rainfall	Barrier	Drainage	Rain Screen
less than 20"	X		
20"–40"		X	
Over 40"			X

Table 2-1
Recommended wall types for different rainfall averages

Several experts on the subject have voiced their opinions on wall types related to rainfall. We have created our own table, based upon a compilation of others, mixed with our own experience, see Table 2-1. In it, we recommend the use of rain screen (cavity) walls wherever rainfall exceeds 40 inches per year.

We recommend that walls designed for use in residential, commercial, and other occupied and conditioned spaces in Florida and most southern states within 150 miles of the coast be based upon a cavity wall system. The 2005 Florida Building Code (FBC) requires in stucco on frame walls the use of, at a minimum, a drainage plane. The drainage plane is created by the use of bond-breaker materials between the outer coatings or finish material and the insulation layer. What is the difference, and why do we use one or the other? In a cavity wall system, there are two distinct parts separated by an airspace. The airspace can be quite small but functions better if it is at least $1^1/_2$ or 2 inches in width. The cavity is designed to provide a pathway for liquid water to drain out of the wall system. Similar to cavity wall construction, the drainage plane has a very small pathway for water to drain down and out of the wall. A drainage plane can be created by the use of Tyvek stucco wrap or one of several other three-dimensional membranes that because of their irregular surfaces make space between the bumps for drainage to occur. These typically get installed right up against building paper, felts or other vapour retarders.

At some points, the two materials are touching, and at others, there is a small (usually less than 1/16 inch) space between membranes (see Fig. 2-8). This still will allow liquid water transmission by capillary action and vapor transmission by permeability. It also reduces the thermal break between materials. Two layers in close proximity still may permit both sides of the drainage plane to be touching, so it cannot perform as well as the cavity wall system. Another consideration is that if the two membranes are installed one on top of the other (touching), then what happens at joints or laps? The extra thickness of material can block the drainage pathway. There is no room for construction tolerances or laps in materials, etc. This equates to an increase in potential liability for the owner, developer, builder, and designer. Liability is bad. Although the codes are becoming more stringent by requiring two barriers behind stucco on frame walls, we do not recommend that you rely on building-code minimums as your recommendation in design. We believe that you need to do more than the minimum, and we believe that you must.

Figure 2-8

Small drainage void
between membranes.

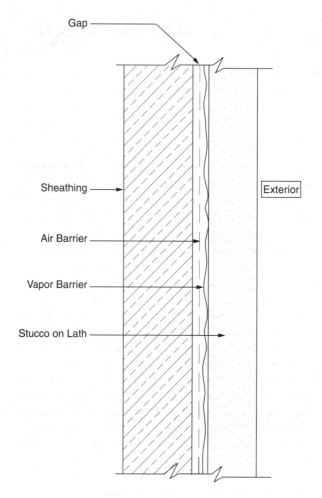

Yes, a cavity wall can have a higher initial cost, but if it is done right, not only can it reduce the risk of mold and mildew, but it also can pay for itself as a result of better insulation values and reduced energy costs. If we work hard and smart, the payback can be as few as 10 years but in every case should result in longer-lasting, better indoor conditions for people using the built environment. In warm climates, the interior face of the drainage cavity should be the place where water and vapor transmission is at a minimum. This is also the point where you want condensation to take place. Regardless of the wall system chosen, the interior face of the cavity should have the lowest permeability of all wall materials (see Fig. 2-9). We believe that this is the best location for the moisture barrier. You want to stop bulk water at the outside face of the exterior walls. You then want to stop air infiltration to minimize moisture in the wall cavity period. If these two steps are done properly and you don't screw up something else, the building should not have mold and mildew problems. Yes, we said it. Stop liquid water and stop wind, and you've effectively reduced the potential for mold in your buildings. Do we think that this is enough? No!

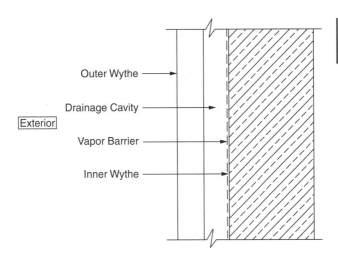

Figure 2-9
Lowest permeability on inside face of cavity wall.

The most important consideration in preventing moisture in the building environment is stopping liquid water. This usually relies on a series of parts, each designed and installed to perform a key functional role. We have to resolve all the obvious natural forces such as sun and rain, as well as other forces such as expansion and abuse from people, plants, and animals. We have to stop water from all six directions. The roof system must stop water from above, the walls from the sides, and the floor system from below. We typically use different products for these applications. You would not expect to use visqueen for a roof or shingles for a basement. Visqueen below grade or below crawl space floor insulation if properly installed is good at preventing moisture from reducing thermal performance of batt insulation.

Visqueen does not resist punctures or tears well, so it cannot be relied on as a roofing system, at least not without protection. This is why we rely on very hard materials such as ceramic roof tile, metal, or concrete for long-lasting roofing materials exposed to the weather. Those products can be relied on to resist UV light without degradation, as well as punctures from small branches or wind-blown objects. Underneath these hard materials, we use more flexible products to stop the water from permeating the system. We rely on gravity to drain the water down and away from our occupied spaces. Many roof underlayments are hygroscopic, which means that they absorb some of the water they come in contact with. These products release that moisture back to the atmosphere after the rain stops.

You may have seen steam rising up from a hot roof after the rain stops on a hot summer day. In hurricanes, we often have rains lasting for several days. In those cases, the underlayment stays saturated and can begin to transmit moisture onto the sheathings below. Many of our roof sheathings are quite absorbent and permit the transmission of moisture through them as well. Most are wood products, which provide food for mold growth.

In walls, we have much the same situation. When wind-driven rain hits the exterior skin of our buildings, even on a porous material such as stucco, on average, only about 1 percent of the water enters the wall through the wetted surface. One small hole in the skin can let in more water than 1,000 square feet of exterior wall sheathing, even assuming that no water-resistive barrier is present. Thus we try to design the wall system so that it can be constructed to have no voids or holes. We typically use a hard material to protect a more flexible membrane. Again, we rely on gravity to drain surface water down and away from our occupied spaces. We use a broad variety of outer skins, ranging from wood to plastic/vinyl, to brick, to stucco, or to plaster.

An exception to this is the use of exterior concrete block as a skin. Some waterproofing consultants tell us to design around breathable block and breathable paints, whereas others say to use the best elastomeric paint at the face. Manufacturers are making special blocks that don't wick water and special foam inserts that allow for vertical drainage in at least part of the wall system. So how do we know which one to use and when?

2.5   GRAVITY, GEOMETRY, TECHNOLOGY

We recommend that you try to use the following simple rule: Gravity first, geometry second, and then technology. Think of the way time-tested installations work. We like to think of lap siding and lapped shingles as a way to explain the first two parts, gravity and geometry. We know to lap the siding, shingles, or membranes from the bottom up. This promotes the use of gravity (see Fig. 2-10), to have water rolling down the materials, and prevents water from getting behind the membranes at a lap. This same principle should be carried over into above-grade detailing at every condition.

Figure 2-10
Gravity first.

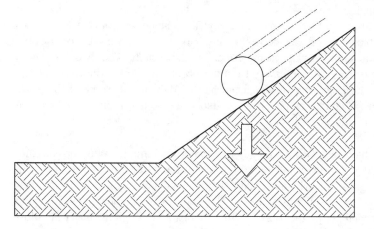

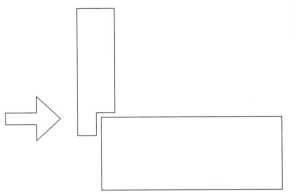

Figure 2-11
Geometry second.

The geometry part comes in to play when we consider the physical fact that water (or any mass) tends to maintain direction and velocity unless and until it is acted on by another force. Thus every time water droplets change direction, shape, or size as a result of our building component geometry, they lose energy. We like to place permanent materials in the path of wind-driven water to prevent their easy entry (see Fig. 2-11).

If you walk up to a wall before sealants are installed and you can see light through a void, this is an easy pathway for wind-driven rain (see Fig. 2-12). This is the main reason that we prefer positive detailing to negative detailing. We do not recommend anyone rely solely upon sealant to stop air and water intrusion over time.

Figure 2-12
Designs should avoid reliance upon sealant.

Figure 2-13

Positive and negative window jamb detailing.

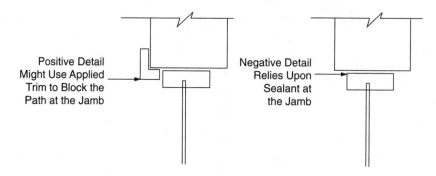

Positive Detail Might Use Applied Trim to Block the Path at the Jamb

Negative Detail Relies Upon Sealant at the Jamb

You can see the difference easily in the two examples provided in Figure 2-13. The geometry of the positive example clearly provides a more difficult to defeat condition for wind-driven rain.

Similarly, in the Positive roof edge example (see Fig. 2-14) one can easily see more pieces of material blocking the path for wind-driven rain to enter the building envelope. In the Negative example, (see Fig. 2-15) materials are abutting instead of overlapping the joints with the next successive layer.

Flashings rely on gravity and geometry. We don't have to extend our flashings more than about 8 or 10 inches vertically behind wall finishes because water droplets hardly ever climb more than that before they slow to where gravity pulls them down and away.

A well-designed and well-installed flashing will go one step farther and stop even hurricane-force winds from driving water droplets beyond the vertical height of the bent metal. This can be achieved by use of another 180-degree bend at the top, this one to redirect water back down (see Fig. 2-16).

Figure 2-14

Example of positive roof detail.

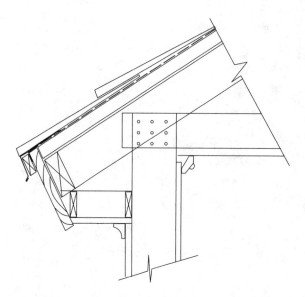

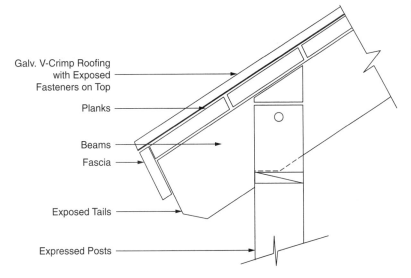

Figure 2-15
Example of negative roof detail.

Galv. V-Crimp Roofing with Exposed Fasteners on Top

Planks

Beams

Fascia

Exposed Tails

Expressed Posts

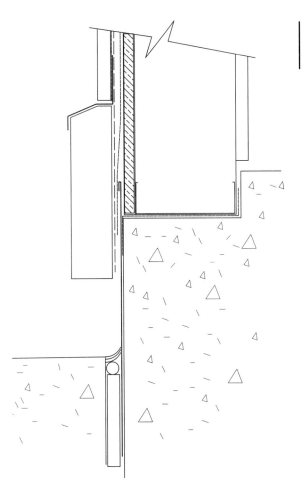

Figure 2-16
Improved slab edge water stop.

Geometry also relates to the seaming and closure at joints in horizontal and vertical materials. We must minimize the potential for water to get around the flashing, whether we weld, rivet, caulk, or bend laps in flashings. This is using technology to improve geometry. Technology also comes in when we add a bead of sealant to the top of this flashing. This will reduce the potential for even the most energetic droplets from getting past, above, or behind the flashing. Adding roofing sealant to a row of starter shingles could be considered adding technology to geometry. The nails and sealants ensure that the geometry will stay in place to take advantage of gravity.

2.5.1   Air pressure control

After we stop liquid water, we have to minimize water vapor intrusion next. Air barriers play the most important role in reducing water vapor infiltration in our buildings. We can calculate the number of grains of water that result from the various kinds of transmission modes to reinforce this statement, but experts assure us that vapor transported by air currents introduces between 100 and 200 times the amount of moisture into our buildings than occurs from vapor diffusion through materials. Airborne water vapor accounts for more than 98 percent of all the vapor movement through the building envelope. The important message here is that we must work diligently to stop leaks in the air barrier at the perimeter.

A certain amount of outside air is necessary to maintain a healthy indoor environment. There are several ways to determine design values for outside air, just as there are ways to achieve the design values. The old American Society of Heating, Refrigerating, and Air-Conditioning Engineering (ASHRAE) standard was 15 to 35 cubic feet per minute (cfm) per person depending on their levels of activity. Some designers prefer to use CO_2 sensors to maintain acceptable levels of CO_2 in the air and connect the sensor output to variable outside air makeup systems. Both systems have their advantages and disadvantages.

We would rather have too much outside air than just barely enough, but we sometimes must consider how much we can afford to bring in. It costs money to provide more than we need because outside air is usually dehumidified and cooled prior to introduction into the building's occupied spaces (summer cooling cooling conditions).

We could foresee a system in the future with a series of integrated differential-pressure sensors, all networked into a series of variable air volume supply systems. In this way, we could sense local differential pressures at multiple points around the perimeter and balance the entire building's outside air and exhaust systems to maintain desired differential pressures at the skin (air infiltration barrier, or AIB). This would assure us that all the pressure-driven water vapors always were moving from the inside out. It is our belief that pressure-driven vapors carry far more grains per cubic foot than vapors moved as a result of differential temperatures (at the same pressure). If we have stopped wind-driven and differential-pressure-driven vapor transmission, we will in most cases have limited indoor mold growth as a result of moisture from vapors successfully.

After vapors are introduced, we need to prevent their movement through the building. Air (and airborne water vapors) has three principal means for movement within a building. They are wind pressure, stack pressure, and differential pressure. Wind pressures create different directions of flow, as seen in Fig. 2-17. To simplify things, wind pressure is positive on the windward side and negative on the leeward side of walls and roof surfaces.

Stack pressures are created by gravity, and by the tendency for warm air to rise and, as it rises to the top, create a relative negative pressure behind it. We need to try to seal vertical wall and horizontal ceiling cavities at floor levels to reduce transmission resulting from stack pressures. Differential pressures typically are caused by the air-conditioning and ventilation systems, ideally creating a positive pressure all over the building exterior skin just strong enough to overcome the wind- or stack-generated negative pressures in order to maintain constant flow (from pressure) from in to out. This will help to keep out new spores and reduce outside air infiltration.

Air barriers are also important so that we can maintain positive pressure in our buildings with the least amount of waste energy. In buildings that are mechanically ventilated, it is important to have the best possible airtight enclosure. This can be achieved by having a continuous and well-sealed air infiltration barrier (AIB) constructed from materials with low infiltration rates (high infiltration resistance).

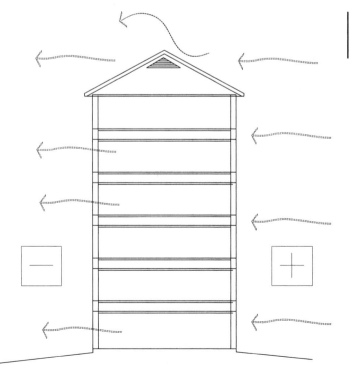

Figure 2-17
Pressures acting on vapors.

2.5.2   Water vapor transmission reduction

Let us now focus on stopping the transmission of water vapor by means other than air movement. The least permeable materials, such as sheet metal, rubber sheets, and polyethylene film, all have a permeability rating of 0.1 or less. These are classified as *vapor-impermeable,* or *vapor barriers.* Little, if any, vapor passes through them. *Vapor retarders* can be grouped into three basic categories based on how permeable they are. A permeability rating is based on the amount of water in grams that passes through a square foot of sample material at an assumed standard pressure differential.

The next classification is referred to as *semi impermeable,* ranging in permeability rating from 0.1 to 1.0. These materials include vinyl wall coverings, oil-based paints, stucco over building paper with glued oriented strand board (OSB), and unfaced polystyrene sheathing about 1 inch thick. Semi-permeable materials include unfaced expanded polystyrene (EPS) board, 30-pound felt, latex paints, and typical plywood and OSB sheathing. They range in permeability from 1 to 10. Permeable membranes exceed 10. Most codes define vapor retarders as materials having permeability ratings equal to or less than 1, dry cup test (0 percent RH on one side, 50 percent on the other). There is also a wet cup test for membranes, where one side is at 50 percent RH and the other is at 100 percent.

Some materials absorb water, whereas others do not. Some absorbent materials actually change their permeability rating as they become more saturated. They are referred to as *hygroscopic.* Plywood is such a material; it is semi permeable when dry and permeable when wet. Bitumen-impregnated kraft paper is another hygroscopic material, but with quite different properties. It is quite vapor permeable when dry and semi impermeable when wet. This lends itself to use in hot humid climates as what is marketed as a "smart membrane." When it is dry, it allows the wall to breathe, allowing water vapor to pass through it. When the humidity increases, the permeability is reduced. These properties have been incorporated into insulating products presently being marketed.

There are many different types of moisture barriers, each with very good characteristics. This is where we seem to find two different schools of thought in the experts we studied. One group recommends use of an impermeable membrane, one that prohibits transmission. In this scenario, moisture inside the building must leave the building via the mechanical system, by exhaust or air-conditioning equipment coils drying out the recirculated conditioned air. The other school of thought is that in certain scenarios we want the moisture inside the building to be able to permeate the membrane to escape. In this scenario, the best solution is the newly developed "smart membranes" that change their permeability depending on how saturated they are. The selection should be based on climate, rainfall, and wind pressures—not initial cost.

Both systems can work successfully. For each building, you need to study the operating modes and maintenance plans and consult with your mechanical designer to make sure that the right decisions are made to create a good system.

The permeability of the moisture barrier must be determined in conjunction with insulation values and temperatures (as well as the permeability ratings of the other wall system components) so as to minimize volume and duration of condensation in the walls and to prevent condensation beyond the moisture barrier. See Section 4.5.6 in Chapter 4 for a discussion of recommended wall types for each climate group.

3

Predesign

3.1 THE BUILDING PROGRAM: A BLUEPRINT FOR SUCCESS

Believe it or not, the single most important step in the prevention of mold- and mildew-related problems in buildings is often skipped. The building program phase (often referred to as *programming*) is often considered to be unimportant by developers and builders alike. Even some architects jump right into the design phase without adequately defining what they are setting out to design. There are many reasons they may use for doing so, but we believe that they should be using their energy to provide the program, a blueprint for successful design. The program can vary in complexity and scope from a simple document containing a few pages to a 3-inch-thick binder with hundreds of pages.

A comprehensive building program will begin with site studies looking at the organization of the intended users and listing area needs, relationships, and all pertinent information from which future decisions will be made. It must include budgetary and timeline considerations but should also provide image statements and performance expectations. By providing such a document using simple terms and abstract diagrams, it can be easier to obtain the first stage of buy-in and approval from the ownership group. Often, design goes forward without getting agreement as to what the building is intended to express or how exactly it is to function. This lack of consensus could lead to disagreement in the processes to come. We have found that even a two-week effort at programming can result in an excellent document, one that serves as a guiding set of agreements and principles for all future decisions.

The building program can set out realistic goals and objectives for the building. This will prevent future disappointment. Rather than letting a client down at the end, we believe that it is important to make sure that every project's goals are achievable—that expectations can be met or, better yet, exceeded. A good program will look at all building and zoning restrictions and evaluate existing transportation and circulation. Setbacks, ordinances, and other applicable regulations should be clearly stated prior to beginning design. In this way, decisions that are made later can be carried out without surprises or stumbling blocks. The program should be presented to the ownership or management group and if possible all stakeholders prior to beginning the next phase. Any objections can be worked out effectively before lines are drawn, building forms are determined, and feelings get hurt.

The building program (or facilities program if more than one building is involved) should spell out achievable goals and objectives for the completed project. Programs vary in size and scope from a simple 10-page summary to a 300-page document that lists each space and what needs to be in it. Perhaps the program elements are not all known when the program is initiated, but the expectations should be spelled out. If both the designer and the developer are experienced with this type of building recently and in a similar location, their expectations will be based on good information. This is the best kind of relationship. Conversely, an inexperienced owner or development group can come in with lofty expectations. Maybe they are using a budget from 4 years ago, or maybe they relied on biased or unrealistic information provided by a real estate agent trying to close a sale. Regardless of the cause, it is important to make sure that expectations can be achieved.

Those expectations apply to the building to be designed as well as to the designer performing the services. In the negotiations for and preparation of a contractual agreement, it is good to state what the owner can expect from the design team, and vice versa. In many countries, architects' obligations are spelled out in statutes. Make them known to the owner by including them in the contract language, do not set the bar so high that you are at risk of letting the client down. For example, do not state that you will be the best architect in the world or provide the best set of documents ever. State that you will make every effort to provide the same level of care that is standard in the industry. Then exceed that, go the extra mile, do extra details. This will establish that you are going to exceed the minimum requirements of your agreement.

Typically, before the program is finished, the project budget needs to be defined. You need to make certain that the project is adequately funded. By *adequately*, we mean that the owner is not counting on some unknown future act to be able to pay the bills. If you have worked with this owner or group before, you can have that experience to draw from. By *adequately*, we also mean that the owner needs to have a sufficient contingency fund and plan in place. For new construction, in a period of low inflation, a contingency fund should be in the range of 7 to 10 percent of construction cost. This owner's contingency budget is to be used for unforeseen conditions, such as soil bearing conditions, and to cover costs that might not have been budgeted, such as threshold inspection. It should not be expected to pay for a series of upgrades or added scope. For renovation or remodeling, a contingency budget should be 15 to 20 percent because there are many more possibilities for unanticipated costs. If you are planning a project and annual inflation or escalation rates are not low, or if materials and labor markets are volatile, you should plan how to cover the risk in the budget plan. If the project is planned for more than 6 months in the future, as many are, we recommend that a separate line should be created in the budget for inflation. This is in addition to the contingency budget. The contingency budget is for unforeseen things; inflation can be predicted. By creating a separate line in the budget, the design and construction teams can see the blueprint for success. They can see that the owner is serious about protecting the integrity of the design and quality of construction from the beginning. This also provides a tracking mechanism for inflation so that bidders might not put as much cushion on their bids because the owner is accepting the risk for inflation. These contractual issues must be worked out, and all parties must buy into the process in order for it to work. However, it also has been proven over time to trim as much as 20 percent off early bids for future work. If funding is in place, the owner may choose to purchase those materials that are rising in cost as soon as the contracts are in place. This may help to limit cost escalation. Quite often storage arrangements can cost far less than price escalation.

A project that is not adequately funded can lead to problems for all concerned. If the project is planned and estimated years in the future, and unforeseen inflation takes place, what happens to the project budget? If steel and concrete go up 50 percent before you finish the design, this may result in a project cost increase that exceeds a low contingency sum. Would the owner/developer require you to substitute lower-cost components, reduce air-conditioning, or leave out the air or vapor barrier, or could the owner raise unit sale prices? It is always nice to know what the contingency plans are for escalation in advance.

3.1.1 Concept statement

The most useful building programs go far beyond functional space needs assessments. They go on to provide a look into the ultimate user's physical and psychological needs. If this information is available to the designers, it can guide them through the myriad of decisions that are to follow in the search for the best building form and expression. One of the keys to a completely successful design is the overriding concept that shapes the decisions. The concept statement should express what the building is to achieve, be, or express. The concept statement gives reason and direction to the design team—why it should be this way and not that way.

Imagine the difference in a building where there is no focus, no concept. Design decisions can be made ad hoc with no rhyme or reason. Consider, instead, the impact of the following concept statement on design: "This building is to grow out of the site, like a large spiraling organic growth of wood and glass that reaches to the sky like a golden telescope." Or the following: "We want this building to be constructed as cheaply as possible." These scenarios would give the design team different directions for building form and expression. Only the first example is the kind of concept statement that really should be contained within a building program. Even if cost is an important consideration, it should not be confused with the concept statement. It should perhaps be listed as the most important objective in the hierarchy of project goals and objectives, but it is far too shallow for a concept statement.

Some powerful ideas for concept statements resulted in buildings that you might be familiar with; for example, consider Le Corbusier's Ronchamps Cathedral, or Utzon's Sydney Opera House or Wright's Guggenheim Museum. Each has a powerful image that was derived as a result of expressing a unique concept. Many of today's themed buildings have a concept behind them as well. The concept is just the big idea, a reason for making decisions that will reinforce the idea. These decisions may be in materials or, more important in public perception, the forms. Humans are always trying to figure out their environment by comparing the thing before them with images stored in their memories. What is it like helps us to figure out what it could be. This is especially helpful in understanding new and unique forms. Image analogies can be familiar shapes such as a sailboat's sail, a bishop's hat, or a pair of hands clasped in prayer. What is important is the appropriateness of the form in leading the designer to a good solution.

Without a reason for selecting one thing versus another, architects can make decisions based on their personal beliefs as to what is right for the building. Programs also may include codes, ordinances, and pertinent design guidelines. Organizational diagrams, numbers of employees by area, and relationships between them can be provided. A group-by-group description of the physical needs and functional roles usually follows.

3.1.2 Hierarchy chart

Within the program, there should be a section in which the many stated objectives are prioritized. All parties should come to an agreement as to what is most important to the project. In the beginning, you may start out with a different set of priorities from the owner or developer (see table 3-1). List them in order. Then ask the owner or developer to do the same. Have the design, construction, and ownership teams work together to compile one list. This becomes the team's hierarchy chart. Without exception, get the building program signed by the project manager for the ownership/developer group before proceeding with the next phase.

The program information that is most important for discussion in this book relates to the building envelope. If indoor air quality, water intrusion, building air-conditioning system performance, and prevention of condensation are important to the owner or developer, as well as low maintenance and an open, inviting atmosphere, the programmer should list those as being important in the program. In order to give the best guidance to designers and builders, the

Table 3-1
Priorities

Building Program Heirarchy Charts, 1 is most Important			How Important are the Following?	
New Image	9	2	Roof Membrane	⊗
Under Budget	4	1	Windows	⊕
On Schedule	6	3	Doors	⊕
Easily Maintained	5	9	Wall System	⊗
Healthy Environment	3	10	HVAC System	⊕
Good Lighting	7	7	Under Slab Membrane	○
Temperature Control	2	6	Grading	⊗
No Leaks, Mold	1	8	Flashings	⊕
Covered Parking	10	5	Sealants	○
Open, Inviting	8	4	QA/QC Process	⊗

Legend	
⊗	Most Important
⊕	Very Important
○	Important

owner or developer can list the most important criteria in order of their importance to him or her. We refer to this as a *hierarchy chart.* By knowing the relative importance of several items, the team can make certain that those top priorities are carried forward throughout design and construction. If a compromise needs to be made in some aspect of the project, it will not come as a result of a reduction in the performance of the waterproofing or air-conditioning system or the open interior spaces. In this way, there is a clear and agreed-on set of objectives that you can be certain are not left out during cost-cutting or value-engineering exercises that have become so commonplace.

3.2 BUILDING DELIVERY SYSTEMS

Different project directors choose their delivery systems based on their own experience and a range of other factors. By *delivery system,* we are talking about the different roles that can be played by designers and builders. In the traditional delivery system, one group designs the building and delivers sets of plans and specifications to the owner. We call these *contract documents* (CDs). Owners then would have *general contractors* (GCs) look at the CDs and send in bids in sealed envelopes.

GCs used to have a core group of full-time employees on the payroll who were skilled in the trades. They would employ their own concrete crews, painters, masons, and carpenters at the very least. GCs might subcontract out electrical, plumbing, and heating, ventilation, and air-conditioning (HVAC) work if they didn't have those tradespeople in their firm but typically would do everything else with their own personnel. On bid opening date, all received bids would be opened, and the apparent low GC bidder would be determined. If the bid was complete and references checked out, that GC firm would sign a contract for the amount of the low bid. This system has several variations, the most interesting, perhaps, is the selection of a lowest and best bidder for award. If the apparent low bidder did not deliver as good a quality building recently as the second or third lowest bidder, he or she might not get the award. If there were concerns about the low bidder's bonding abilities or conflict with personnel, rumors of foul play, or other factors such as minority participation, the award might not go to the low bidder. There are obvious risks associated with low-bidder awards. Some developers accept the risk, others do not.

The bid documents generally are 100 percent complete prior to bidding. The plans and specifications have to show and tell builders what is expected. There are two methods for handling items not shown on the plans: Either the GC submits change orders or, more commonly, the GC is not given change orders. The whole idea behind hard-bid projects is that the owner knows the total cost exposure prior to proceeding. Most firms compile their prices on hard-bid jobs by filling in the blanks for things not shown on the plans. Based on their experience, they know what it is going to take to build the building as generally depicted on the plans. Drawings have more of a systems description content, and details are typical or similar to other conditions. Change orders are approved only for acts of nature, not errors or omissions on the plans. Good contractors put in what is required for a good envelope even if it isn't called out in the details. Others may leave out the detail and try to get away without incurring the cost of doing it right.

3.2.1 Cost-plus GC

A similar delivery system to the preceding example is used where familiarity is beneficial or where there is no time for bidding. In the *cost-plus arrangement,* the owner hires the builder without knowing exactly what the project will cost. The contract is written so that the builder keeps track of all project costs and is paid a percentage for overhead and profit. This takes the risk for bidding a job right out of the equation. A cost-plus contract is based on trust.

Plans and specifications do not need to be full or complete to get started in a cost-plus GC arrangement. Often, the foundation plans are in the schematic design phase when the GC orders the material. Permits are pulled in phases, starting with an early foundation permit, just to get a jump on the schedule. Design progresses to CD phase to get a building permit while work is proceeding on the foundation. Building envelope details can be worked out while the walls are being erected. The owner generally would be kept involved through every phase of design and construction through a representative such as the owner's project manager participating in the decision-making process as decisions are being made.

One very nice feature of this process is the potential for the designer to make informed decisions with input from the owner and builder representatives as the building is going up. This can result in the best-coordinated details and a cooperative team attitude toward the completed project. On most hard-bid jobs, the owner or contractor can react unfavorably to design input as the building is going up and issues arise. On many of them, changes mean that somebody has to pay out of profit. On a cost-plus job, it is seen as improving or fine-tuning the product, that is, value added.

3.2.2 Guaranteed maximum price

The major drawback of the open-ended cost-plus contract is that the owner never knows the total exposure for the project cost until the end. With a *guaranteed maximum price* (GMP) arrangement, a limit is established at the time the contract is written. This also has been referred to as a *cost-plus not to exceed,* but there can be subtle differences in these two approaches. In the GMP scenario, line-item budget limits may be established. If a line item goes over the limit, the contractor pays the overage out of the contractor's contingency budget, if any. Buy savings in any line can go into the contractor's or owner's contingency budget depending on the contract language. In cost-plus not to exceed, these line-item constraints are not usually applied. These are obviously describing one way to contract construction, and myriad deviations and variations on the themes exist.

As it relates to the building envelope, these two approaches are quite similar. They permit the team to decide where to spend the client's money and still end up at the target budget. This is where the hierarchy chart really pays off in performance if, for example, petroleum products rise in cost dramatically, and across-the-board inflation exceeds projections. These approaches allow the team options to keep the project in budget without reducing performance of the skin. Roofing, insulation, and air and water barriers are still included despite rising costs, whereas costs for other line items can be reduced, such as floor tiles or perhaps plumbing fixtures. For the designer, contractor, and owner, there is an opportunity to reduce liability and at the same time end up with a project that performs well over time.

3.2.3 Design-build

In both major examples above, the designer is a different entity from the builder. This can have benefits, such as the specialization of two different professions acting as checks and balances, or it can cause friction and adversarial results. Some people claim that design-build contracts provide the best of both worlds. In *design-build* (DB) projects, the designer and builder are the same contractual entity. Some people theorize that this should result in a reduction in soft costs and an increase in the cost-effectiveness of the design. They believe that the fees for DB total less than the sum of the costs of design and construction firms added together. The logic is that the DB firm would design more cost-effective ways to build the project than the designer might think of. In addition, the fee should be smaller because there is only one overhead component for the DB firm.

Whatever the conclusion or reasons for choosing the DB process, there are several ways that such projects are done. Some have in-house teams that work together in a seamless tandem to design and build projects. In theory, there is a very short and complete feedback loop because things that weren't drawn often result in unforeseen costs. To make things clearer, both groups report to one boss. The client has a one-on-one relationship with the contact on the DB team. There can be no "finger pointing."

In reality, many DB firms do not have in-house design staff members. They rely on outside firms to do the design, at the direction of the build group. The design firm's contract is with the DB firm, not with the client. There may be some tendencies to design what the DB firm has priced rather than design what the design firm thinks the client really wants. This is quite different from the thinking in a traditional design role, wherein the design contract is with the owner.

A more interesting variation on the DB theme has been used recently. With the increase in DB projects, and because of the builder's interest and control over the design in that arrangement, many owners have been hiring their own design firms (referred to as *design-criteria architects,* or DCAs) to develop the program, building plans and specifications to a point where they hand over responsibilities to the DB firm's *design-build architect* (DBA). This point is commonly established when the drawings are sufficient for pricing. In this process, the owner can control the design documents until the image, materials, and methods are generally established. We usually see this point reached when the plans and specifications are complete to the 50 or 100 percent *design-development* (DD) phase. These plans are used to deliver a cost estimate to the owner. The owner then may choose how to proceed, cost-plus, hard-bid, etc. This process yields a compromise that many owners are most comfortable with.

3.2.4   Construction managers

An alternate to GCs was introduced in the late twentieth century, referred to as *construction managers* (CMs). CM firms typically perform little, if any, of the work themselves; they manage subcontractors for all the work. Most CM firms offer preconstruction services to assist owners and designers through the process of design. They are typically paid a fixed fee by the owner for those services. Their role is to guide the process toward the target budget, weighing cost and schedule impacts to the decisions made throughout the process. On request, they will provide cost estimates as DD and CD documents are prepared.

In theory, CM firms are expert at managing projects and hire subcontractors with whom they have completed successful projects and developed good relations. This process is intended to allow competitive bidding by discipline instead of by GC firms as a whole. Some owners feel that this results in a better-quality project because the team can pick and choose from a range of bids and bidders to come up with the "lowest and best" scope bids by division and avoid problems that can result from pure low-bid award. CM projects can be delivered in any of the three scenarios described for GCs, and as such, we will not elaborate further.

3.3 TIME, THE FOURTH DIMENSION

Once we get past image considerations, performance expectations and delivery methods, it all comes down to time and money. The two factors that influence design and construction decisions most are time and money. There may be a few clients who do not care about either, but they are the minority. All the decisions we make potentially can affect project cost, and many of us know and understand the cost implications of design decisions we make with regard to cost. However, we suggest that most designers do not understand or want to know the impact design decisions have on time. Time is the fourth dimension. It is constant and inflexible. We cannot change it.

Owners and developers usually give us timetables, and then designers and builders respond with how we can fit our deliverables to the timetable. We manipulate staffing, arrange project deadlines, and work long hours to meet time constraints that we seldom have any control over. We are seldom provided enough time to do as thorough a job as we would like on plans. Our schedules are often changed, delayed, or cut short with a phone call. Time-management skills are tested as we respond to constant change. The faster design teams can deliver plans, the sooner the building can be built. With inflation pressures, everyone is looking for a way to get their project designed and built faster.

Before the program is completed, the team should agree to the major milestones for project delivery. These do not need to be perfectly calculated masterpieces with pages of linked charts to study every task, but they should define how much time is set aside for design, when bidding is to commence, when permits are expected, and construction duration. Because we believe that the program is so important, we recommend that it be awarded as a separate contract, ahead of the design and construction contracts. The program should be completed simultaneously with contract negotiations so that the information that relates to delivery method and milestones is part of the program and matches with the contracts. Often, programs are referenced by attachment to the design and construction contracts.

If the constructor is under contract during the preparation of *design contract documents* (DCDs), feedback can be provided to the design team as decisions are made and become part of the DCDs. Structural systems, waterproofing, exterior wall and roof systems, and details all impact the construction schedule. The builder typically has best cost data, and it may be that a system that costs more per square foot actually reduces project cost because it has shorter construction duration. Designs that permit partial dry-in of a multistory building also allow interior trades to start earlier. Many high-rise buildings are now permitted by floor so that *certificates of occupancy* (COs) can be issued for some floors while work is ongoing around or above them. This can reduce tenant fit-out by as much as 6 months or more.

This type of design consideration can trickle through all disciplines of design. Life safety and lighting systems need to be installed out of normal sequence for phased occupancies. Temporary dry-in measures can be planned in cost-effective ways so as to be a part of finished systems later. All these time-related considerations need to be spelled out in advance of beginning the DD phase. Another consideration is how long materials may be exposed to the weather. Many materials do not do well in contact to wind and rain or even if exposed to ultraviolet (UV) rays.

Time-of-the-season considerations are also critical. We recommend that design and construction planning take into account the seasons when the building is built, enclosed, and tested. Each of these important phases of construction affects the performance of the building envelope and may affect the way it is designed. Do you need temporary shoring and bracing to resist potential snow loads or hurricane-force winds? Do you need to design the frame to withstand wind loads on interior partitions before the window systems are glazed? What happens to the unbuilt shell spaces if they sit vacant for two years before they are fitted out? Are there sufficient temperature and humidity control measures in phase 1 for a multiphase project? Are differential temperatures between floors going to cause sweating on the mezzanine that will ruin flooring before the building is under air? There are many time-related considerations that we have not touched on that can affect the building envelope performance over time. It is difficult for an overworked architect on a pressure-packed deadline to consider all these factors while trying to finish the drawings. This is made even more problematic if the design also must consider the fifth dimension all the while.

3.4   MONEY, THE FIFTH DIMENSION

Yes, we consider money the fifth dimension. Maybe this is just because it enters into everything that goes horizontal or vertical, but it is more than that. It is safe to say that every decision designers make can affect project cost. From the shape and size of the plan to the color of the paint, everything can have an impact on cost. Now this doesn't relate directly to price. Price is what can be charged others. Cost is the price you paid. Sometimes we increase the cost as a result of adding a line to our drawings or changing a note.

We have already discussed time considerations to be addressed before design proceeds, and most of the money considerations relate to budget issues already touched on. In the program, information as to the owner's intended budget must be presented clearly. Information should be readily discernible and clearly presented. While it should be preliminary in nature, all budget information should reflect the real goals for the project. Included should be an executive-level overview listing building square footage and land areas. It should include anticipated parking count, landscaped areas, and estimates for land development costs, impact fees, and hard and soft construction projections.

Soft costs include design fees, surveys, attorney fees, and costs typically paid for by the owner outside the construction (bricks and sticks) costs. Those are referred to as *hard* costs and often include permit costs, inspection services, and all major systems in the building. Hard costs also tend to include projected temporary water and power, security, supervision, overhead, and profit. Some additional costs often are budgeted as reimbursable, such as printing, travel, postage, and other hard-to-predict miscellaneous costs.

In sum, the program should be your blueprint for success. We caution you against proceeding to design without it and have shown ways to get the program done without extending the design or construction timelines. You would not want to start construction without an approved set of plans. Why would anyone consider going into design without an approved program? List what is important to consider the project a success in order of importance (hierarchy chart) and include expectations of the building envelope.

4 Building Envelope Design

The way a building looks is up to the designer. The form, shape, size, color, and fenestrations all come together to create what we see and what we touch and feel. We presently have more choices of materials available for the building envelope than ever before. Some designers choose to design from the inside out, framing views of the site. Others prefer to work from the outside in, letting the expressive form dictate where openings in the envelope occur. Individual expression is the norm.

Some buildings will be large; others will be small. Some will have flat (low-slope) roof forms, whereas others may have 12-in-12 pitch or more. We may see punched window openings or glass curtain walls. The options are endless. We are limited by our clients' budgets, the amount of time and materials available, the skills of our workers, and by our imagination.

In contrast to this, the conditions we are designing for have much more commonality. Regardless of where we are, certain physical principles are constant. Gravity doesn't change much from Helsinki to Helena. Gravity stays relatively constant from summer to winter. It is one of the most constant of all the physical forces acting on our buildings, and for this reason, it is important to take gravity into consideration in all of our envelope design decisions. Wind and water are two more basic common elements of our physical environment. Wind is the result of cyclic heating and cooling of our oceans and continents as a result of interaction with the sun as our earth rotates. Water makes up three-quarters of our planet. Water is present in all three physical phases in different parts of the planet at different times. It requires energy to change the temperature or phase of water or anything with mass. Velocity, acceleration, momentum, potential, and kinetic energy—all these terms describe real physical properties that affect the building envelope. The laws governing them don't change from Austin to Zimbabwe, just their values.

The evaporation of water from rivers, lakes, and oceans has a huge influence on our built environment. Evaporating water forms clouds, which are the result of liquid water changing phase and turning into gas (water vapor). This phase change reduces the temperature of the remaining water. Warmer air rises because it is less dense than cool air. Temperatures in the upper atmosphere are lower than those at lower levels. When vapors condense in the cooling clouds, they turn from gas into liquid rain that is carried by the wind and drawn back to earth by gravity. If it is cold enough, the droplets change into solid water in the form of snow or ice. This is the way it has been for millions of years.

Designers in a cool climate make different decisions for the building envelope than those in a warm climate. It is logical, then, that designs for a beach house in a hot, humid climate such as Florida are different from those for a mountain chalet in northern Canada. They both share the same approximate gravitational pull. We would expect the two to have vastly different roof and wall sections, insulation, and more. We would design the chalet for seasonal snow loads and the beach house for occasional hurricanes.

We feel that it is logical and appropriate, therefore, to discuss principles in this guide to the building envelope not only by system but also by climate. We have tried to provide a systematic approach for looking at the building envelope that will be of value regardless of the environment for which you are designing. You can see from the Table 4-1 that temperatures vary greatly from location to location. The other thing that we would like you to notice is the difference between the average monthly low and high temperatures and the recorded lows and highs. Which should we use in calculations? If our insulation and/or mechanical systems are not sized to handle the extreme temperatures, what problems might we expect? How can we hope to avoid reaching the dew point in the wall or roof cavity?

This is why we recommend that you hire a good team of professionals to design and build your buildings. Together you can make informed decisions throughout the process of project planning, design, and construction that can result in a completed project that will resist the elements for the long term.

4.1 SELECTING THE RIGHT FIRM

In the process for a building described in Chapter 3, the program was completed in the pre-design phase. The program is usually done by an architectural firm, and it does not need to be the same firm that will be doing the design. In some cases it will have been determined early on that the same firm will do the design. Two good reasons for this are continuity and time. With the same firm, there is less of an opportunity for lost continuity, and relationships that have been established can continue. Any information passed between participants in the program will be retained in design.

Table 4-1

Average temperatures and rainfall

City	Longitude	Latitude	Average monthly		Record temp's		Annual avg. rainfall inches/meters	Annual avg. degree days, htg	Annual avg. degree days, cool'g
			Low	High	Low	High			
Hong Kong	22N	114E							
Degrees F			60	83	41	99	87		
Degrees C			15.5	28			2.2		
Montreal	45N	73W							
Degrees F			16.3	72	−31	95	37.7		
Degrees C			−8.7	22			1.1		
Tokyo	35N	139E							
Degrees F			34	87	23	99	60		
Degrees C			1	31			1.8		
Moscow									
Degrees F			11	71	−44	95	23.6		
Degrees C			−12	22			0.6		
Anchorage	69N	149W							
Degrees F			6.6	64.2	−38	92	16.5	10870	0
Degrees C			−14.1	17.9			0.4	6039	0
Boston	42.5N	71.3W							
Degrees F			14.5	82.4	−30	104	44.5	6520	445
Degrees C			−9.7	28			247	3622	247
Houston	29N	95W							
Degrees F			61.2	91.6	9	106	49	1507	2642
Degrees C			16.2	33			1.25	837	1468

(Continued)

Table 4-1

Average temperatures and rainfall (*Continued*)

City	Longitude	Latitude	Average monthly		Record temp's		Annual avg. rainfall inches/meters	Annual avg. degree days, htg	Annual avg. degree days, cool"g
			Low	High	Low	High			
Las Vegas	36N	115W							
Degrees F			27.7	100.9	8	118	4.3	3191	2036
Degrees C			−2.4	38.3			0.1	1773	1131
Orlando	28N	81W							
Degrees F			69.8	91.4	19	100	54	713	3278
Degrees C			21	33			1.37	396	1821

Tempratures in some cities across the globe also including average rainfall and degree days where available from: www.weather.com

If there is time to be gained by not interviewing and selecting another architect and engineering (A/E) design firm, this might be another good reason to stick with the same firm. Some firms do a better job of programming than they do of design. There are a multitude of reasons why any project manager would do things differently in two different project situations.

As in most long-term relationships, there needs to be a good fit among individuals in the decision-making positions. We have heard of architect selections that have been made based on who the owner would most like to have as a dinner guest. When you think of all the hours that will be spent together and the hundreds of decisions that need to be made together (assuming that all the short-listed firms are nearly equal in competence and experience), then this may be as good a selection criterion as any. When you think of the hundreds of millions of dollars that may be at stake, you might make the selection based on logic or a proven track record of delivering complete documents.

One prominent client (the world's largest entertainment company) chooses to hand many of its development projects to one design firm and has been doing so for more than 15 years. When we asked why, we were told that their documents are more complete than those of any competitors. By getting complete documents, the developer has had far fewer change orders during construction. This has several important benefits. Most important, it allows the developer to tie up less money for contingencies. The second factor was reported to be lower operating and repair/replacement costs as a result of good design at the detailed level. We are talking about building envelope performance as it equates with operation and maintenance. These are powerful reasons for selecting that same firm over and over.

You always should reach a comfort level with the design firm before signing a contract. The same goes for a design firm having a comfort level with the owner. First-time relationships can be troublesome, and references may never tell you the full story over the phone. Conversely, they may tell you that the contractor or owner was not honorable when, in reality, the relationship was soured by the person you are talking to in checking the developer's references. First impressions can be right more often than not, but we wouldn't want to be haggling later over an interpretation of a clause in the contract with a developer that was trying to get the designer to pay for contractor's errors. We have found that the people you feel are generally treating you fairly in negotiating a fee will treat you reasonably throughout the relationship. This is why so many architects and builders like to have repeat business. You know what you can expect.

There are two other ways that architects can be selected. One is based on the fee. Some owners will select the A/E team with the lowest fee. This can lead to a successful set of documents with no problems, or it can lead to the least amount of time being spent on the fewest sheets by the least experienced and qualified firm. This can lead to a series of unanticipated changes which could result in significant construction change orders.

The other common traditional means for selection is based on design competition. Some projects are awarded to the firm that comes up with the best-looking model or drawings. In our experience, this accounts for fewer than 2 percent of all projects. If selection is made based on a design that fulfills the building program, it can result in a terrific solution. If, on the other hand, selection is based on a "beauty contest" held before the program is started, it may not be so wonderful. Trying to squeeze a program into a predetermined form does not often result in a functional product for operation. For most client groups, it is a good idea to choose a firm with local participation, a local branch office (at a minimum), and local project management talent. This will make it easiest for timely responses and on-site representation. You could choose a firm based on merits and attitude or relations and then challenge the firm to come up with an acceptable form based on the program. Provide the firm with a good program, complete with image concepts, and let it come up with several quick solutions. In this way, you will have improved your chances of getting an aesthetically pleasing form from a firm in which you have confidence.

4.2 COMMUNICATION

Following our progression, you have selected an architect at this point. Now begins the process of bringing the ideas to fruition. Throughout this process, communications are important to the success of the relationship. Clear, concise, and complete communications will result in the best envelope for the project. It is not enough to have made good design decisions. Design decisions need to be communicated to the owner or developer. Three-dimensional drawings and models are great communicating tools. We cannot expect most people looking at two-dimensional drawings to be able to visualize what a building will look like in three dimensions.

Design decisions have to be made clear to the builders. The plans and specifications need to tell the contractors what the expectations are. In order to minimize the risk for future problems with the building envelope, the details need to clearly illustrate all building components, their dimension, thicknesses, fasteners, relationships, etc.

Communicating concisely requires accurate and explicit comprehension on the part of the second party. If there is confusion or misunderstanding, it can lead to bad decisions. If the plans and specifications call for a permeable air infiltration barrier (AIB), there should be no confusion as to where in the wall system it goes or how it gets installed. It is no longer enough to rely on standard industry details with a vaguely written note. We must do our best to provide drawings that result in what performs well against the elements.

Complete communication implies continuity throughout the design and construction processes. Complete communication includes more than a set of drawings. It now requires more than the standard set of plan and section views and a couple of details. We must continue working with the builders even after the construction documents (CDs) are done. We recommend participation in pre-construction meetings and looking closely at and providing good drawings and text in answering requests for information (RFIs) and in processing submittals. Two-way communications among designers, owners, and builders can result in the best synergy, benefiting from the cumulative knowledge of all participants.

4.3 CARRYING OUT THE CONCEPT

A *concept* is an overriding big idea, the thought behind the expression. Some concept statements can be powerful guiding reasons why their projects stand out in our memories. A few examples are Wright's Falling water and the previously mentioned Sydney Opera House. In them both, the concepts resulted in the solutions being crafted to express the idea. There are other concepts that result in less powerful expressions. "We just want it to blend in with the neighborhood" can be a concept statement. "We want to build it as cheaply as we can" might be more of a direction than a concept. The best building programs will provide the designers with rich visual clues for the client's image goals, such as a nautilus shell on steroids or a collection of sails in the sunset. Even the briefest programs can offer some guidance as to the intended look, feel, or form. The decision makers in the design process then have reasons for making decisions in one direction versus all others. Without guidance from the client, the designer has more freedom to choose his or her own idea of what the building is to be. We could talk about the importance of concept as the subject for a whole book, but since this book looks at the envelope, we will limit our focus to how the concept can be carried out through the envelope in the process of design.

4.4 SCHEMATIC DESIGN

Going back to the traditional delivery system, the designer now begins the *schematic design* (SD) phase, wherein the overall building areas and volumes are established. Different client groups have varying requirements for the SD phase, but the intent of SDs is to give the client an idea of where the architect is heading with the building. Sometimes designers will provide several different SDs for review and discussion before narrowing it down to one. In many projects, mechanical and electrical systems, as well as structural systems, are then introduced over the architectural framework. Throughout SD phase, decisions are made as to the type of systems being planned. This permits coordination to begin taking place to make sure that all the systems have adequate clearances, etc. Another benefit is the opportunity for material takeoffs in a gross sense. SDs are typically the first opportunity for anyone to compare the estimated cost of the planned project with the target budget established earlier. These pricing checks are typically *rough order of magnitude* (ROM) checks and price systems based on previous experience with similar systems, etc. They are not generally used as absolute facts but rather as general guides. Depending on how complete the SDs are and the expertise of those estimating, the SD price check usually can be accurate to about 2–10 percent of the cost when complete. The most useful estimates are projected to project start dates so that inflation is factored in in such a way that the owner can clearly see the contributing factors, the rates used, etc. SD estimates can let designers know if they are moving in the right direction, if some decisions resulted in cost increases, and so forth. Budgetary control is important to prevent envelope failure that can result from cost-cutting. All too often the performance of the building's skin is compromised because of a budget shortfall. Architects can play an important role in preventing this from happening and should do so to limit their liability.

4.4.1 Avoiding future problems

Architects and engineers typically make decisions in the SD phase that affect performance of the completed building. These decisions include systems-level selections that affect the cost as well. The best way to cut costs if an initial estimate comes in high is by reducing square footage. If this is not acceptable, there are several other ways that do not result in a poor envelope. The worst thing is to confuse cost-cutting with value engineering. In *value engineering* (VE), decisions are made that result in nearly equal performance at a lower cost. We have seen VE result in millions of dollars in savings and actually improve performance over the initial design. An example is the change from driven piles to a mat foundation system that was designed for the National High Magnetic Field Laboratory. The estimated cost for the 140 driven piles was more than $840,000, more than the cost of using a 3-foot-thick concrete mat foundation. The mat also served to reduce vibration transmission, which resulted in better test results in the laboratory experiments. We did not have to use up the owner's contingency budget or reduce the building envelope performance to solve the crisis.

Another building envelope VE consideration could include overflow scuppers in lieu of piped internal overflow drains. There is a resulting lower plumbing cost, as well as a more reliable drainage system in using scuppers if the building height and style allow them. We have seen VE effectively improve creature comfort and dehumidification in office complexes while returning savings to the owners. We also have seen occasions when cost-cutting was employed, thinly disguised and referred to as VE, resulting in terrible lawsuits and poor performance. Cost-cutting should be honest. It can be perfectly all right to accept a lower-cost substitute if the performance is still acceptable to the designer, builder, and owner. Other common costs that are cut are square foot costs of material and labor, accepting a lower-cost carpet or tile, for example. This isn't true VE because the value is not comparable.

What hasn't been stated is the obvious issue of getting a lower price for the same thing. Perhaps there are other potential suppliers with better buying power or somebody who is willing to accept a lower profit margin. If the contractor can save time, he or she might be willing to accept a higher-cost material if he or she can get it faster or install it quicker. Before proceeding to design development (DD), the designer and client should insist on a detailed and accurate estimate. If it exceeds the target budget, scope cuts should be made to get it back to budget, or the owner may have to commit some of his or her contingency funds. It is not recommended that the design moves forward without balancing the budget. An alternative means for balancing the budget might be to identify certain scope items that can be deducted at SD phase in the hope of being able to add them back in as design and pricing are more refined. What one must try to prevent is getting forced into cost-cutting on the building envelope, lower-cost windows, cheaper air-conditioning systems, reduced insulation thickness or average R value, omitted membranes, sill pan omission, or fewer plies of membrane on the roof. Any of these can result in reduced envelope performance and potential future intrusion of moisture or water-related problems. By making adjustments at the end of SDs, the project team should be able to complete the design through every future phase without risk of a poorly performing building envelope.

4.4.2 Liquid water

Liquid water causes the great majority of mold and mildew problems and the largest volume of claims for damages. We have read numbers ranging anywhere from 65 percent up to more than 85 percent of all damage is caused by water in the liquid state. This is why most of our efforts in developing details for buildings are located at the skin. Beginning with the roof and other relatively flat surfaces, such as balconies or amenity decks, we develop wall sections and details to convey water down and away from occupied spaces. At the intersections of roof planes and wall surfaces, we supply enlarged details, providing guidance for each building trade to follow. On walls, we have multiple sheets with plan and section sketches for preventing water intrusion, especially at openings. Window and door openings, louvers, grilles, etc. are the most important holes in the wall where water can be introduced. Then we go on down to the wall-to-floor intersection and floor systems. Each of these conditions has challenges. Each has potential problems that must be addressed carefully and successfully for the building envelope to perform well in normal rain events. We have to step it up a few notches and do extremely well to protect against extreme weather events such as hurricanes and high-wind-speed rain events.

Water normally is expected in the form of rain. Rain typically falls down from the sky in a more or less vertical direction. Traditional design and construction methods perform fairly well in these conditions. Overhangs were introduced thousands of years ago to keep rain from coming in open windows and to shade walls. As buildings got taller and materials became more expensive, fewer windows and doors were protected by overhanging roof planes (overhangs). With more windows and doors exposed to the elements, more leaks occurred. When the rain (or snow) gets blown by high winds, gravity is overcome, and the particles come from every direction. Some rain intensities can exceed design values. Wind-driven rain can build up against vertical planes such as walls or roof parapets, causing unique situations that may not have been planned for. Some maintenance procedures cause water to be blown at high velocity and pressures at buildings from every conceivable angle. How can we prevent problems from all these scenarios?

Our principles are based on three simple words: *gravity, geometry,* and *technology.* We will show you our proven methods for first selecting the right kind of wall for your project and then executing appropriate detailing methods and following them up as the project gets built.

Water has many different ways to move into buildings. The two most common forces moving water are gravity and air. We have already briefly discussed rainfall and water moved by gravity. Whether it is one drop or 2 feet of accumulated water on the roof, gravity is the most constant motive force. We stop it with sloped roofing products that rely on gravity to move the water off the roof.

4.4.3   Airborne water

Let us now discuss the second motive force—air. Airborne water can be moving in any direction. Typically, it moves at less than 45 degrees from vertical. Rain falling at an angle can strike every building surface. Most buildings are designed to convey water down and away from the occupied spaces. The smallest holes in the building envelope can permit gallons of water per hour to enter the envelope. Unfortunately, if those holes occur where horizontal surfaces meet vertical ones, as they typically do, the depth of water can build up, and water pressure can increase, allowing even more water in. We therefore must pay special attention to these conditions.

The best way to prevent airborne water is to stop the air. There are many ways to do this, but the most successful methods are based on a relatively airtight building envelope. We use materials that air cannot move through as an air barrier. Metal and glass are very good; concrete block and wood are not as good. We frequently use a combination of products depending on the condition. Building paper and asphalt-coated building sheets or felts have been used for centuries to reduce moisture and air infiltration.

4.4.4   Water vapor

Water vapor is not so different from airborne water droplets except for size. When the air is warm and dry enough, water stays in the gaseous state. As the air cools, the vapor condenses. The more it condenses, the closer packed the vapor molecules become, until they join one another and form larger molecules. If the temperature is below freezing, it forms solid water (snow or ice). If the temperature is above freezing, it makes drops of liquid water. This takes place in the walls, just like in clouds. When water freezes in a wall (or any other cavity), it expands. This can result in voids in the building envelope. When the ice melts these voids remain which can create pathways for water to enter the cavity. Water vapor can move through solids and air (gas). Vaporous water molecules are so small and light that they can be moved easily. Vapors can move even if no wind is present. They move as a result of temperature differential, pressure gradients, or capillary action. This is referred to as *vapor drive.* Even if there is positive pressure in a building, vapor may be drawn in just by temperature. Energy moves from cool to warm, so if the vapor is cooler than the inside air temperature, it will move inward. It is always trying to reach equilibrium state. Just like water on the roof, it has potential energy based on the height above the ground. It wants to reach the relaxed state with no potential.

Water vapors are more difficult to stop than liquid or airborne water because of the size of the molecules. There are many materials that resist the transmission of liquid water but allow water vapor to move through easily. Materials that permit moisture to move through them are called *hygroscopic.* The more easily moisture moves through them, the more permeable they are. Permeability is measured in perms. A *perm* is a unit of measure equal to the amount of water in grams that moves through a material at a certain temperature and pressure. Glass and plastic have a perm rating of about zero. Construction materials that have ratings lower than 1 (1.0 grams) are referred to as *moisture-reduction barriers,* or *vapor barriers.* Table 4-2 lists the perm ratings of common materials.

4.4.5 Condensation

Condensation is the last of the water-related building envelope issues we are going to address. Condensation as it relates to our built environment takes place when air cools to the point where, much like it does in the clouds, water vapour within it changes state from gas to liquid. Water droplets are formed on cool surfaces or on the face of membranes. This can be the inside painted face of a wall system in the winter or the cold side of insulation. Condensation can form on air-conditioning ducts, grilles, windows, or wherever the temperature is below the dew point. This water can lead to mold growth, just like any other form of moisture. This is why designers must calculate anticipated conditions in buildings and provide adequate insulation, the right membranes, and temperature-control devices. In some conditions, you only need to reduce the temperature of the air or a surface a few degrees to reach the dew point. The more moisture there is in the air to start with, the greater is the volume of water that will be formed by condensation. This is why we try to reduce moisture moving through walls, as well as reduce the humidity of the air in the space. Rooms in which the building heating, ventilation, and air-conditioning (HVAC) system supplies conditioned air that maintains less than 50 percent relative humidity (RH) in the space have been shown to prevent mold growth as compared with rooms that have gone above 60 percent RH for extended periods of time. Keeping rooms relatively dry helps to draw moisture out of the walls and ceiling cavities. This reduces conditions that support mold growth in the walls.

Early in the design process, we must establish the parameters for operation and calculate how to achieve them. Minimal insulation thicknesses need to be

Table 4-2

Perm ratings of common materials

Number	Product	Thickness	Rating
1	Aluminum Foil	1 mil.	0
2	Built-up roofing (Hot mopped)	2 ply	0
3	Polyethylene Film	6 mil.	0.06
4	Self-Adhesive Membrane	0.03	0.08
5	Fluid Applied Elastomeric Topping	36 mil.	1.08
6	Urethane Foam Roofing	30 mil.	2.9
7	Acrylic Elastomer Coatings	10 mil.	8.7
8	Varnish on wood	6 mil.	0.4
9	Enamels on Plaster and Stucco	8 mil.	0.75
10	Latex Paints	8 mil.	5
11	Hot-Melt Asphalt	3 oz/s. f.	0.1
12	Kraft Paper	na	0.4
13	15 pound asphaltic felt	na	6
14	Roll Roofing	0.03	0.25
15	Extruded Poly Styrene board	per inch	1.2
16	Expanded Poly-Styrene board	na	3.75
17	GFRP, glass reinforced polyester board	48 mil.	0.05
18	Plywood, fir, exterior glue	$1/2$"	0.4
19	Plywood, fir, interior glue	$1/2$"	0.95
20	Gypsum Board	$1/2$"	38
21	Plaster on Lath	$3/4$"	15
22	Concrete Block	8" Nom.	2.4
23	Concrete	per inch	3.2
24	Brick	4" Nom.	0.95

Averaged from several manufacturers' product data sheets along with architectural graphic standard (Ramsey and Sleeper).

established in conjunction with mechanical system sizing and air distribution schemes. Window leakage rates, U values, and emittance are determined. Methods of ventilation, building pressurization, and exhausting are decided. Once these essential decisions are made, design can proceed to the next stage.

4.5 COMPLETING THE DESIGN

In the design development (DD) stage, all systems are shown on plans and described in specifications. Our big three ideas—gravity, geometry, and technology—must be carried through the building design. It is in this stage that the designers fully develop the systems-level thinking they expressed in the SD phase. By the end of DD, architects will be providing detailed instructions to the builder as to each component that makes up the chosen systems. Drawings will be developed showing builders how they will be joining the systems together—thicknesses, fasteners, pressures, colors, finishes, textures, dimensions, and all pertinent data for full and complete estimation of costs. This, in our opinion, is the purpose of DD drawings. Of course, it is important for the designer to make sure that there is adequate space in the ceiling cavity for all components, that structures do not stick out of the wall, and that power is provided where it is needed for coordination purposes, but the main purpose for DDs is pricing.

4.5.1 Site design

Beginning with site design, cut and fill sections are very useful. You should have soil reports to define the bearing capacity of the ground, and you should look for groundwater issues, drainage patterns, etc. Utility connections and roads, storm water, landscape, and irrigation issues should be addressed. Of them, drainage and groundwater-related issues are most important. This is where you make certain that wherever you place the building, you are not creating water-intrusion problems at grade. Finish floor elevations are established, drainage patterns are designed, volumes for storm water retention and runoff are engineered, etc. Always make certain that finish floor elevations are at least 6 to 8 inches (15 to 20 centimeters) above finish grade for proper drainage (except for earth-sheltered or basement floors).

Site design issues that affect water intrusion start with conveying surface water away from the building footprint. Slope should be away from exterior walls on all sides. Even if the building is located on the downslope of a hill, a swale should be cut into the uphill portion of the site so as to create drainage away from the exterior wall on that side as well. Soil bearing conditions can affect long-term performance of a building exterior wall system. If you are designing a barrier wall out of concrete block, brick, or stucco, you need to minimize differential settling of the foundations. If excessive settling occurs along any portion of the exterior wall system, cracking can result. Use of a perimeter grade beam can reduce the cracking. If the crack exceeds the elongation of the paint, voids will occur in the barrier. The same is true for drainage and rain screen walls. If you know that the site is likely to have excessive differential settling, you can either limit the length of the footprint or use materials such as wood that allow bending. By reducing building length, you reduce cracking forces. By using a more flexible wall system, you can reduce cracking as well.

4.5.2 Floor system

Building finish floor elevations can't always be that far above finish grade. There are accessibility issues that require many entrances and exits to be located no more than $1/2$ inch (1.25 centimeters) below finish floor. This makes it easier and safer for many people to enter and exit public buildings. This accessibility requirement makes it more challenging for you to meet the building code–required 6 inches

Figure 4-1

Elevations at the door.

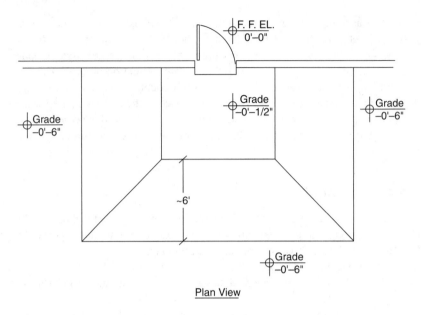

Plan View

above finish grade. You must work closely with the civil engineers (if involved in your project) to make sure that you meet both of these conflicting sets of requirements.

Figure 4-1 shows in plan view how the area directly outside the door can meet the accessibility code. From there you begin to gently slope down and away at less than 4 percent slope for about 6 feet (1.8 meters) in all three directions. You also have a slight step down at the doorway to minimize wind-driven rain water intrusion opportunities at the door. Figure 4-2 shows a section through the threshold. The site must slope away from the building to prevent rain levels from approaching the finish floor elevation, even during a 50- or 100-year storm event. Conveyance devices for surface water drainage need to be reliable. You don't want to rely on a system that is easily blocked or will not work if power is lost. As a last resort, you can rely on closed underground piping, vaults, and/or pumped systems. For these reasons, we tend to prefer gravity as the force to move water in open swales away from the building. For "green" building concepts, we have several swale methods that function to capture rainwater for reuse and purification that work along with gravity draining water away from our building pads. One such scheme uses a series of percolation beds to capture nutrients and pollutants and then relies on select plant materials to reduce the pollution's effects on the downstream discharge off-site. Percolation beds and bioswales are two useful natural processes using free energy to reduce potentially harmful effects of storm water pollution from cars and buildings on the environment.

4.5.2.1 Below-grade floor systems

Assume that the program requires one floor or a basement to be built below grade, and just to make it challenging, consider that the site is located near a lake. We will use the example of a groundwater table located about 6 feet (~2 meters)

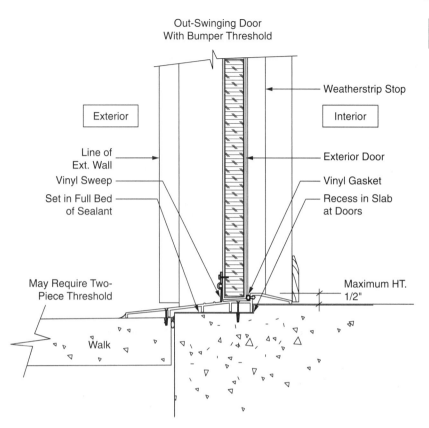

Out-Swinging Door
With Bumper Threshold

Weatherstrip Stop

Exterior

Interior

Line of
Ext. Wall

Exterior Door

Vinyl Sweep

Vinyl Gasket

Set in Full Bed
of Sealant

Recess in Slab
at Doors

May Require Two-
Piece Threshold

Maximum HT.
1/2"

Walk

Figure 4-2
Section at threshold.

below finish floor elevation. Whether it is a tall building or not, the envelope issues are similar. There will be groundwater considerations. The basement floor slab and a portion of the lowest walls will be below the water line. There are three common solution sets for this example. The first is the most reliable. It relies on overexcavation of the wall area so that workers have access to the outside of the wall. You begin by installing dewatering heads (well points), pipes, and hoses with a pumping system. Then you may begin excavation below the normal water table without digging in water. Excavate to a point below the bottom of finish floor, and begin compaction. You may need to bring in some rock or gravel to attain adequate compaction. We recommend using a 4- to 6-inch mud slab. A *mud slab* is a concrete subfloor with minimal reinforcing steel placed just beneath the finish floor slab bottom elevation. In this scenario, machines would have carefully excavated an area beyond the exterior walls sufficient for working access space, say, another 3 feet minimum (6 feet ideally) horizontally (1 to 2 meters). Depending on the soil and how much space is available around the perimeter, this may require sheet piles for soil retention (see Fig. 4-3). Many soils won't retain a high angle of repose.

The designer will have selected an appropriate membrane system to place on top of the mud slab to serve as the water barrier under the finish floor slab. Both sheet membranes and liquid (or fluid) applied membranes can be used.

Figure 4-3
Sheet piles.

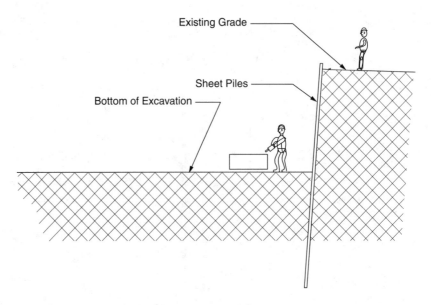

Two of the most commonly relied on sheet membranes are very different in their makeup. The first is similar to plastic or rubber sheet material. This material varies in thickness but is typically in the range of 60 to 80 mils. These sheets are sealed where they lap to prevent water under pressure from coming in contact with the future floor system. The sheets are extended past the edge of the floor so that they can be seamed to the wall membrane later.

The other commonly used materials rely on very fine particles, such as volcanic ash or bentonite, woven into a fabric mat. The mat is installed in a similar manner to the rubber-like sheets on top of the mud slab and extended past the edge. These sheets, however, are not sealed at the laps but rather merely laid on top of one another. The idea behind these products is to use the fine particles to seal the void between the mud slab and finish slab to prevent water from penetrating the bottom surface of the finish floor slab. The fine particles will swell up many times their dry size, effectively filling the space tightly and thereby prevent moisture from moving through the slab.

For a redundant system in a hard-to-reach location, such as a pedestrian tunnel below a highway system, where you will not be able to reach it in the future and where performance is critical, you might choose to use a combination of both systems. Manufacturers offer a hybridized composite with a combination of bentonite and sheet membranes with sealed lap joints. These have higher initial cost but offer the greatest reliability and resistance to groundwater penetration. An active dewatering system would be another potential solution to reduce or avoid hydrostatic pressure after the building is complete.

In some areas, an additional layer of sand or fine stone is placed on top of the membrane and under the finish slab's reinforcing steel. This *blotter layer,* as it is called, reduces the risk of penetration or damage to the membrane and increases drainage potential. The basement floor slab is then placed on top of the membrane materials or blotter. Care must be taken not to damage or displace the membrane during steel and concrete placement. In this example, the wall forms are placed next, and then exterior walls are poured in place. The weak link in this method is the joint between the floor and wall. Water stop systems need to be installed in the detail between the floor and wall (see Fig. 4-4). Bentonite, rubber, and galvanized or stainless steel are all used commonly. After the exterior wall forms are removed, the sheet materials (or fluid/liquid applied membranes) are applied to the cured concrete, lapped properly, and seamed, if appropriate. Backfill material is applied in lifts and compacted properly. Special care must be taken with the bentonite during backfill because it is not fully adhered to the walls and cannot resist damage from careless equipment operation, such as a backhoe. For bentonite to work properly, the backfill must be well compacted against the mat.

A less expensive process does not use a mud slab. The membrane is placed on top of the compacted earthen material below the finish floor slab. Reinforcing steel is put on top of the membrane (and possibly the blotter layer) prior to concrete placement. Quality control typically is not as good in this process. Sidewall excavation might not extend past the slab edge. It is more difficult to fully seal the blind side of a wall system. Wall membranes are applied prior to wall concrete placement.

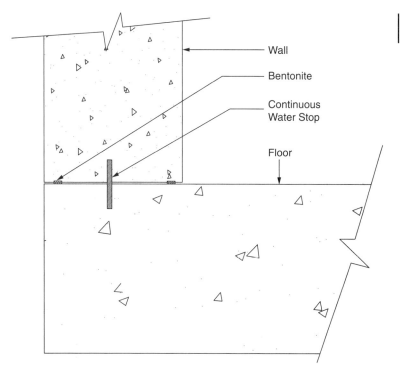

Figure 4-4
Water stop systems.

Wall

Bentonite

Continuous
Water Stop

Floor

The least expensive process would be to put the waterproof membrane on the inside of the concrete floor and walls. There are several products made especially for this application, and they are applied like an epoxy paint coating. Depending on the client, the use, and the exact water pressures and volumes, the designer must choose a system that prevents water (liquid and vapor) from entering the building. If you don't have enough experience to make the decision, hire a consultant specialist or get guidance from the contracting firm. As with all things in the envelope, there is a relationship between initial cost and water intrusion. It is not quite as simple as pay more, get more, but generally, this rule holds true.

In the nonpermeable sheet membrane systems, it is recommended that the wall surface below finish grade (and especially below the water table) uses a drainage board or similar system to promote vertical movement of water. The drainage board gets installed against the membrane after it is applied to the concrete face and extends vertically, where it terminates into a footing drain system. The footing drain is designed to convey groundwater from the foundation system using perforated pipe and filter fabric. The fabric reduces clogging of the perforations and increases the efficiency of the footing drain. It also can lengthen its useful life. Typically, the drain is constructed with coarse gravel surrounding the pipe bed. Depending on site conditions, this drain system may be active or passive. In an underground stream, one might expect an active system with pumps discharging into storm piping or an elevated drain field downstream. For occasional groundwater, a passive drainage system may suffice.

4.5.2.2 Building partially below grade

Earth-sheltered design and construction have at least a portion of the building located below finish grade elevation (see Fig. 4-5). There are ways to deal with the envelope to prevent problems with water intrusion and condensation. You have to carefully consider temperatures on both sides and within the walls. You must stop water from penetrating the *moisture-reduction barrier* (MRB) from the outside and permit drying from the MRB in both directions. The way to achieve that is to have increasing perm ratings for each successive material, starting with the MRB and going in both directions (see Fig. 4-6). In order to protect the integrity of the MRB, we frequently place drainage boards outside the barrier as a part of a composite wall system. The best protection boards have drainage cavities built in. The insulation is placed inside the MRB in warm climates. Some exterior walls are made of block, but formed concrete is better. Calculate temperature gradients for all seasons and operating conditions prior to designing the insulation products and R values. Typically, rigid insulation is used on the exterior of the wall, inside the MRB. Closed-cell insulation is preferred to open-cell foams. Refer to Section 4.6.8 for a discussion of insulation.

Drainage boards and footing drains are commonly used to protect the rigid insulation and to promote drainage. They combine to provide easy pathways for vertical flow of rainwater and prevent it from staying in contact with the membrane long after rains have stopped. Calculations may show that additional

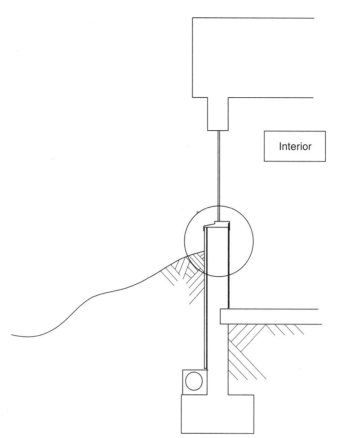

Figure 4-5
Section at earth sheltered wall.

insulation should be added to the interior of the concrete masonry unit (CMU) or concrete wall as a second means of preventing condensation resulting from the dew point having been reached in the wall. Remember, the ground temperature does not vary much. Extreme thermal gradients may take place vertically in exterior walls in earth-sheltered construction, and gradients can cause water and vapor drive. Another important consideration is thermal conductance by materials in the wall. Metal furring and stud framing are excellent thermal conductors. It is always a good idea to interrupt the thermal bridging between exterior masonry and good conductors such as steel. Wood is a good thermal insulator by comparison. If metal framing or furring is to be used, it may be useful to install a thin sheet of insulation material between the concrete or block and the metal.

In cold climates, the thermal insulation should be on the inside face of the wall anyway, so it is in the right place. We recommend using open-cell expanded polystyrene (EPS) boards to isolate the wall from metal framing. Metal framing or furring channels can be fastened right through the insulation with powder-actuated fasteners or screws in such a way that the interior wall sheathing can be installed to the framing. While it can be challenging to keep the framing plumb and true, it can be done with the use of a torque setting on the screw driver. In the

Figure 4-6

Permeability increases
from membrane.

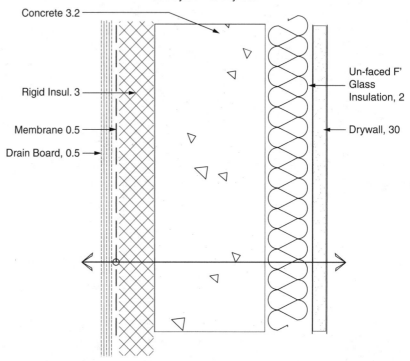

**Permeability of Materials Should Increase from the
Vapor Barrier, in Each Direction**

Moisture Needs to Leave the Walls in Order for the
Wall System to Dry Out

Concrete 3.2

Rigid Insul. 3

Membrane 0.5

Drain Board, 0.5

Un-faced F'
Glass
Insulation, 2

Drywall, 30

cold climate, then add insulation between the framing and install a vapor barrier. We recommend that you always calculate the dew point in the wall for winter and summer conditions before deciding where and how to insulate the walls.

If windows are used in the earth-sheltered walls, the window sills must be flashed carefully to convey rainwater out past the MRB below (see Fig. 4-7). We recommend that interior walls below grade be constructed out of permeable wall sheathings containing only inert materials, such as glass fiber reinforced or cementitious building products painted with breathable paints. Placing vinyl wall covering (VWC) on or near an exterior wall in earth-sheltered construction (or any other) is never recommended. VWC has very low permeability and will cause condensation to form. Do not use epoxy paints or ceramic tile, except after careful consideration and certain steps are taken to prevent mold and mildew formation.

4.5.2.3 Floors at or above grade

Perhaps the most common floor material is dirt. There are still a lot of people living in humble shelters with dirt floors. Concrete, stone, and woods floor systems are all used widely in developed countries. Concrete floors are often cast in place on grade. These are referred to as *slab on grade*. A number of products are used to reduce vapor transmission through the soil and the concrete slab and

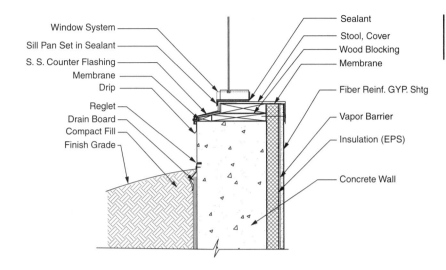

Figure 4-7
Sill flashing on earth
sheltered wall.

to aid in hydration of the concrete as it cures. Plastic sheet membranes are commonly placed under the concrete after soil treatment has been applied. Recently, this membrane has been increased from the old standard 6-mil sheet to a new standard of 10 mil. Reinforced membranes are also available. These reduce the likelihood of rips and tears that can result from steel and concrete placement, workers walking on the chairs, etc. One should inspect the integrity of the membrane prior to placing the concrete. Any punctures, rips, or penetrations should be sealed against moisture movement prior to concrete placement. This includes sealing pipes or conduits that penetrate the membrane. After the concrete has been placed, it gets leveled, smoothed, and finished.

Specifications often recommend different ways to maintain adequate water in the concrete mix for full hydration. Among the most common means are water curing, where water is sprayed on top of the curing slab for a few days, and application of curing agents. Curing agents seal the concrete surface, preventing evaporation. Curing agents trap the water that was in the mix when the concrete was placed. Curing agents also may act like a coat of sealer after curing is complete. This may aid slightly in reducing moisture movement through the top of the slab long after the concrete is fully hydrated. Curing agents may not work well with subsequent finishes, such as ceramic tile, stone, glued down carpet, or vinyl composition tile and therefore must be selected and applied with consideration of future material compatibility.

If non-compatible products are used, there are mechanical and chemical means for ensuring good bonding. Manufacturers' recommendations often include shot blasting and etching with a mild acid solution. Whenever acids are used, you must consider the possible reactions with exposed materials in the vicinity. Metals such as brass or aluminum may be used in wall tracks or door and window systems, and these items should not be installed or stored in proximity of acid etching. Acid fumes will ruin most metal finishes. Floor sanders, grinders, and sand blasting may be acceptable alternatives to acid. Old-fashioned soap and water applied with a nylon brush or pad is another means of final preparation in lieu of acid.

Concrete slabs on grade should be placed at an elevation that will prevent wind-driven water from ever reaching their top elevation (finish floor level). Most building codes require 6 inches (15 centimeters) minimum from finish grade to finish floor. A good rule of thumb is 8 inches (20 centimeters).

Depending on the location and wind and rain issues, you should consider the use of a recessed slab edge detail (see Fig. 4-8). The depth of the recess is normally between $1^1/_2$ to 2 inches and must be coordinated with the wall thickness. The purpose of the recessed edge is to aid in the prevention of water intrusion. It goes back to gravity and geometry. The geometry is such that any water that gets past the first line of defense at the exterior face of the wall then must climb up the vertical face of the backside of the recess before it gets into the building. This is another reason why we prefer 8 inches above grade—we still have 6 inches below the low point of the recess to finish grade.

If subterranean termites are a consideration, we urge you to increase the height above finish grade to 10 or 12 inches. Entomologists teach us that termites cannot survive if exposed to the sun's rays. Sunlight dries them out, and they die. Therefore, subterranean termites construct little tunnels out of dirt to

Figure 4-8
Slab edge recess.

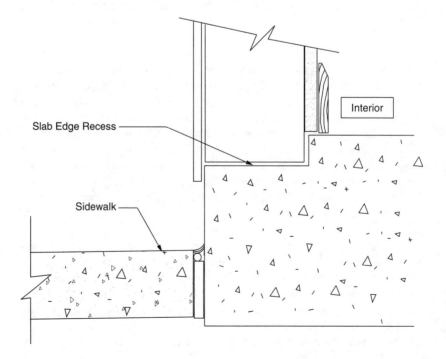

protect themselves. These tunnels can be seen by a quick inspection of the building perimeter and swept away with a broom quite easily. It takes the termites in Florida a little over a year to build these tunnels more than 6 or 8 inches high, so a once-a-year inspection can prevent the termites from getting into the walls. If their tunnels are not destroyed, the termites will make tunnels in the envelope that water and other insects will follow.

4.5.2.4 Elevated first floors

Wood-frame construction typically is built above a crawl space with varying heights above grade. Masonry piers or wood posts are used commonly to support the floor beams and girders. Wood flooring is usually made out of plywood or planks that span over floor joists. Joists are usually installed between 16 and 24 inches (0.5 meter) apart. The crawl spaces typically are ventilated by allowing openings for natural ventilation by wind currents. The purpose of the vents is to (in theory) prevent moisture buildup from decaying wood structural products (joists and decking). In warm climates, they may in fact introduce warm, humid air because the ambient conditions are such. In cold climates, the vents are kept to a minimum or closed off in the winter. An alternative is to ventilate the space mechanically and seal it off to the outside ambient air. This is the preferred solution for moisture control because it reduces vapor drive. In any scenario, we recommend insulating the area below the floor when possible.

The perm rating of the material needs to be considered, much as in a wall or roof system. You want an MRB on the warm side of the insulation and should plan for drying materials both ways from the MRB—inward and outward. In hot, humid climates, we recommend an air and moisture barrier on the outside of the insulation. Introduce enough conditioned air to the cavity to create positive pressure to the outside (outside the crawl space), yet negative pressure relative to the occupied side of the floor. This may be a good place for variable-permeability insulation, kraft-backed fiberglass insulation, or perhaps extruded polystyrene. You must coordinate permeability of the floor finish with the MRB to prevent trapping moisture in the floor. A good rule of thumb is 4 to 1. This goes for walls and roof systems as well as floors. The lowest perm-rated material in the floor should be 4 times less permeable than any subsequent vapor barrier. Therefore, if you are using stone, terrazzo, vinyl composition tile (VCT), or ceramic tile as a finish material, then the membrane outside the insulation should be 4 times more or less permeable. If you are installing finished wood flooring with a urethane finish, the membrane outside the insulation must be 4 times more permeable because urethane has such a low permeability. If carpet is being applied to plywood subfloor, a low-perm membrane should be used. In cold climates, the low-perm membrane should be below the subfloor and inside the insulation. A foil-backed insulation can be installed (foil up) on top of the floor joists before the subfloor is installed.

Floors above grade, for example, second floors and higher in multistory buildings, should be treated much the same as ground-level floors. One difference is that upper-level floors need to stop at the inside face of the exterior walls to prevent rainwater from having an easy pathway to the floor. Water should be conveyed down and away from exterior walls. Exterior walkways should be maintained 6 to 8 inches (20 centimeters) below finish floor. Try to design the building so that occupied spaces are stacked above occupied spaces. It is more challenging and more expensive (not to mention risky) to have occupied, conditioned spaces below outside walkways and decks. In these situations, the outdoor walks and decks must be treated almost like a roof surface, and rainwater must be dealt with. On concrete slabs above grade, with occupied floors above and below, the concrete does not need to be placed on a sheet membrane (air or moisture barrier). Since the ambient conditions are so similar, except for personal comfort set-point differences, there should be very little vapor drive. Whether formed and poured slabs, filled metal deck, or precast slabs, the concrete should suffice to minimize transmitted moisture through the slabs.

4.5.3 Floor-to-wall intersections

The floor-to-wall condition varies depending on the structural and wall systems in use. There are so many that we cannot address each of them in the limited number of pages in this book. We will provide several examples of floor-to-wall conditions that represent the different families of solutions in hopes of explaining the building envelope considerations that affect water intrusion. In the wall sections provided (see Fig. 4-9), you will see several details expressing good, better, and best design conditions for several common wall and floor systems. This example illustrates a concrete barrier wall

Figure 4-9

Floor-to-wall section, good.

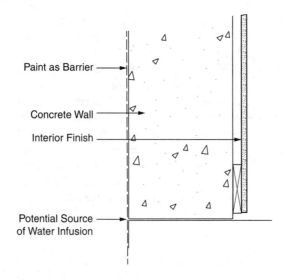

Paint as Barrier

Concrete Wall

Interior Finish

Potential Source
of Water Infusion

without a slab edge recess, utilizing a continuous application of paint on the exterior face to reduce water and vapor transmission. This is a very common condition, however many such walls extend far below finish floor to block intrusion above grade.

You must first understand the conditions for which you are designing. This goes far beyond understanding the climate. You need to know the client and his or her plans for the building in terms of type of ownership, performance expectations, maintenance, etc. You must consider the available budget for the entire project, the owner's experience, the schedule, available work force, and materials availability. All of this should go into the decision. None of it, however important it might seem at the time, is as important as the weather. If you are designing for West Palm Beach, Florida, where there is high wind coupled with more than 40 inches (1.15 meters) average annual rainfall, you must design for the likelihood of wind-driven rain being blown up into the corners and wherever the walls meet the ground. These details must prevent the intrusion of liquid and vaporous water with high pressure behind it.

There are many ways to improve the performance of the earlier example, such as one using an applied closure strip over the joint between floor and wall, (see Fig. 4-10). This example uses an applied vapor retarder behind the applied finish coat of paint. A better design would have the wall sitting in a slab edge recess to reduce the likelihood of wind-driven water reaching the floor elevation, (see Fig. 4-11). As you can see, each successive layer of exterior wall components is lapped over the previous. This has the proven potential to perform better, if well constructed. This detail applies gravity, geometry, and technology all working together. This kind of wall section can not only resist

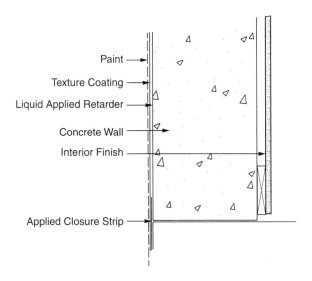

Figure 4-10
Floor-to-wall section, better.

Figure 4-11

Floor-to-wall section, best.

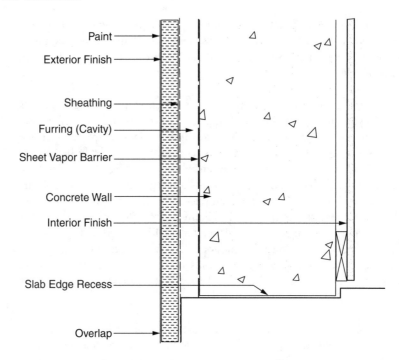

Paint

Exterior Finish

Sheathing

Furring (Cavity)

Sheet Vapor Barrier

Concrete Wall

Interior Finish

Slab Edge Recess

Overlap

wind-driven rain but also works well if water is sprayed on the wall from irrigation systems or pressure washers.

How on earth can you be expected to design a wall system to withstand all this and be affordable? Well, do not despair; Gravity, geometry, and technology are here for your use. The combination of flashings, membranes, finishes, and sealants can prove more than capable to work in concert, over time, to be reliable long-term solutions. You may have to convince the owner not to use the $96 per square foot imported tile on the walls of his or her foyer in order to pay for the membranes and flashings, but real solutions often require compromise and conviction to proven practices and principles. We would like to think that this is why our clients hire professionals, for the benefits of our knowledge and judgment. After we find out the criteria, and hierarchy of needs, we can design an envelope to meet all their needs, aesthetic as well as initial and long-term cost and maintainability. If our buildings are to last centuries, not just a decade or two, we must often choose a system that performs well over the long haul, such as a brick on block cavity wall, (see Fig. 4-12). Depending upon the climate, workforce, image, and other considerations, you may choose to use wood frame exterior walls, with exterior sheathing, in a drainage plane configuration. Figure 4.13 provides an enlarged section indicating a combination of membranes and flashings that should resist wind-driven and even pressure washing water at the floor to wall joint over time.

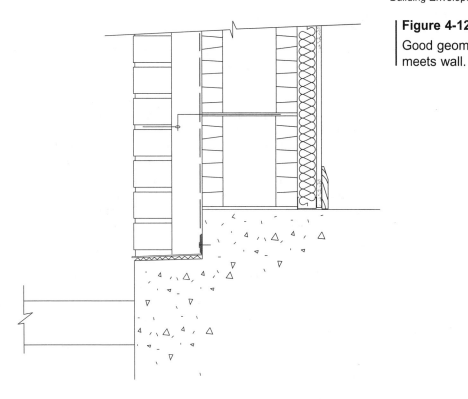

Figure 4-12
Good geometry where slab meets wall.

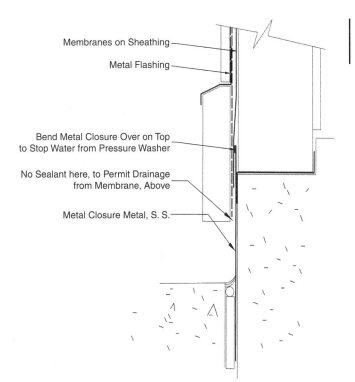

Figure 4-13
Enlarged wall section at slab to wall intersection.

Membranes on Sheathing

Metal Flashing

Bend Metal Closure Over on Top to Stop Water from Pressure Washer

No Sealant here, to Permit Drainage from Membrane, Above

Metal Closure Metal, S. S.

4.5.4 Walls

Assuming that we have applied the lessons learned from earlier segments, we have the floor higher than the grade or walk. We start off by looking at several regular wall conditions, and then go on to look at a door section or two. It is always a good idea to research the applicable building codes before designing a building, even if you are familiar with the historical codes in the area. Codes are changing. Since many areas of North America have adopted the International Building Code (IBC), we will introduce the 2005 changes from the Florida Building Code (FBC) as an example. Florida incorporated the IBC prior to 2004, supplanting the old Southern Standard Building Code. After Hurricane Charley, the state and local code officials hired a panel of experts (including Joseph Lstiburek) to review buildings damaged by the storm and recommend changes to the 2004 code. x. The following are paraphrased changes:

FBC Section 1403.3.2: The exterior wall envelope shall have flashing. The exterior wall must have a water resistive barrier behind the exterior veneer and a way to drain water to the outside (unless water that gets behind the veneer doesn't cause problems). Protect against condensation. A weather resistive veneer is not required on concrete or CMU walls. All finishes shall be installed according to the manufacturer's recommendations. You don't have to drain the wall if water in the wall has been proven by a prescribed testing method to not cause problems.

FBC Section 1403.9: Must have flashings where drainage wall upper stories are built on top of mass (CMU) walls on lower floors to keep water outside the face of the mass wall.

FBC Section 1404.2: Must use water resistive barriers (MRBs) and bond breakers in exterior stucco walls on frame construction.

FBC Section 1404.2.2: You can comply with 1404.2 by using two MRBs, or a plastic house wrap and one MRB, or other methods approved by manufacturers. This can be achieved by using paper backed lath and a MRB such as a 15 pound building felt.

Building codes will continue to change, trying to provide better minimums for future buildings. Remember that the codes are establishing minimums. Even the American Society of Heating, Refrigerating, and Air-Conditioning Engineers (ASHRAE) and the U.S. Department of Energy (DOE) are trying to keep up with the trend toward better building design.

Our designs are perceived by the observer mostly through visual feedback. Our eyes receive reflected light, our nervous systems transmit signals, and our minds process information. We use stored memories as a means for understanding what is in our visual field. Humans look for meaning, and compare what we know with what we see. What is it like? We look for visual clues such as form, size, texture, color, and other information to form an assessment of the building in front of us. The two dominant components of a building in our visual field are the walls and roof. Since the walls are typically located in the most prominent viewing angles and make up the greatest percentage of the visual information we process, they are the single most determining factor in how we perceive a building (for most buildings).

At the next level of analysis, perhaps as we move closer, we begin to study the fenestration of the walls. Fenestration includes the windows and doors, line work, and other differentiating characteristics on the facade. The way these elements of design are composed affects our perception of the whole. It may be a chaotic staccato composition intended to jolt our senses, or the facade could be a rhythmic concert of parts (see Fig. 4-14). We may perceive a smooth, seamless obelisk that reflects light at all angles or a massive dark mass of piers and buttresses. The skin of the building typically impacts our senses with the most visual information and forms the lasting impression in our memories. Perhaps that is why many designers look first at shaping the forms and surfaces in their design process.

The facade and its fenestration also have significant impact on our senses from the inside of the building. Windows and doors are dominant features in our visual field as we experience a building's interior. Even with electric lighting

Figure 4-14

Staccato or rhythmic façade, Perimeter Institute of Physics, by Saucier Perrotte Architects. Photo by Marc Cramer.

throughout most buildings, the contrasting light levels during day or night at window glazing capture our visual interest. The size, shape, proximity, clarity, and views through these portals tend to attract our attention. For these reasons and more, many architects design from the inside out. We consider the views and light to be of primary importance in the process of design.

4.5.5 Some modern examples from across the globe

By skillful manipulation of views, light, shade, and shadow, architects such as the Canadian firm of Saucier Perrotte with offices in Quebec and Montreal, Canada can craft an experiential place (see Fig. 4-15). The company's Perimeter Institute for Research in Theoretical Physics provides us with an exceptional example of design to stir the senses. The window planes are set at a variety of distances from the observer, creating a more nebulous space than would be created by a simple vertical wall (see Fig. 4-16). The designers wanted to create a space where students would ponder everything—from the micro- to macrocosmic. The designers took their conceptual ideas from sketch to reality.

This building is three stories tall, using steel post and beam primary structural systems. Two primary open spaces are the main hall on the ground floor and the garden on the first floor. Offices flank the great spaces to provide visual connection between staff and students. The designers wanted to connect the different levels of the facility through the great garden space (see concept sketch,

Figure 4-15

Perimeter Institute Photo, by Saucier Perrotte Architects. Photo by Marc Cramer.

Figure 4-16
Section at exterior wall, above, by Saucier Perrotte Architects.

1 Roof Composition
  Zinc Sheet Coping
  Water Shield
  16 mm Treated Plywood
  Variable Air Space
  40 mm Rigid Insulation
  Reinforced Asphalt Membrane
  Sitecast Concrete

2 Wall Composition
  25 mm interlock Zinc Panel
  100 mm Adjustable z bars
  10 mm Air Space
  50 mm Polyurethane Insulation
  Blueskin Membrane
  Sitecast Concrete

3 Curtain Wall

4 Floor Composition
  Sitecast Concrete
  Blueskin Membrane
  75 mm Polyurethane Insulation
  25 mm Air Space
  100 mm Aadjustable Double Steel
  Angles Zinc Interlock Panels

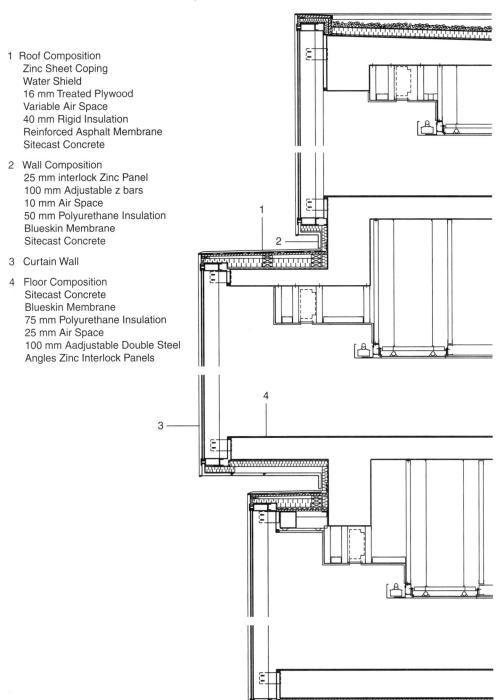

Figure 4-17

Concept sketch.

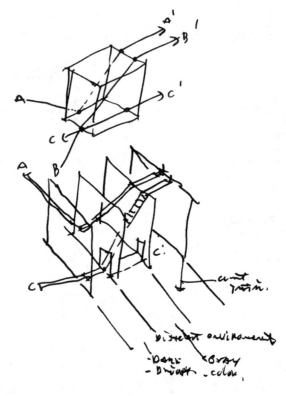

Fig. 4-17 and photo of the finished space, Fig. 4-18), so they crafted three bridge and stair systems that penetrate the north and south facades and all interior planes. The bridges are symbolic and functional connections to people, places, and information. The use of metal wall panels on metal framing was consistent with the desired aesthetic and has the benefit of low maintenance cost.

Figure 4-18

Interior photo of space. Photo by Marc Cramer.

Another Canadian project was completed recently, transforming a fairly low-density collection of older single-family and small commercial buildings into a thriving new world-class resort. The Mount Tremblant development, located in the mountains north of Montreal, has taken the world by storm. The panoramic photo in Fig. 4-19 captures the new look of this modern high-density multi-family resort destination. All the modern conveniences are at your fingertips. The developers used today's technologies and program elements in such a way as to multiply the number of room reservations tenfold over previous seasons. Exterior wall designs, roof edge treatments, and waterproofing for winter and summer challenged their designers and builders. The wall section (see Fig. 4-20) indicates the materials and methods used by a local architectural firm in their multifamily projects in the Mt. Tremblant area. Insulation and vapor barriers have to work both ways to prevent condensation in the walls. The 2" rigid insulation stops at the frost line as a way to conserve cost, yet still prevent condensation in the lower walls.

There are always tradeoffs made between initial and operating costs, particularly as it relates to envelope insulation. We recommend designers permit

Figure 4-19
Mt. Tremblant, Village Panorama. Photo by William L. Walker, AIA.

Figure 4-20

Wall section from Canadian Architects Millette Legare.

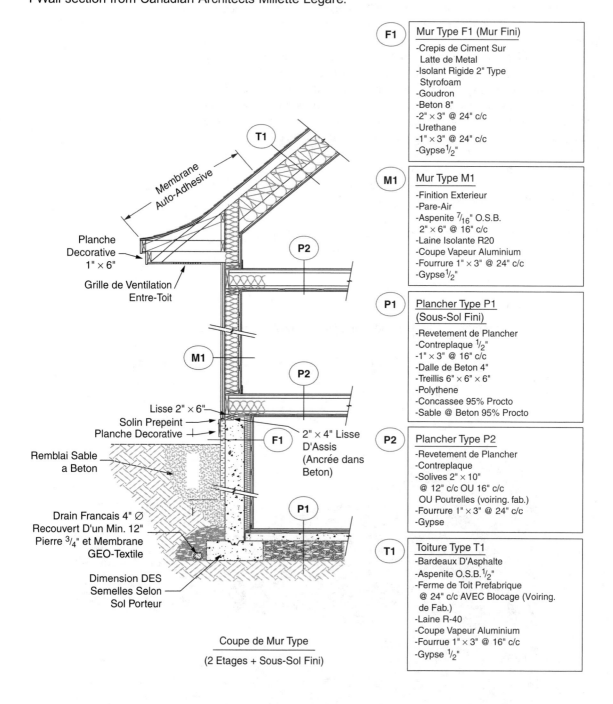

F1 — **Mur Type F1 (Mur Fini)**
- Crepis de Ciment Sur Latte de Metal
- Isolant Rigide 2" Type Styrofoam
- Goudron
- Beton 8"
- 2" × 3" @ 24" c/c
- Urethane
- 1" × 3" @ 24" c/c
- Gypse $1/2$"

M1 — **Mur Type M1**
- Finition Exterieur
- Pare-Air
- Aspenite $7/16$" O.S.B. 2" × 6" @ 16" c/c
- Laine Isolante R20
- Coupe Vapeur Aluminium
- Fourrure 1" × 3" @ 24" c/c
- Gypse $1/2$"

P1 — **Plancher Type P1 (Sous-Sol Fini)**
- Revetement de Plancher
- Contreplaque $1/2$"
- 1" × 3" @ 16" c/c
- Dalle de Beton 4"
- Treillis 6" × 6" × 6"
- Polythene
- Concassee 95% Procto
- Sable @ Beton 95% Procto

P2 — **Plancher Type P2**
- Revetement de Plancher
- Contreplaque
- Solives 2" × 10" @ 12" c/c OU 16" c/c OU Poutrelles (voiring. fab.)
- Fourrure 1" × 3" @ 24" c/c
- Gypse

T1 — **Toiture Type T1**
- Bardeaux D'Asphalte
- Aspenite O.S.B. $1/2$"
- Ferme de Toit Prefabrique @ 24" c/c AVEC Blocage (Voiring. de Fab.)
- Laine R-40
- Coupe Vapeur Aluminium
- Fourrure 1" × 3" @ 16" c/c
- Gypse $1/2$"

Labels on drawing:

- Membrane Auto-Adhesive
- Planche Decorative 1" × 6"
- Grille de Ventilation Entre-Toit
- Lisse 2" × 6"
- Solin Prepeint
- Planche Decorative
- Remblai Sable a Beton
- 2" × 4" Lisse D'Assis (Ancrée dans Beton)
- Drain Francais 4" Ø Recouvert D'un Min. 12" Pierre $3/4$" et Membrane GEO-Textile
- Dimension DES Semelles Selon Sol Porteur

Coupe de Mur Type
(2 Etages + Sous-Sol Fini)

clients to participate in the decision making process as to how well to insulate the perimeter. This does not mean how little insulation can be installed, but how far in excess of minimal energy or building code compliance the walls will receive in R-value. The location and type of insulations should be determined solely by the designer. Calculate dew points for summer and winter conditions, and use insulation values to prevent condensation resulting from dew point being reached in the walls. We are seeing more and more owners using longer return on investment periods for calculating payback on insulation and other energy related products such as air-conditioning equipment and lighting especially. While it used to be about 7 years, it is not uncommon to find 10 to 30 year planning horizons nowadays.

In my travels around the Canadian countryside, my wife and I observed many buildings in the process of construction. We found it very common to observe combinations of batt and spray-applied wall insulation in exterior wall and roof systems, (see Fig. 4-21).

Halfway across the world we find still more examples of buildings creating a dynamic statement. Previously (until July 2007) the world's tallest building, Taipei 101 (see Fig. 4-22), is over 1,670 feet (509 meters) high and was constructed with 101 floors. Completed in 2004, the design was inspired by

Figure 4-21

Photo of wall insulation, spray applied. Photo by William L. Walker, AIA.

Figure 4-22

Taipei 101, world's second
tallest building. Photo by
Dan Felice.

traditional Chinese pagoda design and incorporates the segmented bamboo
form for reinforcing each segment of the tower and as a model of beauty in
organic elegance.

In contrast, the Guang Zhou Pearl River Tower makes quite a modern silhou-
ette among other tower projects in the area, (see Fig. 4-23). Its grand scale is
softened at the street level by the spherical podium, a landscaped terrace above
the street level (see Fig. 4-24).

These projects are but a few examples of the many buildings being built
across the globe as we continue to look for new and exciting ways to design
and construct buildings. We will talk about some of them in more detail later
in this chapter, focusing on the glazing. With advances in science and technology, you can expect to see new products; thinner, stronger, and lighter
skins; improved coatings; and new insulators. The possibilities are not limited
to our imagination anymore. With continued integration of computers into the
design process, we have exponentially expanded our realm of possible per-
mutations and combinations of solution sets. With space exploration, we are
not limited to building on earth with our natural forces to respond to; we have
a whole new future of designs and building to ponder. However, there will
be some commonality to all building on earth, and for the present, we will focus

Figure 4-23
Pearl River Tower, Aerial View. Image by SOM.

the remaining pages of this book on ways and means you can use—for the future is now.

4.5.6 Wall performance categories: Barrier, drainage, and rain screen

We will classify walls into the three different wall performance categories and then provide some examples of variations within each. Depending on the climate, the program, and initial cost versus long-term maintenance considerations, one wall type may fit best with your planned project. Figure 4-25 shows wall sections constructed of wood frame, concrete block, metal stud, stone veneer, and other systems in each of the three basic categories. The three wall performance categories based on performance are (1) barrier, (2) drainage plane, and (3) rain screen or cavity wall.

As you have seen, water, vapor, and air intrusion can lead to leaks, condensation, and increased potential for mold growth. Designers are faced with countless conflicting criteria. Your clients may have limited knowledge of building envelope performance, yet many of them try to provide you with directions as to what they want. More important, some try to tell you what they don't want:

Figure 4-24

Pearl River Tower Terrace.
Image by SOM.

"Oh, we don't need any of that membrane stuff in the walls; that's a waste of money!" We have faced the same difficult situations with informed clients, who tell us: "We would like to have cavity walls, but we just can't afford them. Just do it in tilt concrete and forget about it." Are these the same clients who will come after us if the new offices leak in five years or if the condensation we warned them about begins to create strange smells in the boardroom? What is a designer to do? The first thing is to build a good relationship, and the second is to try and teach your clients the scientific and mathematical reasons on which you are basing your recommendations. If all this fails to bring them around to your point of view, bring out the big guns. The best ally we have is the building code. Recent changes have been made in many codes that require better wall system design and performance. "We would love to leave out the air and vapor barrier as you wanted, but the building code won't allow it" is an excellent reason to support your preference. It maintains your camaraderie with the client. If the codes do not support your recommendations, quote the best experts in the field.

A respected expert in building design and construction, Dr. Joseph Lstiburek, with the Building Science Corporation, has authored several articles and books on the subject. Table 4-3 was derived from his recommendations and was expanded based upon our experience.

Figure 4-25
Three types of walls; barrier, drainage and rain screen.

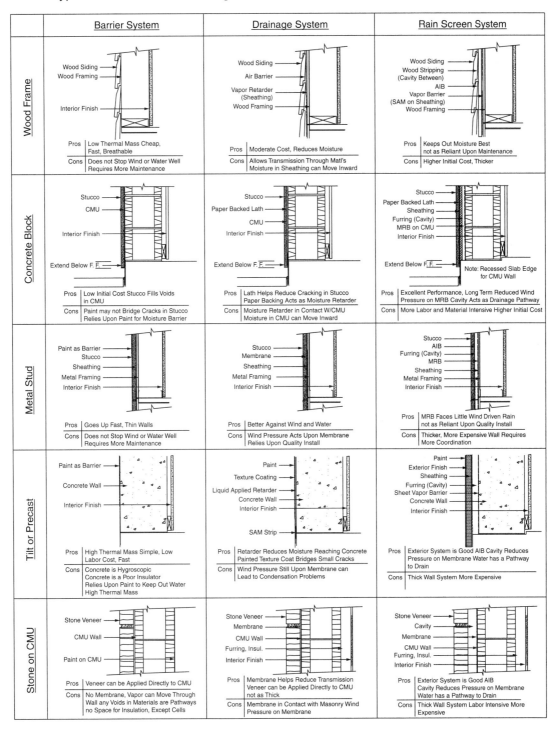

Table 4-3

Rainfall with systems

Rainfall amounts	Barrier	Drainage	Rain screen	Insul. CLG	Insul. roof	Ventil. attic	Ins. Abv. roof
Extreme (>60")			X	X	X	X	X
High (40"–60")			X	X	X	X	X
Moderate (20"–40")		X		X	X		X
Low (<20")	X			X			X
Mixed humid			X	X		X	X

Barrier walls can be acceptable in areas with less than 20 inches of annual rainfall. Barrier walls, as a general rule, have lower initial cost than rain screen walls of the same system. Barrier walls rely on the paint, stain, vinyl coating, aluminum, or surface treatment to stop all water at the face. If it doesn't rain much, or if you don't mind the wall materials behind the surface getting wet on occasion, this may be all you need. Some barrier walls rely on paint or other coatings to stop water. These products typically need maintenance and reapplication over time. If, for example, you have a west-facing barrier wall built using painted plywood to stop water, this plywood may crack and split over time as the sun's heat bakes it at more than 125°F. Cracks and splits often exceed the bridging ability of paint. The void could allow water in, so it needs to be filled and paint applied. This is what we are referring to as *maintenance*. Barrier walls rely on the skin to stop wind and water. In hot, humid climates with a lot of rain, we would try to get the most flexible coating with the lowest perm rating. In a colder climate or an arid area, we like a breathable exterior coating such as a latex paint or perhaps a penetrating stain.

Drainage walls are different from both barrier and rain screen walls in that you are allowing water into the wall and hoping it drains out before it causes problems. The old standard for many years was what we call a *mass wall,* constructed out of thick layers of stone, brick, block, or a combination of them. Mass walls can absorb a lot of water before it reaches the inside face of the wall. As long as the rain stops before the wall becomes saturated all the way through to the inside face, and as long as vapor drive is working in your favor, this type of wall should perform adequately. The table indicates that drainage walls are acceptable for use in areas where average annual rainfall is between 20 and 40 inches; however, it is really the intensity and duration of the rain event that matters. Since temperature and pressure differentials will drive vapor through a wall, you should consider the rates of transmission for the sum of the selected materials and thicknesses before relying on it. Because these walls need to dry to the outside, permeable coatings are recommended. Plaster cement coatings are commonly applied to the interior and exterior faces of mass walls. These provide permeable exterior wall coatings that reduce air transmission by sealing most of the irregularities in the stone, brick, or block. At the same time, plaster cement coatings are quite durable. Mass walls may be built without insulation if temperature differences do not exceed the thermal lag caused by the mass of the composite whole. If it doesn't stay too cold for too long, the temperature in the wall may never reach the dew point.

Drainage walls can be built out of the most porous construction materials. Many of our example sections show stucco as the hygroscopic material that permits moisture to be absorbed, but it could be almost anything. Face brick, concrete, and wood are all porous. For a modern wall built in the drainage category to perform well in hot, humid climates, it will need a moisture barrier. The lower the permeability of the membrane, the less water gets into the interior of the wall. The less water that gets into the wall, the fewer chances there are for mold growth. The barrier system needs to restrain both air and vapor in most walls. This point in the wall is the only low-permeability vapor barrier product that we use in the entire wall section. A combination of insulation and HVAC system modulation should minimize the potential for the dew point being reached inside the wall. If well detailed and well constructed, the wall should keep liquid water out.

Rain screen walls or, as we like to call them, *cavity walls* are the most expensive of the three (as a general rule) and also perform the best in areas with a lot of rain. The choice of wall type depends on many factors, but climate and contents should be considered first. Rain screen walls are not required for most industrial uses, for storage of durable materials, for unconditioned spaces, for seasonal-use buildings, etc. Depending on what the building is used for and who the occupants will be, a barrier system may suffice. If average rainfall exceeds 40 inches per year and/or the units are to be sold as condominiums, then rain screen walls are the only wall type that should be used. This is what we have been recommending for years and is what many of the world's leading experts recommend.

Rain screen walls require more three-dimensional planning because of their increased thickness. Rain screen walls also perform far better in high-wind and rain events than any other wall types (in the same material category). The cavity in rain screen wall construction has three key advantages in hot, humid climates: (1) It separates the outer wythe from the inner wythe, preventing moisture from being transmitted through materials hygroscopically, (2) it serves as a thermal break between planes, and (3) it reduces the pressure and force of any water in liquid or vapor states that reaches the membrane. *Before we go into the more detailed review of their differences, we need to let you all know that the graphical examples provided in the book are intended to illustrate differences in systems and wall types. They are not intended to be used for construction as they are depicted herein. We might have left out some important sub-component in order to more clearly make our point with what is shown and discussed. Please don't copy them and paste them into your plan sets. We would be glad to talk with you about a possible review of your details, or develop some especially for your projects. (Author)*

4.5.6.1 Wood frame construction

We start off with a wood frame construction example and then go on to look at concrete block, metal stud, concrete, metal panel, stone veneer, and glass wall systems. Regardless of the type system, you have to stop water from causing problems in your built environment. In the barrier system, you try to stop it at the face, for example, with paint on wood siding (see Fig. 4-26). Its

Figure 4-26

Wood frame barrier wall.

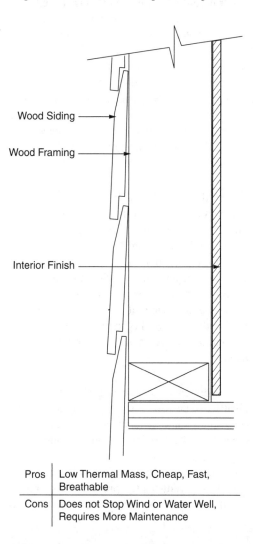

Pros	Low Thermal Mass, Cheap, Fast, Breathable
Cons	Does not Stop Wind or Water Well, Requires More Maintenance

performance depends totally on fit. In order to stop high winds, it needs to be installed so that no space exists between the many pieces and parts. This is highly unlikely.

The better drainage system version relies on the combination of sheathing as a vapor retarder and an applied air barrier to prevent any water that defeats the paint and lapped siding from getting into the wall behind the moisture-reducing membrane. The continuous membrane extends down past the floor level toward grade. The best system uses a multitude of components, each playing a role in stopping air and moisture, whether liquid or vapor. Rain screen or cavity wall system performance is far better than that of the drainage wall because of the addition of the air cavity between the sheathing and siding. This cavity provides many benefits. It provides a drainage pathway for any moisture that defeats the siding to drain down, and perhaps more important, it reduces wind pressures acting on the air moisture barriers, reducing the amount of movement through any voids or a permeable membrane component. This particular example uses a self-adhesive membrane (SAM) as an air and moisture barrier applied to the exterior face of the sheathing, (see Fig. 4-27).

Since typical wall sheathings allow moisture transmission through them, we feel that it is beneficial to stop moisture from reaching the sheathing. This is

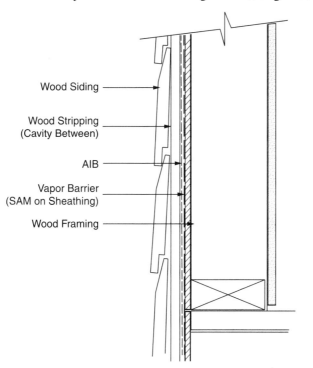

Figure 4-27
Wood frame rain screen wall.

Wood Siding

Wood Stripping
(Cavity Between)

AIB

Vapor Barrier
(SAM on Sheathing)

Wood Framing

Pros	Keeps Out Moisture Best, not as Reliant Upon Maintenance
Cons	Higher Initial Cost, Thicker

what makes this the best performing of the wood frame systems. If you wanted to take it a step further, you could add a separate air infiltration barrier (AIB) as well. In our opinion, it is not necessary if the SAM is well sealed, except in warm climates with more than 80 inches (2.5 meters) of annual rainfall. In cold, humid climates, we would not locate the SAM on the outside of the wall framing. We would want to stop moisture from moving through the wall from the inside face toward the insulation (not shown) and toward the outside in the winter. This would mean that the MRB would be on the interior face of the wall insulation. Depending on the design conditions, the MRB might be vapor permeable, such as a coat of paint on drywall, or vapor impermeable, such as foil-backed batt insulation or closed-cell styrene products.

4.5.6.2   CMU walls

The general conditions described previously are similar for each of the sample walls. What is important is matching the wall type to the requirements. In CMU barrier type wall section (see Fig. 4-28), you will see that the example indicates paint over stucco on concrete block. The paint serves as the air barrier and

Figure 4-28

CMU barrier wall system.

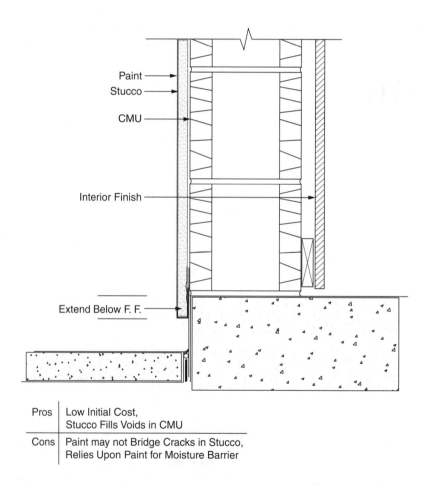

Pros	Low Initial Cost, Stucco Fills Voids in CMU
Cons	Paint may not Bridge Cracks in Stucco, Relies Upon Paint for Moisture Barrier

water-reducing membrane, stopping wind and rain to the best of the paint's ability. This is where we frequently see an elastomeric coating specified because of many beneficial properties. Among them is its elastic qualities, to span and bridge small voids or cracks over time. It is relied upon to stop as much air and water penetration as possible. If it rains less than 15 inches (0.5 meter) per year, and the temperatures are mild, this might suffice. Moreover, if there are no interior finishes and some moisture moving through the wall is acceptable, a barrier system with a breathable paint is fine. There are pros and cons of using non-breathable paints such as epoxy, oil-based enamels, and elastomeric coatings. The selection and application should be based on a careful evaluation of all factors, most important of which are vapor drive and temperature/pressure differentials. We have seen misapplied elastomers cause large blisters on expose exterior wall surfaces as a result of condensation taking place on the backside of the paint. These blisters or bubbles are unsightly and point out the bigger problem—moisture migration and trapped condensation in the wall. We have never seen this condition on a rain screen system, mostly in barrier walls.

If there are more than 20 inches but less than 40 inches (0.5 to 1.2 meters) of rain per year, then perhaps the drainage system may suffice. This is well-suited to a cool, dry climate and works adequately if moisture is permitted to drain down and out slowly through the stucco. In humid climates, it may be necessary to place an MRB behind the stucco on the outside face of the CMU. This can be liquid or sheet products (if self-sealing) and typically would have expanded metal lath fastened to the block. The lath reduces cracking, thereby improving the wall's performance over time.

The rain screen version of the CMU wall can work well in either warm or cold, wet climates. The rain screen wall is recommended where rainfall exceeds 40 inches (1.2 meters) per year or where tropical rains are likely to last longer than it takes to saturate the block. The cavity permits drainage and effectively reduces the wind-driven rain pressure on the concrete block portion of the exterior wall system. If you want to limit moisture transmission, we recommend a sheet or fluid-applied MRB applied to the block. In Fig. 4-29, the exterior finish again is stucco, this time applied on lath over fiber-reinforced sheathing. We typically see this done with an air barrier on the sheathing. Paper-backed lath does not function as a sealed air barrier unless the laps are sealed, and we have never seen this done successfully.

Paper-backed lath functions as a moisture-reduction barrier and is part of a bond breaker system. More important, it interrupts capillary action through the stucco. It creates a slight but effective drainage plane between sheet materials. Studies have shown that when not in contact with adjacent materials, stucco or any hygroscopic material does not transmit moisture. Thirty-pound building felts are suitable for use in a wall as an MRB because they are more self-sealing than the lighter 15-pound versions. The void between the lapped felts permits air to aid in drying after rain events.

Figure 4-29

CMU rain screen wall system.

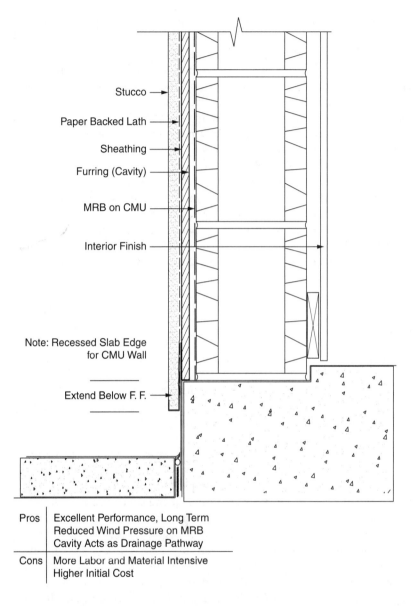

Stucco

Paper Backed Lath

Sheathing

Furring (Cavity)

MRB on CMU

Interior Finish

Note: Recessed Slab Edge for CMU Wall

Extend Below F. F.

Pros	Excellent Performance, Long Term Reduced Wind Pressure on MRB Cavity Acts as Drainage Pathway
Cons	More Labor and Material Intensive Higher Initial Cost

4.5.6.3 Metal stud

The third type of a wall system (see Fig. 4-30) is the metal stud exterior wall system. In the barrier version, you see a section example constructed with stucco on sheathing. As in most barrier systems, the paint is supposed to stop the water. In the drainage version, the stucco is intended to absorb water, and gravity is supposed to convey it down and away. MRB is required between the stucco and the sheathing. The J-bead at the lower limits of each stucco plane is required to let water escape from the stucco. We refer to these specific types of specialized J-beads as *weep screeds*. They have a series of

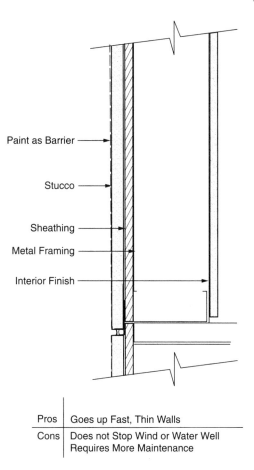

Figure 4-30
Metal stud barrier wall system.

Paint as Barrier

Stucco

Sheathing

Metal Framing

Interior Finish

Pros	Goes up Fast, Thin Walls
Cons	Does not Stop Wind or Water Well Requires More Maintenance

small holes in them to promote drainage. When applying sealant to a weep screed, always install the sealant bead behind the most remote of the drain holes. If you do not, you will effectively trap moisture behind the sealant (see Fig. 4-31).

At the base of the wall in this example you can see the introduction of a piece of closure metal to close off the potential pathway between the bottom of the wall sheathing and the slab edge. In Fig. 4-32, you can see a blow-up of the closure metal taken to a new level. This was designed to combat the pressure-washer situation described earlier. Many public buildings and entertainment or resort facilities have as a part of their routine maintenance procedures weekly cleaning of exposed surfaces with pressure washers. The closure metal indicated in this section has been bent 180 degrees and installed in such a manner that if any water is forced past the bottom of the wall (stucco on J-bead, weep screed), that water will be deflected back down again and not be permitted up into the building or even the wall cavity.

Figure 4-31

Apply sealant behind weep holes.

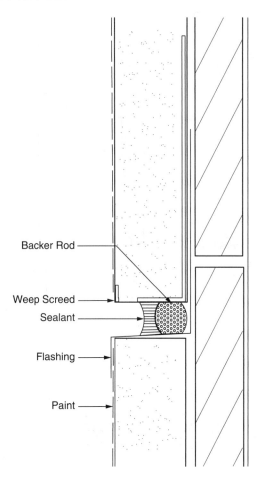

Backer Rod

Weep Screed

Sealant

Flashing

Paint

We recommend 304 or 316 series stainless steel, preferably welded at the joints, installed before the J-bead and membrane. If stainless is too expensive, galvanized metal, foil-backed self-adhesive membrane (SAM), or even thick plastic is better than nothing. Notice also that there is no sealant at this joint! We want any water that gets to this point in the wall to be able to drain out.

In the next example, the metal stud wall uses counterflashing behind the sheathing to convey water out and beyond the face of the next-lower sheet. In the barrier system, you are counting on the paint and sealant to stop water at the face. The drainage system uses membrane behind the stucco to stop water from reaching the sheathing. It is designed to drain through capillary action in the cementitious stucco itself. The membrane laps over the counter-flashing. As with all wall types, the cavity wall system has the most reliable performance period and is recommended wherever average annual rainfall exceeds 40 inches (1.2 meters). In the cavity wall, we build the interior wall and apply sheathing,

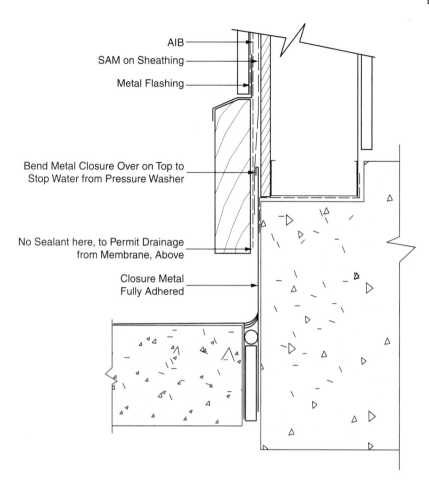

AIB

SAM on Sheathing

Metal Flashing

Bend Metal Closure Over on Top to Stop Water from Pressure Washer

No Sealant here, to Permit Drainage from Membrane, Above

Closure Metal Fully Adhered

Figure 4-32
Closure metal at wall edge.

appropriate membranes, and insulation depending on the climate. In the cold climate, we apply vapor retarder on the inside face to prevent moisture from migrating toward the insulation from the occupied side in the winter. In hot, humid climates, we apply moisture barriers to the outside of the insulation. In the graphic example, we install fiberglass sheathing products to the metal studs and apply vapor barrier membrane to the outer face. Then we create the drainage cavity by applying furring members and an air barrier and the stucco on lath. We prefer nonpaper products as the air barrier. On the outside of traditional three-coat stucco, we like elastomeric paint products. An excellent alternative might be white stucco because stopping air and water at the face is not important to the overall performance of the composite wall system.

4.5.6.4 Concrete

The next example is for concrete exterior wall systems, such as formed and poured in place, tilt, or precast. Figures 4-33 through 4-35 show three levels of performance, with the best once again employing the drainage cavity. As tilt walls have become more prevalent, resulting from increased labor costs across the board, more and more client groups are choosing them. Many of these

Figure 4-33
Concrete barrier wall.

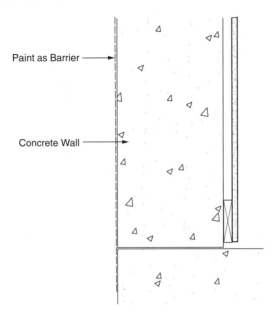

Paint as Barrier

Concrete Wall

Pros	High Thermal Mass
	Simple, Low Labor Cost, Fast
Cons	Concrete is Hygroscopic
	Concrete is a Poor Insulator
	Relies Upon Paint to Keep Out Water
	High Thermal Mass

Figure 4-34
Concrete drainage wall.

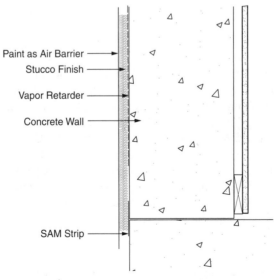

Paint as Air Barrier
Stucco Finish
Vapor Retarder
Concrete Wall

SAM Strip

Pros	Retarder Reduces Moisture Reaching Concrete
	Painted Texture Coat Bridges Small Cracks
Cons	Wind Pressure Still Upon Membrane can
	Lead to Condensation Problems

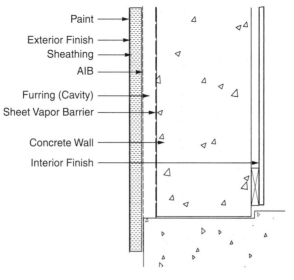

Paint
Exterior Finish
Sheathing
AIB
Furring (Cavity)
Sheet Vapor Barrier
Concrete Wall
Interior Finish

Figure 4-35
Concrete rain screen wall.

Pros	Exterior System is Good AIB Cavity Reduces Pressure on Membrane Water has a Pathway to Drain
Cons	Thick Wall System, More Expensive

clients have no previous experience with this type of construction but make the choice based on initial cost considerations. Unfortunately, the cost information they are using may not be a fair comparison with previous systems. Many clients are choosing the tilt wall based on the price of a barrier system in tilt (see Fig. 4-33) and comparing that with drainage or rain screen material and labor costs in frame or block walls. One can only hope that these decisions are not regretted years from now when the exterior protective coatings need replacing and a big storm event hits the area. In the barrier system in tilt concrete, we often rely on a coating to prevent water intrusion. Many of these are based on elastomers with a binder. Water that may penetrate the coating gets right into the concrete wall.

As long as the intensity and duration of the rain event do not exceed the wall's capacity to hold and store water molecules and, more important still, the molecules do not penetrate all the way through the wall to the inside face (see perm ratings for concrete in Chapter 3) where it is more likely to fuel bacterial growth, this incidental moisture should cause little concern. If, on the other hand, the moisture exceeds the wall's ability to store water and the rain continues, then water will exit the interior face of the wall. These scenarios can change with temperature and pressure differentials as well.

The other important consideration that we feel is often overlooked on all wall systems is the issue of condensation from dew point conditions being reached in the wall. Most clients want the tilt wall to be exposed on the outside face.

They expect durable coatings to be applied to the outside. This means that any MRB needs to be applied under or with the coating. This basically prevents the use of sheet-applied membranes with low permeability. This usually results in the insulation (if any) being placed on the inside of the wall system, the conditioned side. Any moisture that works through the wall must be removed by the building HVAC system, if it is operating.

Tilt concrete in barrier systems is probably much more suitable for warehouses (nonconditioned but well-ventilated or nonoccupied spaces) in the hot, humid climates than for classrooms or offices. In the cold climates, tilt concrete panels often get insulated where it is cost-effective and energy-efficient. This is on the cold side or interior face of the wall. In mixed climates, you must consider condensation from vapor drive wherever you place the insulation and MRB. Some concrete panels have been constructed with integral rigid insulation foam between inner and outer concrete layers. This is seen as an improvement in thermal resistance and dew point and could be considered in hot and humid climates.

Tilt wall construction can be built in the drainage wall (see Fig. 4-34), and rain screen (also called cavity wall) form (see Fig. 4-35). In the drainage version, a vapor retarder is applied to the outer face of the concrete wall surface. The lower the perm rating, the more moisture is prevented from entering the concrete. The stucco acts as the drainage medium. This might make sense in hot, humid climates if the drainage cavity were located on the outside of concrete panels. In the rain screen scenario, the vapor barrier and insulation would typically be located on the inside face of the cavity in hot humid climates. The rain screen version has the advantage of having wind pressures reduced outside the wall, and keeping the elements off the membrane. It will outperform other versions of concrete walls, and is recommended if average rainfall exceeds 40 inches per year, and when interior spaces are conditioned and occupied. One way to achieve this would be with rigid insulation such as expanded polystyrene adhered to the outside face of the concrete panel. This would be installed using furring members to space the insulation from the concrete to make the cavity. Air and vapor barrier material would be applied to the outer faces of the EPS board.

Another method would be to use extruded polystyrene and a liquid or sheet membrane. In the drainage wall, an AIB would be installed with lath and stucco. In the cavity wall, furring would create the airspace depth desired. Stucco could be installed over paper-backed lath or on fiber-impregnated exterior sheathing (preferably with lath). Insulation could also be placed inside the wall sandwich with concrete on both sides. This section works reasonably well in heating or cooling mode and has several other advantages. It protects the soft insulation from impact and allows easy fastening to both inner and outer faces, (see Fig. 4-36).

Obviously, concrete wall systems come in many other shapes and composites than these. We have seen the popularity of foam and concrete walls increase in the past 20 years as energy costs continued to rise. They use hollow foam shapes as forms for site-placed concrete and reinforcing that results in a well-insulated

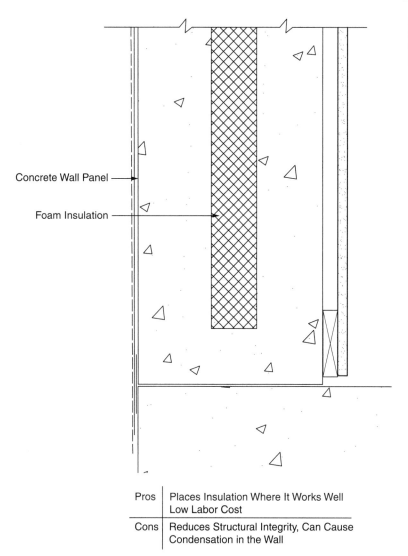

Figure 4-36
Internal insulated concrete wall.

Concrete Wall Panel

Foam Insulation

Pros	Places Insulation Where It Works Well Low Labor Cost
Cons	Reduces Structural Integrity, Can Cause Condensation in the Wall

and durable wall system. They perform well in missile impact tests owing to the inherent strength of concrete. Thus it is easy to see that concrete can be used as an exterior structural system with no added insulation, as an internal core in foam composite sandwich construction, or with interior or external insulation depending on the climate. It is truly a versatile product.

4.5.6.5 Metal wall systems

Metal panels come in several shapes and forms. These military-, industrial-, or agricultural-based engineered metal buildings have made their way into mainstream society. For over a decade in the late twentieth century, metal buildings were one of the most popular commercial building types based on cost and time considerations. The system shown as an example in Fig. 4-37 uses metal-clad

Figure 4-37

Metal panel system, rain screen version.

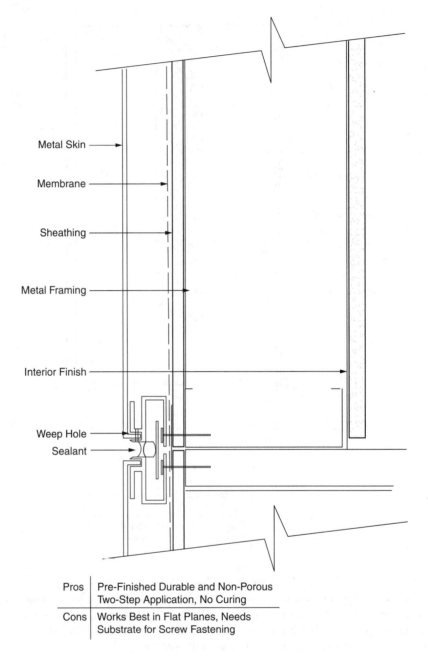

Metal Skin

Membrane

Sheathing

Metal Framing

Interior Finish

Weep Hole

Sealant

Pros	Pre-Finished Durable and Non-Porous Two-Step Application, No Curing
Cons	Works Best in Flat Planes, Needs Substrate for Screw Fastening

composites that are a little more expensive and used more commonly today in commercial construction than the purlin and girt–based ribbed wall panels. There are many recent examples of metal-clad wall systems winning design awards throughout the world. One of the reasons for this is the clean lines and concealed fasteners available, but the systems go up fast as well. Saved time means saved money.

There are three common types of metal wall panel systems, too. We have indicated three common expressions basically consisting of the dry joint, wet joint, and rain screen systems. The main difference between the dry and wet joint products is the addition of backer rod and sealant used in the wet system. The dry system lets water get behind the face plane to the bent-metal rout and return fasteners beyond. The wet system is really a barrier system. The sealant makes up a part of the barrier. The rain screen system employs an MRB on top of the sheathing and under the metal composites. This has the best performance against air and water intrusion.

4.5.6.6 Masonry veneer

The stone or brick on CMU example (see Fig. 4-38) is probably the highest-cost example illustrated to this point. It takes more labor and time to build but typically lasts longer and requires less maintenance. It possesses a much higher thermal mass than most other systems. This can be a positive or a negative feature depending on your climate. It requires you to look at thermal (time) lag and moisture transmission as they affect the dew point and condensation. The barrier system depends on the stone veneer face to stop water. This system is suitable for areas with low rainfall, less than 15 inches (0.5 centimeter). Perhaps if you specified nonpermeable grout and nonporous stone, you could stop rain at the face, but this system is better suited to low rainfall and low humidity.

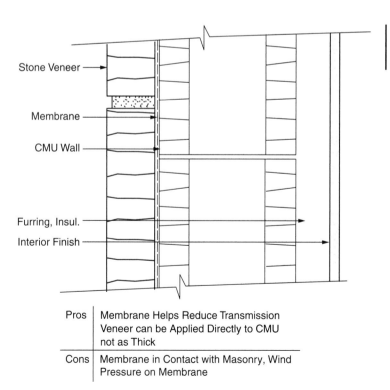

Figure 4-38
Stone veneer on CMU, drainage wall type.

Pros	Membrane Helps Reduce Transmission Veneer can be Applied Directly to CMU not as Thick
Cons	Membrane in Contact with Masonry, Wind Pressure on Membrane

Figure 4-39

Stone veneer on CMU, rain screen wall type.

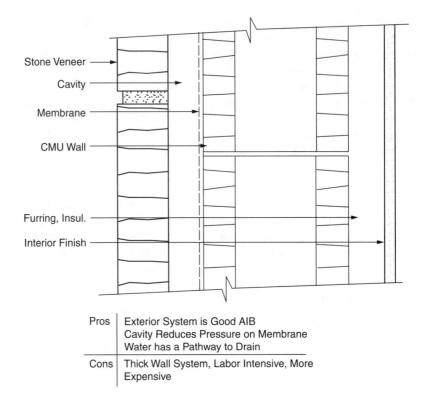

Stone Veneer

Cavity

Membrane

CMU Wall

Furring, Insul.

Interior Finish

Pros	Exterior System is Good AIB Cavity Reduces Pressure on Membrane Water has a Pathway to Drain
Cons	Thick Wall System, Labor Intensive, More Expensive

The drainage system assumes that voids exist in the materials and that moisture can move through mortar that gets saturated and conducts water down and away. We would recommend an MRB on the face of the backup wall if rainfall exceeds 15 inches (0.5 meter) per year. More the rainfall, the better the MRB needs to be. If you get more than 25 inches (0.6 meter) of rain per year, we would anticipate possibly using a maximum 1.0 perm rating liquid or sheet product and lath behind the scratch coat of stucco. Then mortar the stones to the scratch coat. Again, the rain screen system (see Fig. 4-39) performs better than the others and is recommended in areas where rainfall exceeds 40 inches (1 meter) per year. For hot, humid climates, we would recommend closed-cell foam insulation on the outside of the block and an MRB outside the insulation. In cold climates, the insulation might be inside the CMU wall. As always, the climatic data for the specific site should dictate what insulation to use and where it needs to go.

4.5.6.7 Structural brick

A final opaque wall construction method is the structural brick type of wall system. This system is in a niche of its own and does not fit into the same categories very easily because of the material properties. You may put such a system in between barrier and drainage cavity systems. In order to present this system in an "apples to apples" comparison, we will discuss the brick wall system as fitting into the three wall performance categories, whereas their physical properties prevent them from performing the same. A single-wythe wall made of structural brick could be thought of as a barrier system because the face of the brick does a fairly good job of stopping liquid water penetration. It is composed of vitreous clay material like face brick and is fired at 2,000°F for several days in a kiln.

Structural brick are slightly hygroscopic and, as such, could be thought of as a drainage system. Water that gets through the face can work its way into the cores, where it can be drained vertically down and away from the wall. A double-wythe wall made of brick could be considered a cavity wall or rain screen system. All these structural brick examples would have the potential to use the brick as facing material for both interior and exterior surfaces. This precludes the need for paint, sheathing, membranes, furring, and drywall finishes. These systems are available for use with internal insulation to achieve R values around 10 to 11. Coupled with its inherently high thermal lag, structural brick is well suited for use where temperatures fluctuate greatly from day to night and where maintainability is important.

4.5.6.8 Glazed wall systems

There are more window system manufacturers today than ever before. This promotes competition, which leads to advances in products. Many of these advancements are related to the performance of the glass, but a lot has to do with frames, extrusion shapes, and fastening methodologies. Regardless of the manufacturer or shape, there are certain constants that we will discuss that hold true for most systems. Let us take this opportunity to recommend that you draw your window and door details carefully. You should show the extrusion at large scale on the basis of the design. Show all fasteners, where they are likely to be installed, what material the screws go into, the shim space, where the backer rod and sealant go, and where water drains out of the sills and/or covers. Take special effort to show two-piece systems where one piece fastens to the jamb or sill framing, block, concrete, etc. (see Fig. 4-40).

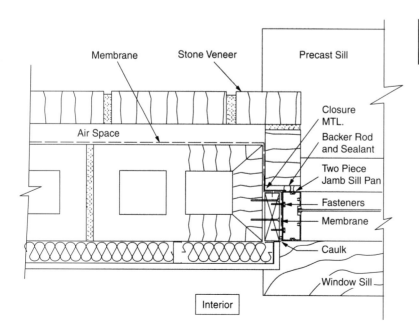

Figure 4-40
Show shapes and fasteners.

Storefront and curtain wall systems are not the same. Curtain wall systems can go to greater unsupported lengths and heights and, as such, usually cost more. Curtain wall systems come in a variety of shapes and sizes, some with internal stiffeners (concealed within the extrusion, where they are not visible) and others with visible bracing such as Kawneer's truss-style system. Curtain wall systems range in depth from 4 inches (10 centimeters) to more than 12 inches (30 centimeters). They can easily span more than 30 feet (9 meters) in height. New advancements in technology have allowed manufacturers to offer photovoltaic curtain wall systems that generate electricity and reduce heat gain. Glass is available in many colors and in variety of thicknesses. Storefront systems start at about $2^1/_2$ inches (6 centimeters) in depth and span more modest openings. Owing to their differences in heights and resulting loads, their profiles will be correspondingly different. There is also a difference in their fastening. Most transfer wind loads at the head and sill only. The jamb deflection can exceed $1^1/_2$ inches (4 centimeters), which requires special detail considerations.

At exterior perimeter conditions at floor level, both should be detailed with the recessed slab-edge detail discussed earlier. This enables any water that may pass through the sill fasteners or along side the sill or jamb to drain harmlessly out and prevent it from reaching finish floor elevations. If possible, coordinate the pocket depth and height so that the sill flashing extends just past the outward edge of the concrete recess so that workers can apply sealants from the inside to fully seal the window systems. Metal sill pans can be difficult to install with most curtain walls because the fasteners in sills are around $1/_2$ inch in diameter, which can result in more than eight big holes in the sill pan. This is why we recommend the slab-edge recess for curtain wall systems. No sill pan is required at a recessed slab edge, but it is still a great secondary protection.

Curtain wall sills that are not at floor level are more difficult to seal. Most occur at the top of internal red iron structural steel, metal frame box headers, or perhaps a concrete bond beam. You must get any water that penetrates the face sealant or that drains down the glass into the coverplate area out past the wall in order to prevent it from getting into the wall. In a rain screen wall, you just have to get that water out past the vapor barrier on the inside of the cavity. This can be done much more easily than getting it to the face of the finish wall surface.

Since these systems typically get shimmed at or near fasteners with short pieces of shim material, they rely on sealant to fill the voids between and around shims. Require the sills to be set in a bed of sealant, and make certain that the drain pathway in the extrusion or sill is not impeded by sealant placement.

Among the many manufacturers' products, there are some important differences. Some of them rely on concealed fasteners (F-clips and T-clips) for their mounting supports (see Fig. 4-41) and are difficult to seal. Grommets, sealant, or SAM patches can be used, but it is difficult to be sure that they are working right, and they are even more difficult to maintain over time. We have found several ways and means for improving the seals at window jambs, sills, and

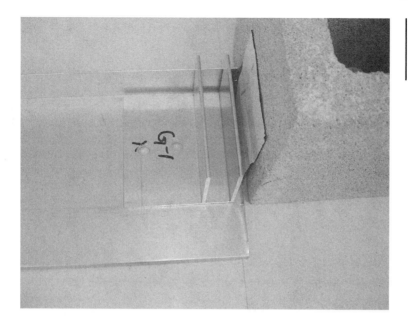

Figure 4-41
Photo of sill pan with holes for fasteners through Clips (YKK).

heads. One of the most successful ways we have found to provide long-lasting closure at the jambs is to install bent metal closure strips under the pressure plates. These pieces of metal close off the void between substrates and window systems. If the closure metal is adequately fastened and set in a bed of adhesive sealant, then we have formed a long-lasting seal well behind the finish system (brick in this example, see Fig. 4-42).

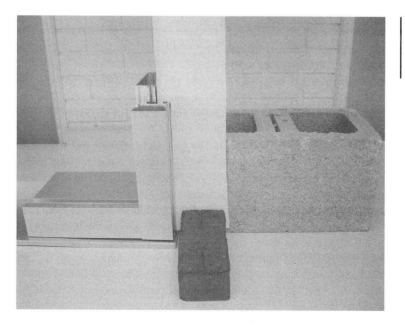

Figure 4-42
Curtain wall mockup with metal air and moisture barrier.

Figure 4-43

Window jamb and sill photo with sealant (EFCO System).

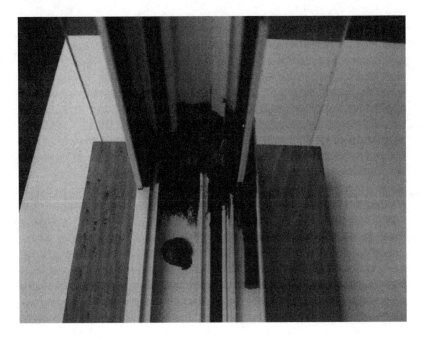

One of the companies we frequently see in competitive bidding situations depends on installers to apply sealant to fasteners that protrude through the sill extrusion that can be inspected visually and resealed over time (see Fig. 4-43). While we are still relying on sealant, we have a better opportunity for quality assurance of completed work than if nothing were done at all. The sealant effectively reduces opportunities for wind-driven, or gravity induced water to move through the extrusion and enter the wall cavities.

4.5.6.9   Windows in walls

Punched openings and strip windows are treated differently from storefront and curtain wall systems. Concrete-formed sill pans can be cast into tilt or pre-cast wall panels to help limit water intrusion. These should be constructed at no or little cost to the owner and provide long-lasting benefits in terms of reducing water intrusion. If well designed and well constructed, these shapes (see Fig. 4-44) function like three-dimensional dams to keep wind-driven water out of the walls when (not if) sealants fail. It would be nice if there were no fasteners through the sill into structure below. Most manufacturers offer fixed and operable windows for punched openings. Many of them can be fastened at the jamb. This allows a sill pan to be used without fastener penetration. Depending on spans, wind loads, and extrusion strengths, there are limits to the width of a window system that does not require fastening at the sill. If all wind loads were positive, we might be able to avoid holes in our sill pans or precast sills, but we usually design for positive and negative forces on our exterior surfaces.

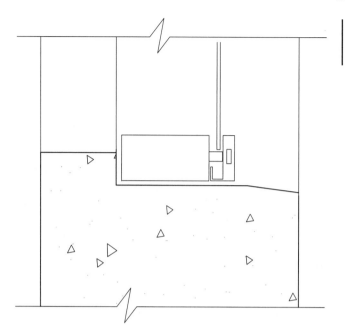

Figure 4-44
Sill pan formed of concrete in tilt wall.

4.5.7   Sill flashings

A sill flashing is nothing more than a means to reduce water penetration behind or under a wall, door, or window sill. Wall sill conditions are similar. In traditional wood frame construction, we see termite shields or similar metal flashings. These served two important functions. First, they acted as a capillary break between floor or foundation and wall systems. Second, they serve to make it more difficult for tunneling insects to penetrate the sole plate for the wall. In concrete floors, especially at grade, we see the use of recessed slab-edge pockets discussed previously. This is another form of sill flashing. The depressed concrete forms a sill of sorts for the wall.

Sill flashings take on many shapes and are made of many materials, but they play the same important role. Their job is to make it more difficult for water to get into the occupied spaces, wall, floors, etc. Many window manufacturers provide sill flashings that are designed to be integral to their structural sill components. The simple isometric drawing provided in Fig. 4-45 illustrates the geometry of a window sill flashing. There is a continuous piece of sheet material that extends from under the window to a point where it turns down the face of the exterior wall. There is no vertical face on the rear or sides of sill flashing. The front (exterior) face of the flashing should extend vertically down to provide a way to cover the void beneath the window sill and also to keep water out past the face of the finishes below. Ideally, the horizontal portion of the flashing is sloped slightly toward the front and is not penetrated by fasteners. Only if the window systems transfer all wind loads to the jambs can you avoid fasteners through the sill flashings.

Figure 4-45

Simple sill flashing.

4.5.7.1 Sill pans

A sill pan is an improved version of sill flashing. Sill pans have vertical components on the jamb sides, as well as the rear. A good way to show these in construction plans is an isometric drawing with dimensions for fabrication (see Fig. 4-46). These three-sided vertical flanges keep water from dripping off the sides of the sill flashing if it accumulates. Most sill pans are constructed out of bent metal, and the preferred way of sealing the joints is by welding. Lower-cost alternatives include sealants in the seams or pieces of SAM applied to close them off. There are inherent challenges to sill pans, in that they must be installed behind and under subsequent finishes (see Fig. 4-47). They must be installed before the windows or doors and perhaps before air or moisture barriers are complete (depending on the wall system). In the ideal world, the rough opening is framed in and sheathed, and then MRB is installed and sealed. This is followed by the AIB installation, and then the welded sill pans are installed. Coordinated with J-beads and other trim pieces, the opening is then stripped in from the bottom up with SAM, making sure that the jamb legs of the sill pan are behind the SAM, (see Fig. 4-48). In this way, any water that gets to the SAM is carried down into the sill pan and causes no harm.

Sill pans play a very important role in moisture control in areas with heavy rain and snow fall. Sill pans have three different levels of performance over time, and they are closely related to initial cost. The lowest-cost sill pan is formed out of a flexible membrane material that is bent into shape. A piece of plastic sheathing or SAM would work better than nothing. Shower pan material would perform well over time. The second level of performance is achieved by the use of cut metal that is bent to shape. The joints or seams would be sealed with SAM stripping or perhaps a good sealant. These are not

Figure 4-46

Sill pan isometric.

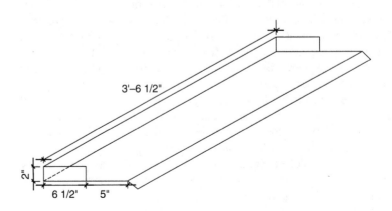

Figure 4-47
Sill pan for door coordinated with other materials.

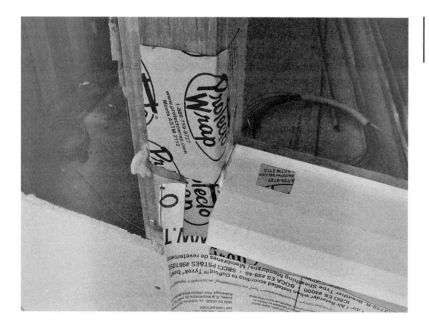

Figure 4-48
Sill pan installation in progress.

as good in the long term as bent metal with welded seams. We recommend minimum 0.05-inch aluminum or stainless steel sill pans. The minimum vertical height of the legs depends on the wind speed to be experienced. We have found that a minimum of 2-inch vertical leg stops most wind-driven water that a sill pan might see in a well-designed and well-constructed building with less than 50 mile per hour winds.

Another key element to the overall performance of a sill pan is proper fit with the window and rough opening. Given the thickness of folded SAM strips and the flashing itself, you have to take those dimensions into account in framing the rough opening. After the sill is installed, it should be checked for positive drainage to the front. A well-designed sill pan slopes down at $1/_8$ inch per foot from the front face of the window sill extrusion to the face of the wall and beyond by $1/_2$ inch or more. The drip leg bends on kick-out flashing will then minimize staining on the wall below, as well as reducing incidental water behind the wall membrane. Sill pan flashing must be coordinated with brick vents and other relief details at window sills in brick or stone cavity wall systems. See Figs. 4-49 and 4-50 for detailed examples of sill conditions for several of the wall types.

For sliding-glass door systems and folding-glass wall systems, the details must be done differently. The point at which water is discharged from the Nanawall system, for example, is about 2 inches (~5 centimeters) below finish floor. In the example in Fig. 4-51, you can see that the drain point is coordinated with the installation of a hot liquid applied membrane system well below finish floor elevation. In this condominium example, the finished walking surface is

Figure 4-49

Sill pan at CMU and stone rain screen wall.

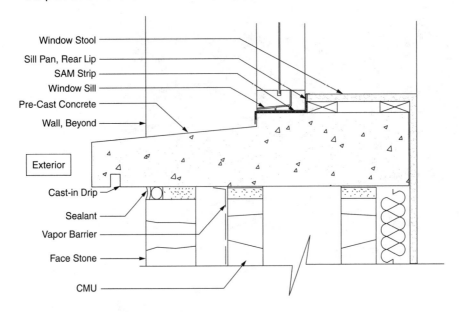

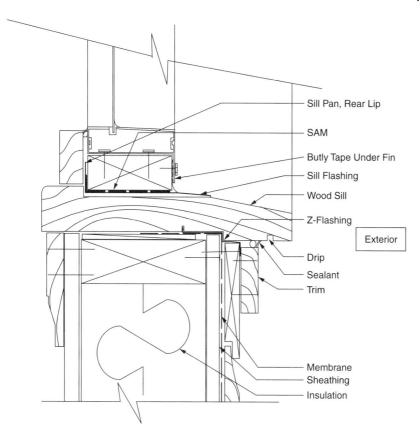

Figure 4-50
Sill pan at wood frame
wall.

Sill Pan, Rear Lip

SAM

Butly Tape Under Fin

Sill Flashing

Wood Sill

Z-Flashing

Exterior

Drip

Sealant

Trim

Membrane

Sheathing

Insulation

brick pavers set about $^3/_8$ inch (1 centimeter) below the interior floor elevation to get as much of a barrier to water as possible and still be less than the accessibility codes permit.

Since we are still very concerned about wind-driven rain in this detail, we sloped the pavers at about $^1/_4$ inch per foot (2 percent) away from the opening. In addition, the pavers were set in very porous screenings from a local concrete block plant to maximize the porosity and drainage. Bi-level drains were installed, one at the surface of the pavers and the other at the top of the post-tensioned structural slab. As an added precaution, we placed overflow scuppers through adjacent exterior walls and located them so that they were always at least 2 inches below finish floor elevations. This required coordination with the drain elevations of the paver-level drains but was seen as the minimum level of protection by the lead designer on the architect's design team. The plumbing engineer was not certain the scuppers were necessary, and the owners tried (in vain) to talk us out of spending the money for eight scuppers, but we felt the obligation to future owners. Sometimes we believe that we have to protect owners or developers in this case, from themselves. They can get so caught up in trying to cut costs that they lose sight of the cost-benefit ratio of critical components. All they had to do was omit a few amenity deck-level plants in pots to pay for the incremental added cost for the scuppers (about $6,000).

Figure 4-51

Sill pan detail for sliding wall at pavers.

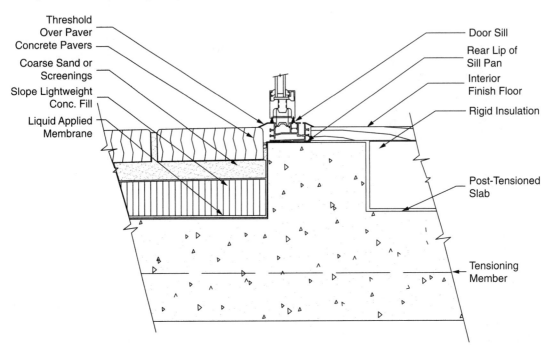

4.5.8 Jambs

We have talked about sill flashings and pans, so let us discuss the second important location for window and wall moisture intrusion considerations—the jamb. Whereas you often have a barrier to wind-driven moisture in sills, it is not as common in the jamb. An exception to this is the use of fin-type windows. Fin windows (and doors such as sliding-glass doors) are supplied with integral flanges that effectively reduce the path for wind-driven rain along side jamb openings. Fin windows were used commonly in wood frame construction. Some manufacturers provided them with full corners, whereas others offered the corner covers as an option. These were common in vinyl and aluminum. They typically would be installed after the AIB and MRB. Many window systems do not offer fin product lines. With non-fin windows, the jambs are more difficult to close off from wind and rain. Jambs come in one- and two-piece systems. In the one-piece systems, exposed fasteners get installed through the extrusion into wood, metal, or concrete alongside the jambs. The rough openings are oversized to accommodate construction tolerances, and shims are placed strategically to tighten the jambs to the structure in proper alignment. The voids between the window system jambs and the wall openings are never filled completely with shim material. Shims usually take up less than 20 percent of the jamb length. This leaves a large void to be filled in some manner or left open (see Fig. 4-52). In this example, bricks were to be returned back toward

Figure 4-52
Shim space at window jamb.

the frames, and sealant was expected to fill the voids. Window installers in the 1960s began to use an expanding foam product to better seal the voids. Most of these canned foam products are open-cell foams that are temporary air barriers at best. We do not recommend reliance on foam fillers or sealants for long-term solutions. They have been shown to deteriorate over time. Wood windows may be constructed using wooden jamb and applied trim pieces to create confining pathways for double- or single-hung wood windows. The fasteners typically are exposed, unless they are installed in such a place as to be concealed by another piece of wood, such as casings, moldings, metal tracks, or stops. In wood window detailing, there are often removable closure pieces such as brick mold that effectively seal off the opening between jamb and wall (see Fig. 4-53).

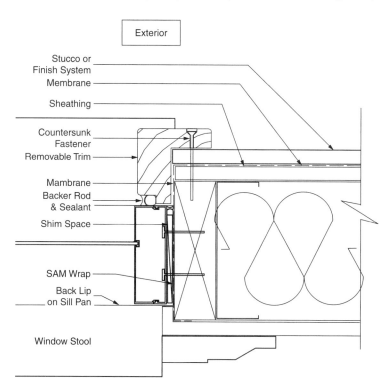

Figure 4-53
Removable trim pieces.

Removal of the casing can be accomplished by setting the finish nails and prying off the old piece of trim. Whenever you are designing or building opening protectives, you must consider future repair, maintenance, and replacement. A future owner should be able to replace a broken window without removing interior finishes such as wall sheathing or exterior finishes such as brick, block, or stucco. Ideally, screw-type fasteners are used in such situations. Metal or wood trim pieces can be installed so as to allow future access to repair damage. Sealants should be installed similarly so that it does not have to be removed in order to reglaze a window. In condominium designs, take extra precautions to seal window against high winds. The detail illustrated in Fig. 4-54 shows a high-rise project's solution to close off the shim spaces at the jamb. It uses redundant sealant applications and a strip of SAM. The sealant selected must be compatible with the SAM, or the sealant will react with the SAM, causing it to degrade.

In two-piece aluminum jambs, the outer piece gets fastened into the structure first, and the second piece gets snapped on afterward. In this system, the fasteners are concealed. Different manufacturers have totally different extrusions and dimensions, so it is important to have a basis of design that is well detailed as to dimensions and methods of closure. We recommend drawing the window and door details at a sufficiently large scale that the fastener sizes and depths, as well as what they are to be fastened into, are readily visible. The details also

Figure 4-54

Redundant sealant in condominium jambs.

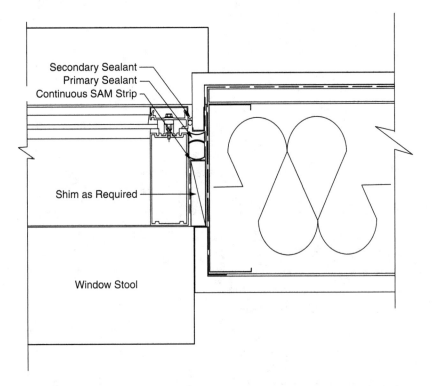

Secondary Sealant
Primary Sealant
Continuous SAM Strip

Shim as Required

Window Stool

should extend beyond the window to illustrate how the window ties into adjacent wall materials and systems. Show shim spaces, and show membranes and sealants as you want them placed. In this way, you make sure that the structural and waterproofing considerations can be solved in concert.

When shop drawings are provided, take care to review attachment materials and methods proposed, and see that they do not deviate substantially from that which was shown on design documents and specifications. Make sure to avoid potential galvanic action between dissimilar materials, such as steel and aluminum. Look at the particular makeup of the materials submitted, and make sure that you're getting 304 or 316 stainless steel if it is to be in contact with other materials such as aluminum or copper and not a 400 series stainless, which has more reactive characteristics. Another important consideration in jambs is where in the wall section they occur, how far back from the face of wall, etc.

Several wall sections are provided, employing the different types of walls and performance levels. Make sure that there are no breaks in the air barrier, thermal insulation, or moisture-resistant barriers. For example, in Fig. 4-55, you don't

Figure 4-55

Mis-applied sealant in rain screen brick wall.

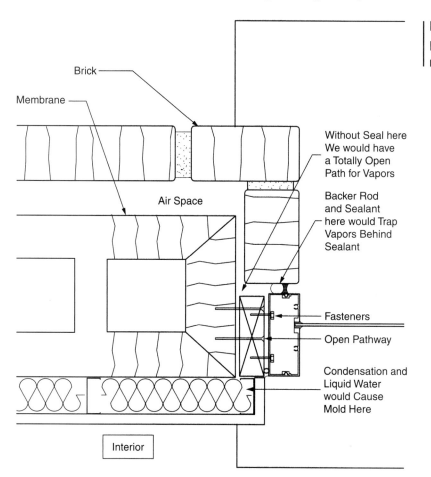

want to seal the jamb to the face of the brick in a rain screen wall system if the MRB is on the face of CMU backup masonry wall. The sealant at the face of the brick could be a secondary barrier. The sealant in a cavity or rain screen wall should seal the face of the backup wall to the window extrusion. This is where the MRB is applied, that is, where (in hot climates) the moisture will be.

4.5.9 Heads

In wood frame construction with lap or bevel siding on a barrier wall, we used to install a simple water table at window heads. The function was the same in masonry, where masons placed protruding stones or bricks out past the face of the wall to get water from above to drip out further than the face of the window head. This also helps to minimize the amount of rain striking the head joint and possibly getting into the wall. Head flashings in drainage and cavity walls do the same job. Head flashings should be installed last because the systems are all designed to keep water from getting behind layers below. In a rain screen stucco-on-metal-frame wall (see Fig. 4-56), you can see how wall membranes should be lapped over the head flashing to avoid backwater laps

Figure 4-56

Rain Screen stucco on metal framed wall.

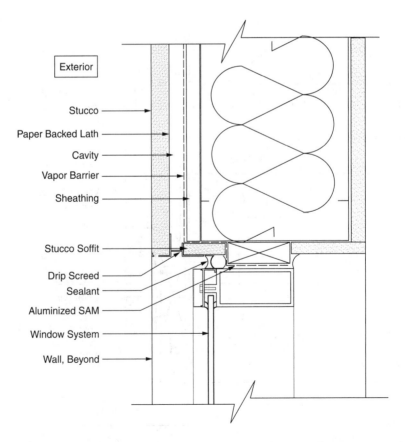

Exterior

Stucco
Paper Backed Lath
Cavity
Vapor Barrier
Sheathing

Stucco Soffit
Drip Screed
Sealant
Aluminized SAM
Window System
Wall, Beyond

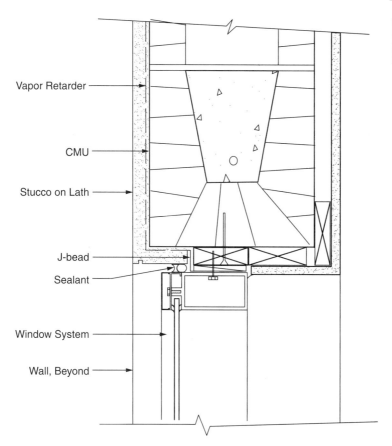

Figure 4-57
Head detail, stucco on CMU wall.

Vapor Retarder

CMU

Stucco on Lath

J-bead

Sealant

Window System

Wall, Beyond

and problems associated with them. Since we have heard of numerous projects where stains were observed long after sealants were applied directly to the bituminous face material on SAM products, we began using aluminized SAM products where in contact with sealants. The cut ends of the aluminized sealants should be behind the point where sealants will be in contact, and we believe you can avoid future stains in this manner. We have been using them in heads, jambs, and sills where in contact with sealants. Since leaking head conditions are not as common as jamb and sill leaks, we will not spend as much time focusing on them. The same issues discussed in terms of jambs apply. We have illustrated other types of head conditions in other common materials (see Fig. 4-57).

4.6   MATERIALS

Now that we have briefly introduced the common wall types, we will now go into the materials that make them up in more detail. Let us begin with the outer skin and work our way into the building. You have already seen the main components listed in the wall sections. Starting with siding, there are several material sources and shapes available. Among them, wood, metal, and plastic are the most common. The most common shapes are bevel and tapered lap siding. V-joint and shiplap are two other shapes that seal better against wind and water intrusion between subsequent boards when applied. They do not dry as quickly owing to the tighter joint geometry. In wood, you typically see rot-resistant woods such as cedar, cypress, or redwood used. White pine, yellow pine, fir, spruce, and other products can be purchased, many of them pressure-treated to make them more resistant to damage from exposure to moisture. Paint and stain, like sealant, are temporary and need reapplication to be effective in preventing moisture from entering wood. In order to minimize warping or twisting, prepaint the wood on all sides prior to installation. Treat all cut ends before installing the next piece. Seal and paint holes from fasteners, if exposed, and then apply another coat of finish product.

Plastic has become much more popular lately because of improved chemistry and cost comparison. Vinyl siding is available in various colors and faux wood grains that seldom need painting. They are close-cell plastics and, as such, are more resistant to water penetration, dirt, and organic materials. This also makes them easier to clean. We have seen some vinyl products come loose during hurricanes, so it is important to make certain that they are fastened according to manufacturer's recommendations for the code-required wind speed in the locale. Aluminum siding is not as common as a horizontally lapped product but has great strength-to-weight properties.

Sheet goods and boards are also installed as exterior finish materials. Texture 1-11 and 6-11 plywoods were common on low-cost projects in the late 1960s and 1970s. Those numbers identified the spacings on scored lines in the sheathing. Cedar and pressure-treated pine were common. Joints often were closed with sealant and painted or covered with thin batten strips. Board and batten applications were common in rural areas where trees were plentiful and affordable. In board and batten installations, 1 by 12s were nailed to horizontal wood stripping, leaving a narrow gap between boards. Battens, in the range of 1 by 3s, were applied to cover the gaps. Reverse board and batten siding is just the opposite, with the boards exposed when finished. As you may know, none of these are low-maintenance, long-term solutions to keep out wind and rain by themselves. They work nicely in conjunction with other products, if the desired look is rustic.

Cementitious coatings, such as stucco or *portland cement plaster,* as it is sometimes called, are very common finish materials. Although they are similar, we will not include synthetic plaster products in this category, such as are used in exterior insulation and finish systems (EIFS). Basically, cementitious coatings are spray- or trowel-applied coatings that consist of various sand and cement products that have water added on site and dry to a hard finish. They can have integral colors or just take on the color of the sand and cement. Our favorite among them is white stucco (see Fig. 4-58), which is made from

Figure 4-58
Photo of 15-year old White Stucco residence, Walker Castle. Designed and built by W. L. Walker, AIA.

clean white beach sand, white portland cement, and lime, which is also white. This creates a very workable mixture that never needs painting. The amount of lime affects how hygroscopic the finished product is. Lime effectively reduces the ease by which water moves through the cured stucco. Depending on how well it is installed, the climate, the chemistry of rainwater, the amount of plant material and other staining agents that come in contact with it, roof drainage and overhangs, etc., white stucco can last up to 50 years without any maintenance other than cleaning every 5 to 10 years and possibly light bleaching with a dilute chlorine and water solution (1 part chlorine in 10 parts water).

In the middle of the twentieth century it was common to see siding materials that contained asbestos because it was so durable and resisted the elements. Late in the century, a new kind of thin panel was introduced that had the same kind of weather resistance but was less hazardous to health. Cementitious planks and panels can be used in much the same way as wood, aluminum, or asbestos. You see them used commonly in horizontal lap siding to replicate wood siding (see Fig. 4-59). Column build-outs and suspended ceilings are other common applications of the fiber-reinforced cement boards. They can be cut, nailed, and painted much like wood. Some are available in wood grain. They are also used as facings in exterior wall diaphragm systems with foam cores. They are dimensionally stable, but they are not nearly as hygroscopic as formed-in-place concrete, CMU, or wood.

Stucco typically is installed over CMU walls or over frame construction when combined with sheathings, membranes, and lath. As a rule, the minimum

Figure 4-59

Photo of hardie siding, replicating wood.

thickness of stucco ranges between $^7/_8$ and 1 inch (2 and 2.5 centimeters) and requires three coats to build up properly to the required thickness. The first coat is referred to as the *brown coat*. It is applied as a general leveling coat. This also serves to fill voids in the CMU or irregularities in the lath. After it is dry, a second coat is applied to further prepare for the finish coat. This second layer is referred to as a *scratch coat* because it is deeply scratched with a tool before the mix sets up (see Fig. 4-60). These scratches aid in the mechanical adhesion of the finish coat(s). Depending on the desired texture, the next one or two coats are applied using different techniques with a steel trowel. Smooth textures typically are referred to as *sand finish,* the easiest to paint and keep clean. There is a multitude of expressive ways to give character to the final coat. The rougher the final texture, the easier it is for dirt and insects to take root, and the harder it is to keep clean. The rougher, thicker textured coats also trap more air at the surface, slightly improving thermal performance.

We recommend applying stucco over expanded metal lath. The lath acts as reinforcement in every direction, reducing cracking over time and improving the bond to a substrate. In the drainage wall, we use stucco over an air and water barrier to reduce the amount of moisture that enters the wall material. Remember, the less water entering the wall, the lower will be the likelihood of mold and mildew growth period. Several techniques are used to limit cracking in stucco, but the most important is to prevent the moisture in the mix from leaving the stucco and going into the block or concrete substrate. This can be achieved by pre-wetting the substrate. Do not retemper the stucco or make it too wet in an attempt to prevent the moisture from leaving—wet the wall. Paper-backed lath helps here. In many building codes, membranes are required to be used behind stucco on frame walls.

Figure 4-60
Scratch coat.

In EIFS systems, the synthetic plaster coating is most often relied on to minimize water and vapor penetration of the surface. The foam beneath does allow hygroscopic action from molecule to molecule over time. The use of reinforcing fiberglass mesh makes the foam less susceptible to damage from light contact. It does little to reduce moisture transmission. We have not shown EIFS details as one of our illustrated wall types, but you can anticipate excellent performance of the rain screen version of EIFS, one with cavity drainage behind the foam and an effective air and moisture barrier in front of that. We would not hesitate to use an EIFS-based system in the right application. It should prove to be a cost-effective system where barrier-type systems can be used, such as in areas with low amounts of annual rainfall, say, in the range of 10 to 15 inches (0.4 meter) per year.

The structural system can serve as a finish material by itself depending on the product. Concrete or CMU walls, for example, have been used as the exposed finish material since their inception. Architecturally, exposed natural concrete can be a very attractive finish. There are several civic structures in most big cities that rely on the aesthetic of exposed concrete as part of the intended effect. This works well in modern, classic, and brutalist forms, as well as in certain organic expressions, such as the Orlando Public Library (see Fig. 4-61). Here, rough-sawn form boards were planned to be part of the finished image of the place. From the moment the forms were stripped, the addition from the late 1970s blended in with the timeless look of the original edifice constructed in the 1960s. The biggest negative of exposed concrete is that in wet climates the concrete is always wet. You can deal with this. It requires additional dehumidification by the building HVAC system and careful selection of wall materials behind the wall. The biggest drawback is the dew point issue and where to put insulation in hot, humid climates.

Figure 4-61

Orlando Public Library,
photo by W. L. Walker, AIA.

Good design would use concrete outside the air cavity, then the air and moisture barrier on the interior side of the cavity, and then wall insulation. Since condensation in a hot, humid climate is likely to occur at the MRB, that plane would need to have planned drainage to the outside. Setting the drainage plane of the cavity and MRB up so that it drains any condensation down and away past the lowest-level slab is critical. In this scenario, you dry toward the outside from the moisture barrier, as you have been taught. In addition, from the MRB inward, you need to permit drying toward the interior wall finishes for removal by the building HVAC system. No problems. In cold climates, the insulation would be installed on the warm (inside) face of the concrete. The MRB would be at the inside face of the insulation. Condensation would form on the MRB and would need to be dried toward the inside by the building HVAC system. In order to minimize the amount (volume) of the condensation, the building humidity set point should stay as low as practical and healthy for the occupants, say, in the 30 percent RH range.

4.6.1   Glass and glazing

Some of our favorite skin materials are glass and stone. The physical properties of glass now can be modified to achieve things never before possible in construction. Spans, reflectivity, insulation, colors, refractance, thicknesses, joints, and other factors that used to limit applications are no longer obstacles. We can do anything. Our only limits are our imagination and our pocketbooks.

Glass now can be engineered to fit the needs of your project. Manufacturers offer a range of colors and thermal performance, a variety of support and joint systems, and many thicknesses. Many of the standard insulating glass projects are based on two layers of $^1/_4$-inch-thick glass with an evacuated void in between. These range in U values from 0.5 to less than 0.29. The lower the U values the better the insulating R values. Some of the better glass has very low ultraviolet (UV) transmittance values, some as low as 1 percent. These can have very low shading coefficients as well. For cold climates, UV values can be more than 85 percent transmittance, and solar heat gain coefficients can be in the 90 percent range. By fine-tuning the insulating and heat gain coefficients you can reduce energy consumption as well as potential condensation in the inside face of glazed systems.

4.6.1.1 Projects pushing the limits on glass

We want to share with you two outstanding examples of what can be done—in fact, has been done recently—in glass. The first is the Kendall Physics Laboratory in Cambridge, Massachusetts, by Steven Ehrlich, AIA. This project, completed in 2003 uses European terra cotta panels and channel glass (see Fig. 4-62) in an exciting interplay of overlapping planes and cubic mass seen from the outside and from within the space (see Fig. 4-63). A design paradigm was developed to reflect the new technologies emblematic of the biotech world and also to relate to the existing architectural fabric of Cambridge. A kinetic interplay is achieved through planar massing of contemporary materials from Europe. Terra cotta was chosen for its harmonious fit with the traditional brick architecture of the city and its lighter, softer qualities in mass.

The material's warm earthiness, in counterpoint to the translucent, fluid quality of the channel glass, forms a composition of Modrianesque syncopation between weight and weightlessness. The project boasts North America's first large-scale panelization of an energy-efficient terra cotta rain screen wall system

Figure 4-62

Exterior, Kendall Physics Laboratory in Cambridge, Massachusetts, by Steven Ehrlich, AIA. Photo by Christopher Lovi.

Figure 4-63

Interior photo of Kendall Physics Research Lab, by Steven Ehrlich, AIA. Photo by Peter Vanderwarker.

that covers 40,000 square feet of the exterior in panels of up to 12 feet, 6 inches by 40 feet in size and 10,800 pounds in weight. The surface patterning of the terra cotta rain screen subtly alludes to the nature of the research taking place within the building. Four textures of the extruded terra cotta tiles represent the four sequencing gels of DNA molecules: adenine, thymine, guanine, and cytosine. This pattern, in taut extruded clay, changes character as the light changes at different times of the day, (see Fig. 4-64). Providing additional variations in light, shade, and shadow are the structural braces that function to support the large overhanging roof plane, above (see Fig.4-65).

The second reference project pushing the limits in glazing is the new Beijing Poly Plaza by S.O.M. in China. This project also was designed using a large glass panel system in a contextual manner, as expressed in the study sketch shown in Fig. 4-66. Each facade was planned in response to sun angles and adjacent building forces. As seen from the inside (see Fig. 4-67), this huge expanse of glass provides a unique connection between inside and outside, creating an image statement of clean lines and dynamic expression. This is believed to be the world's largest glazed panel system at more than 100 by 150 feet (30 by 42 meters).

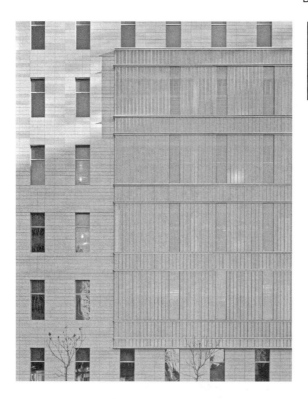

Figure 4-64
Variety of exterior finishes represent the physics inside. Photo by Chuck Choi.

Figure 4-65
Rain screen glazing system and braces. Photo by Paul Warchol.

Figure 4-66

Plans and Solar study, Poly Plaza, by SOM.

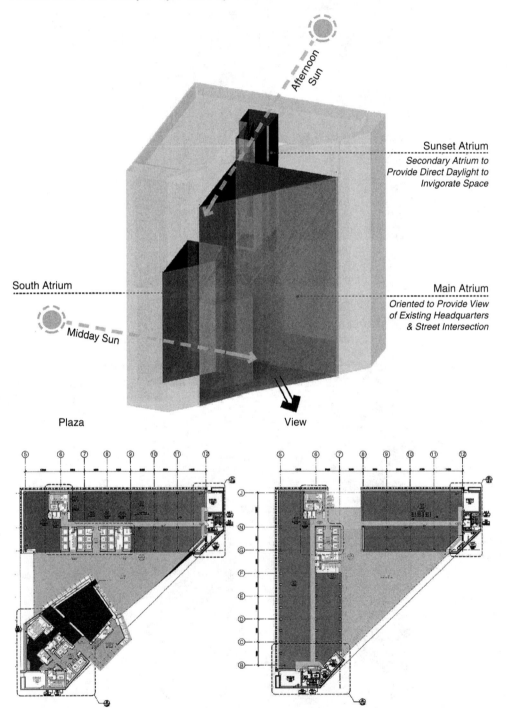

Figure 4-67
Interior photo of space created, as seen from Walkway. Photo by SOM.

China Poly, a major state-owned company with influence in many market sectors, wanted to create a new landmark headquarters complex that, through its quality and mix of public and commercial uses, would establish a grand civic presence in Beijing, It provides functional and symbolic access for its citizens. The new 100,000 square meter headquarters is located opposite to the existing headquarters building on a prominent intersection along the Second Ring Road, Northeast of the Forbidden City. With its program of office space, retail, restaurants, and the Poly Museum, the new headquarters reflects the project's public mission. The Poly Museum houses one of the most important collections of bronze and Buddhist antiquities in the country.

The building's simple monolithic triangular form is based upon an L-shaped office plan enclosed by an expansive, glass cable-net wall. The bars of office space align with the surrounding development while the large atrium looks outward to the intersection and the existing China Poly building beyond, (see Fig. 4.68). The design takes full advantage of the natural day-lighting, with the Northeast facing atrium, which is one of the largest cable-net enclosures in the world. This is roughly four times the size of Time Warner Center's cable-net wall in New York City. The use of the cable-net system maximizes the transparency of the glazed wall system (see Figure 4.67) as compared to a truss or column and beam structural system.

Figure 4-68

Exterior photo of Façade by SOM.

Due to seismic considerations, a V-cable system was engineered to allow the main cable to accommodate movement that might result from an event with a specially designed rocker mechanism. The counter-weighted rocker responds to movement caused by wind or earthquakes, giving more or less slack to compensate for movement of the glazed panel. The Museum is the counter-weight, attached to the other end of the cable. The suspended lantern's delicate and luminous qualities call attention to the Poly Museum framed within the main atrium. Public circulation areas and custom-designed lighting occupy the space between the interior and exterior, adding to the play of light, shade and shadow. Through innovation in technology and engineering, a unique architecture capturing the prominence of this stalwart company is created. The rainscreen aspect of the project is almost overshadowed by the prominence, however it will function well as a thermal and water separator to protect people and places inside. Now back to more common applications and solutions.

4.6.2 Membranes

Behind the skin system, whether glass, stone, stucco, or wood, both the drainage system and the rain screen system rely on additional components that form a second line of defense. Rather than count on the coat of paint to stop air and moisture at the surface of the wall, you have additional parts and pieces to perform specific tasks. In the quest to stop liquid water, we recommend the use of a continuous membrane.

Membranes come in two main types—air and water. Air barriers are intended to stop or retard the flow of air through them. We refer to them as *air infiltration barriers* (AIBs). Water molecules can be carried through some AIBs in the form of vapor. The gaseous water molecules of water vapor can move in an airstream through microscopic openings in the AIB. To stop water molecules, both liquid and vaporous (gas), you can use one or more of a very broad family of products referred to as *moisture reduction barriers* (MRBs). For a chart listing air leakage rates for commonly used air infiltration barrier materials, see Table 4-4. The number, placement, and performance of these membranes will be of paramount importance for the performance of the building envelope over time. Building codes should be consulted as a minimum criterion for stopping water. Engineered and computer-calculated performance models are only as good as the information being input into them. Designers need to weigh all available data, consider their experience with previous projects, think about the client groups, liability issues, and initial and long-term costs, and make the right decisions.

The minimal perm rating of the appropriate membrane for a project can be determined based on the amount of rainfall and the duration of anticipated rain events. The greater the intensity and longer the duration of rain events, the lower is the perm rating selected; therefore, the less water will pass through it. Another consideration must be the type of use for the building and how important is it to you to minimize water intrusion. Is it going to be a laboratory or a hospital? High-end condos on the beach might require a moisture barrier (lower than 1 perm). There is a debate going on as to breathable versus non-breathable wall systems in moist, humid climates. It is not as simple as choosing one over another. Many factors contribute to the choice, and initial cost never should be the only factor.

Another consideration is the finish going over it. If the surface is metal panels, the only exposure to moisture is that which might get between the panels. For the wet rout and return panels, the risk is minimal. Sealant at the face of each metal panel reduces exposure to and pressures from surface rain. A higher perm rating might be acceptable. For a rain screen system in stucco on block, you might use the best membrane (lowest perm) that you can find. More important than matching the MRB to the budget is matching it to the climate

Table 4-4
Air infiltration barriers

Number	Product	Thickness	Air leakage rate, cfm/sf	Tensile strength	Tear resistance
1	Dupont Tyvek	1 mil.	0.04		
2	Grace Perm-a-Barrier VP	2 ply	0.04		
3	Johns Manville ProWrap		0.017		
4	Closed Cell Spray Polyurethane foam	1.5 inch	0.001		
5	Polyethylene sheet	6 mil.	0.0015		

From manufacturer's webpages product data

and rainfall data. Other considerations may include the mechanical equipment, insulation, overhangs, available work force, and maintenance.

4.6.3 Air infiltration barriers

AIBs can take many forms. A coat of paint or a sheet of plywood can be considered a barrier to air. An air barrier function is to resist the movement of air through a material, thereby stopping air pressure. Depending on the system chosen, the AIB must fit the physical requirements of the application. In hot, humid climates, for a rain screen system you are talking about a sheet of thin material that gets fastened to the skin. A 1-mil-thick visqueen sheet stops air movement quite well but has very little resistance to tearing if it is stretched tight. Therefore, it does not meet the physical requirements. For an AIB to work, it must be extended continuously from floor to roof. This means stretching over corners, where puncture resistance is important. Reinforced AIBs, such as Typar, effectively reduce punctures owing to the fabric fibers in their makeup.

The roof needs an AIB sealed to the wall membrane. For a crawl-space first floor, the AIB must extend under the floor area and be sealed to the walls, including penetrations. The slab on grade condition can be detailed with a 2-inch overlap of material taped or otherwise sealed to the concrete below the finish floor. For the AIB to perform to its fullest potential, the fastener penetrations should be sealed as well. Several means for sealing the fasteners are used, including special nails with an oversized washer that closes off the penetration. This is more important in coastal zones with high wind speeds and in cold, wet climates where snow can build up against exterior walls. Any voids in cold climates can allow water vapor penetration, which can freeze. This freezing action causes water to expand, further enlarging the voids.

The main purpose of an AIB is to help create an airtight seal around the exterior. By controlling leakage, you can efficiently control humidity, temperature, and creature comfort. Drafts can be especially troubling in cold climates. The doors, windows, and other components that interrupt the AIB need to be considered as parts of the AIB system. Louvers through the envelope need to be ducted tight to the building air-conditioning system or they become points of admission for air. Attic vents, soffit vents, and similar openings should be closed to the indoor environment. The intersection between the AIB and other components must be an airtight seal as well. Tapes are available from most manufacturers to seal between the AIB membrane and other materials such as metal. Depending on the design, you may choose an AIB that allows vapor diffusion through it. This can help drying in some conditions. An AIB, if used, should be at least four times as vapor permeable as the vapor barrier.

Roof membranes that serve as continuous AIBs are being used more commonly in hot and cold climates. Self-adhesive membranes (SAMs), which were developed specifically for roof underlayment, such as W. R. Grace Ice and Water Shield, are also being used in wall installations as air and vapor barriers. The self-sealing aspect of SAM products makes them desirable.

4.6.4 Moisture-reduction barriers

In Florida, especially near the coast, many designers try to create barriers to water and vapor transmission. They rely on continuous and well-sealed membranes with low perm ratings. The goal is to limit the number of grains of water that enter the envelope to the lowest total. One approach is to try to seal the envelope and pressurize it from the inside with the building air-conditioning system. Therefore, you must strive to seal from the lowest point of the pressurized envelope to the highest and around all four sides. Other designers choose to use permeable wall systems that permit moisture through the wall system, just in some limited designed quantities. One rule we can agree on for all climates is that the permeability should increase as you move away from the MRB. There should be only one low-permeable material in the wall section, and materials should increase by a factor of 4 to 10 in both directions from there. For a table showing perm ratings of stated products refer to Fig. 4-113.

There is no one way that works well for all building materials; however, you can group all MRBs into two major headings—sheet or liquid-applied membranes. It is obvious what the apparent differences are—their physical states are different. Sheet membranes are solid when applied, and liquid-applied membranes need to cure before they become solids. Sheet products are made in factories with controlled environments, and thus they have very consistent thickness and composition. Their quality-control practices are quite good. Sheet membrane's perm ratings are achieved in the field consistently and can be relied on regardless of the installer. There may, of course, be differences in the joints, cuts, and seams from individual to individual, but the sheets themselves are quite dependable. For these reasons, sheet membranes typically are preferred over liquid-applied membranes in hot and humid climates. Liquid-applied membranes in warm climates are mostly used on horizontal surfaces where they can flow to fill difficult to reach areas, and are seldom exposed to the direct heat of the sun to avoid creep.

Some sheet membrane materials you may be familiar with are tar paper and visqueen. Liquid-applied MRBs you might know include paint, sealers, and bituminous and rubber coatings. These typically are applied with roller, brush, trowel, or sprayer. Liquid products need to be applied over the right kind of material in a uniform thickness in order to have a consistent perm rating. There are many advantages to liquid-applied products, including their ability to flow into voids, corners, and tight spaces. Since they are applied in a continuous coat, there are no laps and cuts to worry about. Each MRB has different benefit-versus-cost considerations, so designers and specifiers must fit the product with the client's needs and budget.

Over the years, manufacturers have continued to improve their product lines to meet the ever-growing need for moisture-control products. SAMs were developed in the 1990s in response to the need for easier application of membranes over large vertical surfaces. A very small crew can install SAMs without having to fasten them as they go and at the same time avoid sagging. For applications over nonporous materials, manufacturers recommend using their own specially formulated primers. These primers significantly increase adhesion to almost any material, including lapped edges of SAM to itself. Penetrations from fasteners seal themselves. Imagine how many nails, screws, and staples get installed in a building facade. Assume that there are about 4,800 per wall. If you multiply 4,800 times an average tear or rip of $1/8$ square inch, you would have a total opening size of 600 square inches or just under 5 square feet (1.8 square meters) per wall. This is especially meaningful near window or door openings, where you frequently get a concentration of fasteners and where so many of the leaks originate in buildings. The self-adhesive and self-sealing qualities of SAMs (also referred to commonly as "peel and stick") provide the construction industry with a whole new solution set for tightening up the envelope. Just like everything else, though, it must be done right. In order to take advantage of the adhesive properties, the surface below must be dry and clean. If it is dusty or porous, prime it first to remove loose particles. Then, after every application of SAM, it is very helpful to use a special roller created by the manufacturer to apply pressure evenly in an attempt to force out bubbles and complete the adhesion process. It is not enough just to smooth the SAM with your hand and walk away because it looks good enough. To take full advantage of the inherent properties, use the roller at every joint and over strategic portions of the entire surface, (see Fig. 4-69). This will minimize sagging over time. At least one manufacturer now offers pre-primed glass fiber impregnated sheathing. This will prevent you from having to prime sheathings, but needs to be protected from dirt and dust to maximize adhesion to the SAM.

Improvements in the SAM family have been well received. SAMs now have such refinements as foil facing bonded to them. The foil-faced SAM can be used when you expect it to be exposed to UV radiation or for aesthetic purposes. Aluminum-faced SAM can be used in the corners of sill pans to be more dimensionally stable and resist puncture better. Another good place for foil-faced SAM is where sealant will be in contact with the SAM. To continue on with the theme of the right way to apply SAM at windows, please review the next two photographs beginning with Fig. 4-70 showing the right way to install SAM stripping at a window opening. We begin with this example of a fin-type aluminum window. Note the plywood sheathing around the perimeter to accept screw fasteners along all four sides. Ideally, these screws also penetrate the metal framing, however that is not necessary if jamb or head and sills are fastened through the extrusions.

Figure 4-69
Tool for applying SAM.

Figure 4-70
SAM window wrap, step 1.

As work progresses, pieces of SAM are applied over the primed surfaces, being careful to extend past the edge of wood sheathing onto the fiber reinforced gypsum sheathing a minimum of four inches (10 cm), (see Fig. 4-71). Make sure sharp edges and fasteners are smooth and will not tear through the membrane. Take your tool, and work out all voids and bubbles in the applied membrane.

Figure 4-71
SAM window wrap, step 2.

For best protection, install head flashing and strip it in with another layer of SAM. Now you are ready for application of air barriers, and finish materials, in many cases leaving space for a sealant joint around the frame. Due to the fin-type window flanges we have a redundant air and water barrier system that will perform well for decades to come, even without sealant.

Depending on the wall type, climate, budget, and client (again), you may choose to use the MRB as an AIB as well. Several recent articles mention their acceptance of the use of an MRB on only a portion of the envelope. The articles go on to discuss the fact that the total volume of water in the building is a function of both the surface area of membrane and the perm rating. What they fail to discuss is that anyplace the membrane is not installed, you have created a concentration of water molecules, not to mention vapor-driven dynamics resulting from the pressure gradients along the border. Once in the walls, that moisture will be able to move to locations where the conditions may be ripe for condensation. If you are going to limit your SAM applications, we recommend you use it at windows, doors, and all other locations with concentrations in the fasteners or in proximity to grade.

In cold climates, where your concern is snow piled up against a wall, this may make some sense to some of you. The approach would keep the moisture in that location from moving through the wall, but it still doesn't make sense to me. In cold climates, you place the MRB on the inside of the insulation, so that scenario won't work well. Perhaps in mixed climates in the winter time it would make more sense, but in either cold or hot, humid climates, we recommend that the MRB be extended to every part of the envelope. For this reason, in temperate, humid climates with fewer than 20 inches (0.5 meter) of average annual rainfall, with a good HVAC system and good insulation, it may be acceptable to use a partial MRB to save a few dollars on initial cost (if you have to). We are just not proponents of doing anything halfway. If you're going to use an MRB, use it everywhere. This is, in our opinion, just as important as insulating the complete envelope.

4.6.5 Both membranes working together

As we have mentioned previously, liquid water does most of the damage to buildings. Historically, designers and builders did not try very hard to stop air or vapor penetration in the building envelope. As recently as 40 years ago, you were lucky to see a window installer fill the voids around his or her products with a can of open-cell foam. It was rare to see weather stripping seals, and nobody worried much about infiltration. Asbestos shingles were installed over impregnated sheathing. Interior walls were made of wood lath and plaster. All these materials (except for the siding) were breathable. Most buildings were operated at negative pressure, out of ignorance and for economic reasons. It was the way it had always been done! As labor costs and the demand for buildings increased, builders started using paper-faced gypsum boars in lieu of lath and plaster. This was just the beginning.

Changes in building envelope design continued with the energy crisis and rising costs for electricity. People began to care about wasting energy. Sealing the building envelope was seen as a must; it had to be done in hot or cold climates. As a result, designers and builders came to rely more on building air-conditioning systems than ever before. They introduce outside air, don't they? How much? Is it enough to be cool? Few occupants open windows except for those few days in the fall or spring (assuming that they have operable windows). As building envelopes got tighter, it seems more and more people complained about the air in buildings. Well, surprise! The inside smells worse than the outside in most small cities. People started reporting illnesses and blamed them on the air in their buildings. The term *indoor air quality* (IAQ) started to take on negative connotations.

It seems that buildings were designed and/or being operated after modification by owners and operators in a negative-pressure condition. Even if the architects, engineers, and builders provided enough outside air in their designs, the professionals began to get named in lawsuits at astoundingly increasing rates. Negative-pressure buildings tend to suck in outside air (often hot and moist in those climates). This air gets drawn in at the points of least resistance—at windward windows and doors or at intersections of systems. This moist air seems to always be at a different temperature than the indoor set points for HVAC systems. Pressure and temperature gradients caused this air to move through walls and corridors, condensing in places that occupants could not see or clean. The cycle continued until such a time as a trigger event occurred, such as a hurricane dumping rain for days at a time coupled with a loss of power—and boom!—mold growth increases exponentially.

The best way to prevent mold growth is to stop it before it grows. Minimize the number of spores, and then prevent moisture from dissolving food sources that fuel its growth. Thus the AIB plays a very important role. It permits you to effectively keep out humid air that even may contain new spores and at the same time allows you to cost-effectively maintain positive pressure on the envelope. In some systems, you will see that there is a separate, dedicated sheet material that acts as the AIB. In others, the MRB is used as the AIB. In still others (see Fig. 4-72), you might see a layer of paint over CMU or applied directly over sheathing for the AIB. If a wall sheathing is to be used as an air barrier, the joints must be properly sealed. There are several products on the market, most of which must be protected from UV exposure for long-lasting adhesion. There are many reasons to choose one over the others, but it all comes back to the three big C's—climate, clients, and cash. How much rain is expected? What are the temperatures of the outside air compared with the inside set points? How much does it cost? These are the issues that really matter.

In mixed arid climates, there may not be a need for moisture barriers. In these situations, you might wish to have the entire wall system breathe. This entire discussion is based on the assumption of air-conditioned interior spaces. In a warm, dry scenario, an AIB that breathes might be a great solution. Locating this AIB inside or outside the insulation would be determined based on heating and cooling day considerations, as well as individual occupant comfort

Figure 4-72

Paint as AIB.

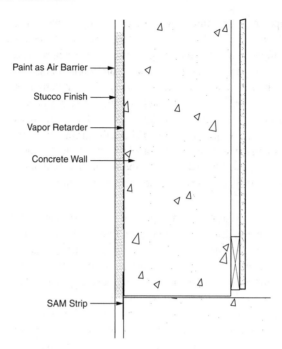

Paint as Air Barrier ——→

Stucco Finish ——→

Vapor Retarder ——→

Concrete Wall ——

SAM Strip ——→

(for single-family buildings). High-thermal-mass masonry on block wall systems could provide a good solution, if coupled with the right sun exposure, for cool, dry climates, where temperatures vary greatly over a 24-hour cycle. In other areas, where you don't want to store the heat energy for long periods of time, low-thermal-mass wood frame wall systems would be better. You would want a low-permeability AIB for when the difference between inside and outside temperatures or humidity is greatest. There are some variable membranes that allow less air and moisture through them when the humidity is high than when it is low. These "smart membranes" are also manufactured in conjunction with insulation as the facing material. We do not recommend their use in hot, humid areas.

There are many differing views on where the AIB gets installed. This is particularly applicable to multicomponent wall systems such as the metal or wood frame examples with sheathing in the rain screen system. In warm climates, AIB's are installed outside the insulation, just like the MRB; we know that. But where exactly does the AIB go? As a general statement, the AIB should be installed wherever the installers have the best opportunity to complexly seal the envelope. In the framed wall examples shown in Fig. 4-73, the AIB goes on over the SAM. This permits the SAM (acting as the MRB) to have reduced pressure on it. The AIB effectively reduces ambient air pressure on the MRB. Another reason is that the SAM adheres better to raw sheathing, such as DensGlas or plywood. You don't really want the SAM over the top of the AIB, especially if a sheet AIB is used. Wrinkles in the AIB make it difficult to install the SAM without potential leaks where the wrinkles are below. Finally, the fasteners from the AIB will seal themselves as they penetrate the SAM. In this scenario, we have created two effective

Figure 4-73
Photo showing AIB outside MRB.

air barriers because the SAM also functions to prohibit air movement through it. For the AIB to seal against air penetration, all seams, fasteners, laps, and penetrations need to be sealed with the manufacturer's approved sealing tape.

We need to detail roof and floor wall joint geometries for sealing the AIB and SAM to slab and walls. Roof membranes need to relieve moisture and pressure by venting out at relief vents or under flashings at parapets (see Fig. 4-74). Note in the photo that we cantilevered the ladder supports over the face of the roof coping. This prevented roof sidewall membrane penetrations as well as holes in the coping itself. Hot gases can escape under the coping and cleat system through the small voids in the membrane. All our membranes and air vapor and moisture barriers need to be designed to work effectively in concert with the wall and roof skin systems to control pressure and limit infiltration. In the section provided (see Fig. 4.75), we show a roof edge detail with ventilation designed for relief under the metal flashing. This lets the hot gases out, and keeps wind-driven water out along the edges. Good ventilation leads to a longer lasting roof since the sheathing and membrane stay drier beneath the roof.

4.6.6   Sealants

We don't use caulking on the exterior of our buildings very often. Caulking is limited to use where joints do not move. There may be an occasional case where caulking is appropriate on the building envelope, such as . . . well! we really can't think of a good one. Caulking is for painters and generally is limited to the interiors of buildings where temperatures are relatively stable. As an experienced designer, we consider sealants to be an important part of the building envelope system. We like to think of the skilled worker applying sealants as waterproofing

Figure 4-74

Photo of roof membrane that will vent at coping.

Figure 4-75

Roof membrane will vent at wall receiver, detail.

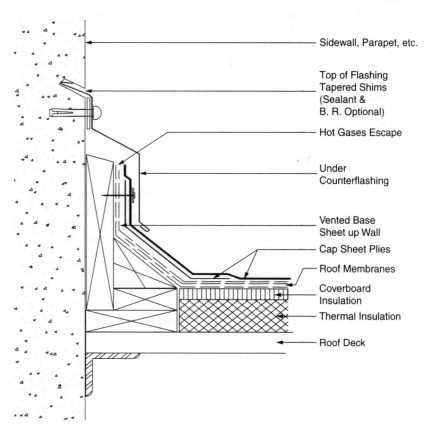

Sidewall, Parapet, etc.

Top of Flashing
Tapered Shims
(Sealant &
B. R. Optional)

Hot Gases Escape

Under
Counterflashing

Vented Base
Sheet up Wall

Cap Sheet Plies

Roof Membranes

Coverboard
Insulation

Thermal Insulation

Roof Deck

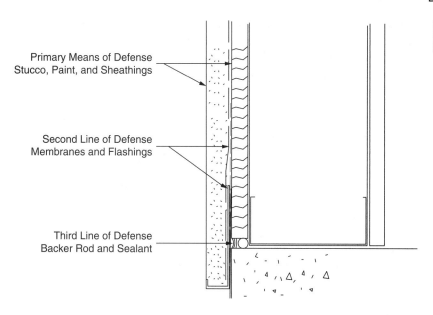

Primary Means of Defense
Stucco, Paint, and Sheathings

Second Line of Defense
Membranes and Flashings

Third Line of Defense
Backer Rod and Sealant

Figure 4-76
Three lines of defense.

experts. We think of sealants as the third line of defense against water and vapor intrusion. The building skin, with coatings, veneers, and sheathings, is the first line of defense. Membranes and flashings are the second (see Fig. 4-76). Sealants generally are used to reduce the sizes of openings exposed to the weather and to fill voids. We urge you to never rely on sealants by themselves to stop water intrusion into a wall or roof cavity. They are only a part of the entire system.

Sealants are temporary. If selected and applied properly, a good sealant can last for 5 to 10 years without significant reduction in performance. Sealants should be inspected annually and removed and replaced if they are seen to be cracking or separating from one surface or another for (rule of thumb) more than an 1 inch per 10 feet of length (2.5 centimeters per 3 meters). If more has separated than this, the entire area needs closer inspection.

If sealants are seen to be coming loose from a surface, this often can be the result of several possible root causes. If both edges are still fully adhered, the sealant did not have enough elasticity. It could be the wrong product for the job. You must calculate the expansion and contraction of the materials being sealed, looking at total movement as well as differences in adjacent materials. Then you should select a sealant product that far exceeds the calculated movement. A factor of 2 is minimum; 4 is not uncommon. If the materials are going to move $^1/_{16}$ inch (0.15 centimeter), the sealant should be able to stretch (and compress) $^1/_8$ inch (0.3 centimeter) without coming loose from either of its two adhered surfaces. The higher percentage the material elongates, the less it fatigues and cracks or pulls loose from its bond.

Thermal coefficients of common materials range from 0.000003 inch per degree Fahrenheit for pine to 0.000007 for Portland cement and 0.0000128 for soft metals such as aluminum. Glass has a coefficient equal to 0.0000047. To get the total expansion, multiply the span in inches times the coefficient for thermal expansion times the ΔT (difference from low to high temperature the material may see in a year) or, as a rule of thumb, 120°F. Note that this is not air temperature, but material temperature exposed to the sun.

Let's work a sample problem. For a 100-foot-long (30 meter) masonry wall (see Fig. 4-77), this would be 100 × 12, (to get total inches) × 0.000034 × 120°F = 0.49 inches (1.27 centimeters). Let's call this $^1/_2$ inch. Let us imagine that we are trying to minimize the appearance of the sealant joints, so we might choose to limit them to $^3/_8$ inch (1 centimeter) in size so that they would be the same size as the mortar joints in our typical masonry wall.

We prefer to design the joints to move about one-quarter of their width so that we can't see them bulging out noticeably in the summer months when materials are at their largest. In the example, the structural system is steel columns and beams on a 25-foot (8-meter) grid. We could introduce three joints along the entire length, giving us vertical sealant joints at the center of interior column lines *B, C,* and *D.* We recommend keeping the masonry unit corners laced, without a movement or sealant joint, for both aesthetic reasons and for structural integrity. In this scenario, each joint would move about a third of $^1/_2$ inch, or $^1/_6$ inch (0.4 centimeter).

Figure 4-77

Plan showing 100' wall.

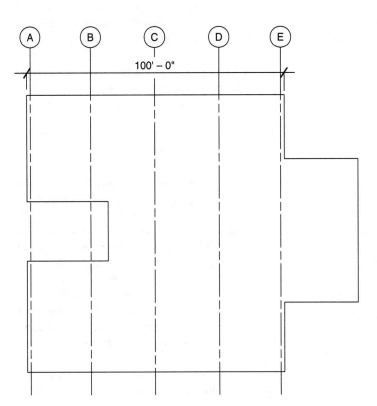

We would need to specify a sealant whose material properties exceed $1/6$ inch times our factor of 2, or $1/3$ inch (0.85 centimeter). This requirement is easily exceeded by most sealants. A good silicone sealant will be able to stretch five to seven times its installed length (500 to 700 percent). If our joint is $3/8$ inch (1 centimeter) wide, the product could stretch more than $1\frac{1}{2}$ inches (4 centimeters).

This leads us to the second possible cause of sealant separation—bad design. Sealant joints are not to be confused with expansion joints; rather, they should work in concert with them. Expansion joints are designed where movement is excessive. Long buildings require expansion joints. The conditions that require expansion joints generally include: (1) new building meeting existing building, (2) different systems coming together, (3) long wings meet main structures, and (4) tall buildings transition to shorter roof areas or any geometric configuration where excessive differential settling is likely to occur. This book does not address expansion joints; however, in many projects, expansion joints are not required, and cracking must be minimized through the use of control joints (typically with sealant), to be referred to hereafter as *sealant joints* or *joints*.

There are three principal areas where design decisions must be made relative to joints: frequency, location, and geometry. Frequency can depend on the primary structure, soil-bearing capacity, temperature differential, etc. Joints should be located so as to minimize cracks in exterior walls. A rule of thumb for stucco is to place joints every 20 to 25 linear feet (7 meters) or 250 square feet (20 square meters). Manufacturers and industry associations will publish their recommendations for maximum distances between joints. Location depends on the type of material, support conditions, and many other factors. In brick veneer, we typically place vertical control joints where support angles are fastened to the primary structure, at the center of column lines, for example. In a tall wall, we often locate horizontal joints at places where ledger angles are required or where bond beams exist. The idea is to minimize cracking in the finish materials that could result from movement related to thermal energy, vibration, or differential settling. It is also a good idea to place joints where forces are concentrated, such as in line with window or door heads and sills. Another recommended location is where materials or systems change, such as CMU walls to floor or roof slabs (see Fig. 4-78). We recommend joints in the $1/2$- to $5/8$-inch-wide range (1.25 to 1.5 centimeter) in most materials. You can work this backwards to determine how far apart the joints need to be. We try not to ever design sealant joints over $1\frac{1}{2}$ inches wide (3.75 centimeters).

Joint geometry is also important, as discussed in the preceding paragraph. There are three common kinds of sealant applications. A typical butt joint is perhaps $5/8$ inch (1.59 centimeters) wide. The depth of the sealant should range between half and two-thirds of the width (see Fig. 4-79).

It is common to use foam backer rod material at the back side of the joint. The backer rod also should be clean and dry when installed. It should be compressed to about two-thirds or three-quarters its full size in the void. Backer

Figure 4-78

Sealant at roof to wall joint.

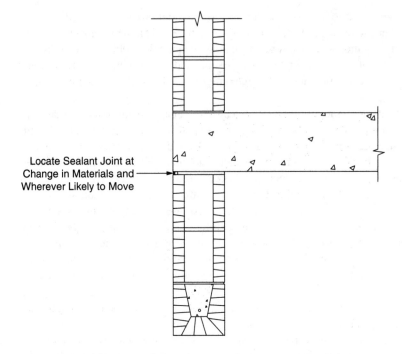

Locate Sealant Joint at Change in Materials and Wherever Likely to Move

rods should be installed so that the remaining depth for the sealant is about half the width at the center. You should have more depth for bonding at both ends where the two materials are joined, for example, in a butt joint (see Fig. 4-80). Use a $^5/_8$-inch or maximum $^3/_4$-inch (1.5 to 1.75 centimeters) backer rod for a $^1/_2$-inch-wide (1.27 centimeter) joint. The depth should be constant. If the depth of the joint is insufficient for the backer rod, an alternative is bond-breaker tape. This tape adheres even better than most sealants when applied properly. It can be used in shallow joints to ensure that only two-sided adhesion takes place. In most cases, the tape is applied to the backside to prevent three-sided adhesion. In cases where the movement exceeds half the elongation, an expansion joint should be used, or a different sealant should be selected.

Figure 4-79

Joint depth-to-width ratio.

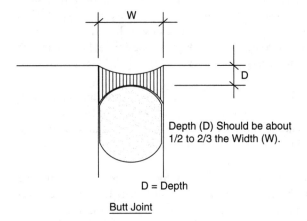

W

D

Depth (D) Should be about 1/2 to 2/3 the Width (W).

D = Depth

Butt Joint

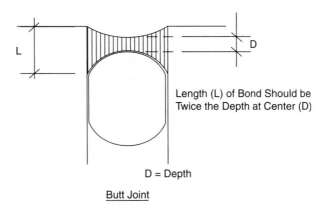

Figure 4-80
Hourglass shaped sealant at butt joint.

Length (L) of Bond Should be Twice the Depth at Center (D)

D = Depth

Butt Joint

Poor preparation can be another cause of joint failures. The most common cause of sealant adhesion problems is insufficient surface preparation of bonding surfaces. Most sealants adhere best to dry surfaces, and all surfaces to be in contact with the sealant need to be clean. By this, we mean free of all loose contaminants such as dirt and dust, oxidation, oils, and most paints. Some painted surfaces, when the paint is adhered sufficiently to the metal, such as shop-applied kynar-coated aluminum or powder-coated or baked-on enamel, may not need the paint removed prior to application of the sealant. The sealant selected must be reviewed carefully to make sure that it is right for the materials with which it will be in contact. Some sealants contain materials that will react with solvent-based paints.

We do not recommend applying a sealant over another trade's liquid- or fluid-applied material. If, for example, the vertical joint in a tilt wall panel comes in contact with a roofing detail involving sealant, it is best to make the transition with a metal cover plate, counterflashing (see Fig. 4-81), or similar separation/isolation of trades. Another solution might be to make certain that the two sealant products that come in contact are made by the same manufacturer. It is always a good idea to try to get all sealant products in a single project from a single source (manufacturer, if possible) so as to not reduce or void warranty issues.

Sealants should not be used as adhesives, as a general rule. Materials being joined generally should use mechanical fasteners to resolve forces acting on the joint. For a sliding lap joint connection, one side is fastened fixed, and the other side of the joint is permitted to move as forces are applied. Sealants should be used in either a fillet joint, lap joint, or butt joint configuration (see Fig. 4-82). In no case should there be three-sided adhesion; the two sides being sealed preferably are parallel to each other. While some of the better sealants have great adhesive properties, up to 25 or 30 pounds per inch, they should be using those properties to stay in place, not to hold window jambs in place or copings to the parapet wall.

Figure 4-81

Avoid applying two sealants in contact.

Joints need to be tested in order to ensure anticipated performance. There are two steps to sealant testing. The first step is in full-scale mockups. Wall and roof segments should be built to mock test the most challenging conditions. These typically include window and door openings and wall-to-grade, wall-to-soffit, and roof details (see Fig. 4-83). We cannot overstress the importance of full-size mockups. Even the best-intentioned designers with time-tested details should make certain that the contractors build the mockups well in advance of wall framing and sheathing. There may be a quarter of an inch one way or the other that could make the details work better. Or a sequence-of-construction tip could be learned. You can have pull tests done on sealed joints

Figure 4-82

Three kinds of sealant joints.

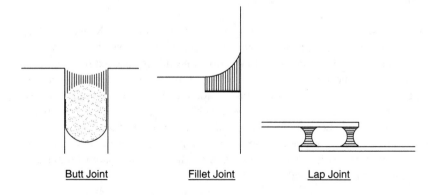

Butt Joint   Fillet Joint   Lap Joint

Figure 4-83
Photo, mock-up of roof crown element.

(see Fig. 4-84) and penetration tests done on the representative systems as mocked up.

In nearly every instance, there are tweaks that can be done to improve the details (at least one of them). Assuming that everything finally passes the tests, the contractor now has a great idea of your expectations. After the final details

Figure 4-84
Sealant pull testing on a mock-up.

are worked out and construction is complete, additional tests should be performed on a portion of the completed building to make sure that the subcontractors who performed the work in place did so at the same level of competence as the mockup. Final thought: *Insist on mockups!*

4.6.7 Flashings

Another of the very important skin components we rely on to minimize water intrusion is the family known as *flashings*. Flashings come in a wide variety of shapes, sizes, and materials. They play a very important role. We believe that the first flashings were used in roofing, such as valley flashings where two roof planes slope toward a common intersection (see Fig. 4-85). Valley flashings were used in shake and shingle roof systems to minimize water flowing down one roof plane from getting behind the membrane at laps. Metal valley flashing helps to bridge the gaps between sheathing materials on both sides of the valley. This can function as a conductor for water that gets behind the membranes, as well as a moisture barrier.

Valley flashings typically are light-gauge sheet metal made of galvanized steel, lead, or copper. Exposed metal valley flashings also function to reduce friction of organic material such as leaves and branches that tend to build up in valleys. A buildup tends to make small dams in the valley that can cause water to flow up and behind the membranes placed in the valleys, thereby causing leaks. It is important to maintain barrier-free valleys so that owners can clean the valleys when material accumulates.

Flashings also were common at roof-to-wall conditions, where a piece of L or Z metal (see Fig. 4-86) was placed behind wall finishes and on top of roofing materials to prevent water from coming down the wall after having gotten under the roof membranes. This flashing also makes it more difficult for wind-driven rain to get behind the wall membranes. Roof-to-wall flashings are used at the tops of the roof planes, as well as at any roof-to-sidewall intersection (see Fig. 4-87). Chimney flashings fit into a similar condition, where vertical surfaces meet sloping roof planes. The level top-of-roof-plane flashings are often simpler to install than sloped-roof sidewall flashings. Sidewall flashings need to be coordinated with finish materials. In our example (Fig. 4.87), the kickout flashing which is required in many jurisdictions is not yet installed.

Figure 4-85

Valley flashing.

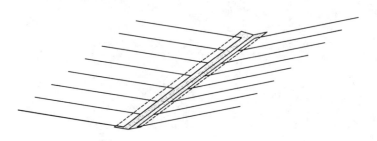

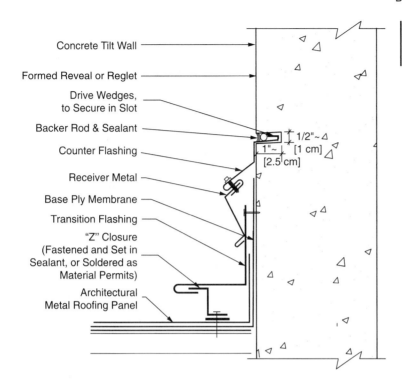

Figure 4-86
Metal flashing at wall to roof.

Concrete Tilt Wall
Formed Reveal or Reglet
Drive Wedges, to Secure in Slot
Backer Rod & Sealant
Counter Flashing
Receiver Metal
Base Ply Membrane
Transition Flashing
"Z" Closure (Fastened and Set in Sealant, or Soldered as Material Permits)
Architectural Metal Roofing Panel

1/2"~ [1 cm]
1"~ [2.5 cm]

Figure 4-87
Roof to sidewall ready for membrane.

Kickout flashings reduce potential for leaks when water coming down a roof surface terminates into a gutter or similar condition at the low end. The kick-out flashing forces water away from the face of the wall reducing amount and force of water striking the wall-to-roof flashing.

Bricks are small, rectangular masonry units that are laid on a level line. The flashing for brick walls to a sloped roof are usually cut to horizontal lengths that coincide with the size of the bricks. This is referred to as *step flashing*. The horizontal wall must be sheathed and membrane applied, as well as the roof. Short segments of horizontal flashing are coursed in with each brick from the bottom up. The step flashing is fastened in such a way as to prevent water that might get through or behind the brick from getting behind the wall membrane. If this is a brick-on-CMU (or brick) backup wall, the flashing should be laid up with the backup wall, installed approximately 8 inches (20 centimeters) above the elevation of the finished brick. Each successive piece of step flash-ing is bent tight to the face of the finished brick. The low side of the flashing then is bent to fit with the sloping roof and fastened above the roof membrane (see Fig. 4-88). Many installers recommend installing another piece of roof membrane over the step flashing, continuous from bottom to top.

There is one thing about the preceding that does not protect the joint in wind-driven rain. Do you know what that is? What about the rain or snow that is blowing up the roof? What keeps wind-driven precipitation from getting behind the laps in the step flashing? As usual, it is a question of how far you want to go with your protection.

Figure 4-88
Chimney flashing to roof.

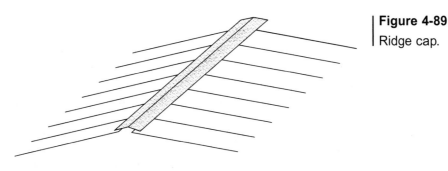

Figure 4-89
Ridge cap.

There are several other flashings used in conjunction with sloped-roof systems. Starting at the high point, there is *ridge flashing* (see Fig. 4-89), also called a *ridge cap*. A ridge cap is designed specific to the roofing material and function it plays. In a ventilated ridge cap, air is expelled under the metal. This requires a special water trap so that wind-driven rain doesn't enter the roof system or ceiling cavity below. At the bottom edge of a roof plane, drip metal and perhaps fascia trim flashing pieces are used. For a look at all common flashing shapes, please refer to Fig. 4-90.

Figure 4-90
Common flashing shapes.

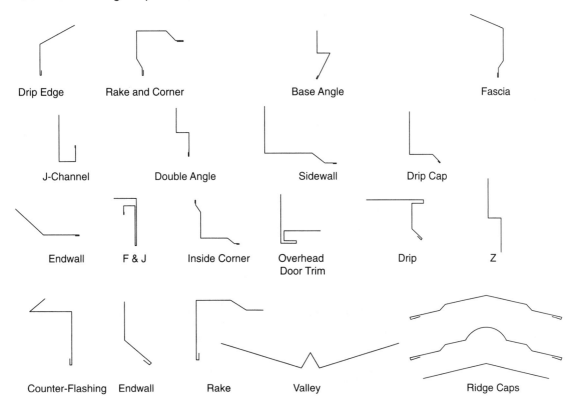

4.6.7.1 Window flashings

Window flashings are also common. The most important window flashing is probably the *head flashing,* also referred to as a *drip cap.* It functions to keep water coming down the wall from getting behind the window head. Head flashing gets installed behind the wall membrane above the window opening. Window sill flashings are becoming more common. The best sill flashings are three-sided welded or molded sill pans. Sill pans keep water that may defeat sealants from getting into the wall cavity. These are commonly made from stainless steel. Stainless steel is weldable and does not react with most other metals. Stainless steel also resists rust and corrosion well, especially 304 and 316 series. Figure 4-91 shows a sill pan for a window. This photo shows it being checked for fit, however the air and vapor barriers would be installed prior to pan installation. Then the sides were to be stripped in with SAM, over the vertical sill pan lips at the jambs.

One of the challenges of sill pan installation is how to fasten the window system through the sill pan without allowing it to leak. Many window systems, especially curtain wall systems, have large-diameter fasteners through the head and sill that transfer wind loads to the primary structure. Fastening a sill pan without allowing it to leak can be done by fastening it at the sides into jam framing. The fasteners can be located more than 1 inch (2.5 centimeters) above the bottom edge of the sill pan. Water seldom, if ever, will accumulate in the sill pan to this depth. The front (outer) edge of the sill pan should be the low point of the pan, allowing water to drain out owing to the force of gravity.

Figure 4-91
Photo, sill pan.

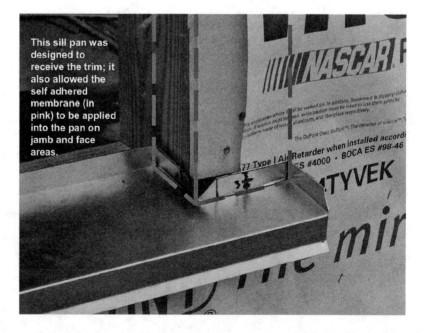

This sill pan was designed to receive the trim; it also allowed the self adhered membrane (in pink) to be applied into the pan on jamb and face areas.

Figure 4-92
Photo, large bolt holes on
curtain wall sill.

The more difficult challenge is sealing the large bolt holes (see Fig. 4-92). We recommend a combination of SAM to the top side of the sill pan and application of a sealant under the head of the bolt. Another solution places rubber washers, or O-rings, under the T-clips and F-clips.

Many manufacturers have begun to develop their own sill flashings and will warrant their performance with their window systems. The difference between a sill pan flashing and a sill flashing is the side and rear vertical lips on sill pans. Which should we trust? Would you rather mix concrete on a sheet of plywood or in a wheel barrow? Think about it!

Through years of evaluation, we have come to recommend a minimum of 2 inches (5 centimeters) of vertical leg height on all sill pans. In a holistic solution, we would design the details so that installers put a three-sided bead of sealant in the bottom inside corner of the sill pan prior to installing the window (see Fig. 4-93). This sealant will make it more difficult for wind-driven water to defeat the sill pan system and blow into the wall cavity, where it can provide moisture for mold growth.

Sill pans need to be well fitted to the opening they are going to protect. On most projects, we try to limit the number of window opening sizes so that the fabricator makes a few standard sill pans and uses them throughout. This places

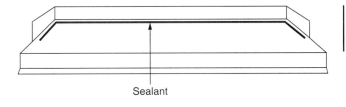

Sealant

Figure 4-93
Isometric showing sealant
at rear of sill pan.

importance on the accuracy of layout and framing. If the openings vary by more than $^1/_2$ inch (1.27 centimeters), the integrity of the detail can be compromised. It is important for the trades to be well coordinated and sequenced properly. We prefer the AIB to be complete, outside the exterior wall sheathing first. Then the MRB, in this case, a SAM, goes on the surfaces. Again, we like the self-sealing aspect of a nice SAM to seal fastener penetrations, etc. Then the sill pans are installed. Ideally, there is a very small space between the vertical lips of the sill pans and the SAM. This void should be about $^1/_8$ inch (0.25 centimeters) or less. Then SAM stripping is applied to close off the void, making a pathway for any water that may reach the jamb to drain vertically into the sill pan, where it should drain out past the finished face of the wall system (see Fig. 4-94). If the sill pan and related membranes are installed as directed, you will have effectively water-proofed the bottom edge of the window opening. It should not need face sealants to perform well. Once the jambs are flashed, the final application of finish materials then can go forward.

Jamb flashings are not yet common. Except where we specify fin-type windows, we seldom see jamb flashings. In our opinion, far too many designers rely on sealants to close off the jamb openings. In the old days, we had wood windows and mostly wood frame construction. After the windows were installed, sometimes after the finish skin materials were installed (such as brick or stucco),

Figure 4-94

SAM strip over sill pan lip, plan view.

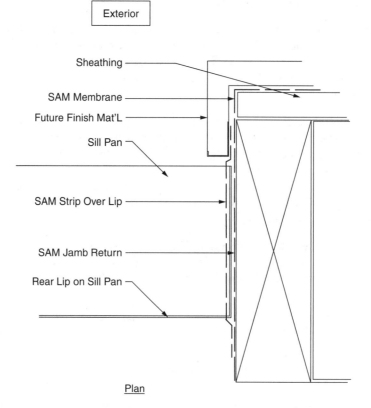

a piece of wood trim was installed to close off the void. This was done to reduce drafts through the void, as well as for improved appearance. This piece of wood trim, often quarter round, or casing would reduce the pressure and volume of wind-driven rain. If you had to replace a window, you simply would set the finish nails using a nail set (driving their heads through the depth of the trim) and pry off the trim. The windows then could be removed by unscrewing their fasteners. This was the typical condition; some builders applied stucco or brick or wood sheathing right over the window jambs, making replacement much more difficult.

In today's construction methods, wood and applied trim are not as common. A large percentage of the commercial, industrial, and government jobs we see use sealants for closure between walls and window jambs. This goes against our first rule of envelope design and detailing: Use gravity, geometry, and then technology. In our opinion, you need a piece of something solid, such as wood or metal, to close off the potential pathway at the jamb. In modern metal windows, many manufacturers use two-piece sill and jamb construction. It is incumbent on our designers to draw the extrusions as they really are. Show all the fasteners, all materials being fastened into, the shims, and shim space to scale. If windows are being fastened to the walls, many of these two-piece window jambs use a pressure plate that gets screwed into the vertical wall framing members. In this way, jamb fasteners are not exposed. In order to seal the jamb, you must close of the void between the window and wall. The location of the window system in the depth of the wall is very important. Figure 4-95 illustrates one way to close off this void, improving the joint geometry. In it, we use a small piece of closure metal to close the gap between the two primary systems.

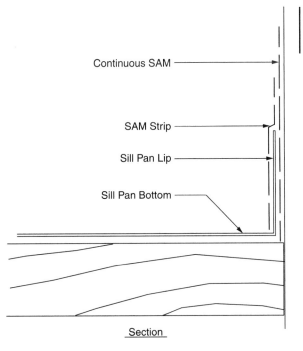

Figure 4-95

Section through sill at jamb.

Continuous SAM

SAM Strip

Sill Pan Lip

Sill Pan Bottom

Section

You will note that we show the shim [usually about 1 inch (2.5 centimeters) in total width, one half on each side] with backer rod and sealant behind the closure. Depending on the ultimate geometry of the window system, this may have to be a Z-closure piece to make up for nonaligned surfaces. In our detail, the closure metal would be installed prior to a window set from the inside or after one set from the outside. The embedded portion of the closure metal should be outside the MRB and AIB. It should fit tightly to the face of the window jamb. To make it function as a wall opening air barrier, the closure metal should be installed over a continuous bead of flexible sealant. After the skin is finished, a final fillet sealant should be applied between the closure piece and wall material. The closure metal can be fastened to the window jamb with rivets or machine screws, manufacturer permitting. Head flashings should go on last. Make sure not to void warranties if attaching to a window.

4.6.7.2 Other wall flashings

We recommend that wall louvers be treated similar to window openings. Louvers that are part of an outside air makeup system need special treatment, not at the exterior face of the finish wall, but inside. Owing to the negative pressure (and velocity) of an outside air louver, it can bring in more moisture than a passive louver. Depending on where in the section these louvers exist, you must plan for the increased amount of potential moisture. In the best case, these louvers are protected by long, overhanging roof planes. This will effectively reduce water droplets and the volume of water that will need to drain out.

The worst case is where a gable louver is high up on a building facade and unprotected. Water separator blades alone are insufficient in even a moderate rain storm. Imagine that you are bringing in 100,000 cfm of outside air makeup into a large building. First, you have to get the water past the wall cavity without it entering the cavity, and then you have to remove the moisture from the air and drain it back out again. A good solution is to start by creating a deep sill pan, sump, or basin just inside the louver section. This sump needs to be treated like a shower pan or small swimming pool. Depending on the amount of air being introduced, this pan could measure more than 50 feet wide by 10 feet (15 meters by 3 meters) deep. In this scenario, the vertical flanges would need to be more than 6 feet high (2 meters).

Now you need to use gravity and applied physics to remove the large droplets from the air prior to it coming in contact with filter or heat-exchange media. Figure 4-96 illustrates how you trap the moisture—by making it go down and then up. As it goes up, you increase the cross-sectional area of the plenum, thereby slowing the velocity. This aids gravity in pulling the heavier droplets from the airstream. After the air climbs vertically more than 6 or 8 feet (1.8 meter or 2 $1/2$ meters), most of the water droplets will have been removed. This water drains down into the sump, where it is collected and discharged out

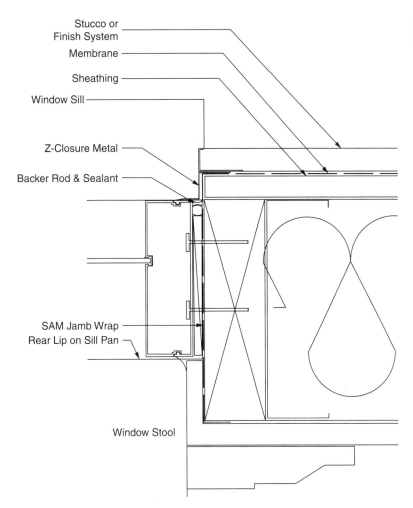

Figure 4-96
Closure metal at jamb.

Stucco or Finish System

Membrane

Sheathing

Window Sill

Z-Closure Metal

Backer Rod & Sealant

SAM Jamb Wrap

Rear Lip on Sill Pan

Window Stool

past the face or, even better, into the storm drainage piping system. In our section, you will see that the discharge piping is about 8 inches (20 centimetres) higher than the drains, acting as an overflow drain for intense rain events or if the drains get clogged. Another component of the detailed system is a fiberglass screen at the face that reduces the size and energy of droplets reaching the louvers. *Note:* This also adds significantly to the required surface area of the opening owing to increased static pressure loss of the screening and, as such, may not be aesthetically pleasing or desirable. The good news is that it also reduces bugs and large particles that could clog drains and filters.

Flashings have proven beneficial in a variety of other skin conditions. One of the most common is through wall flashings. Such flashings are used in many places. In single-level buildings, flashings are used near grade. Masonry walls have flashings installed so as to drain water that gets behind the outer wythe. Wood exterior sheathing relies on flashings, such as Z flashing (also referred to as *double-angle flashing*), to keep water from getting behind the sheathing. These flashings are used every 8 feet ($2^1/_2$ meters) vertically or where sheets are butted. During the hurricanes of the 2004 season, many Florida buildings failed where poorly conceived wall flashings between block ground floor walls and frame second-floor walls allowed water to get behind the membranes.

4.6.7.3 Roof flashing

On simple V-crimp roofing, one of the most important flashings is called a *rake and corner flashing*. It very effectively prevents wind and rain from getting behind the metal roofing or membranes at the roof edges. In addition, it provides for closure between the roof and fascia framing (see Figs. 4-97 and 4-98 for a photo and section view), and because of its tensile strength, helps keep the roof and fascia tied together in hurricane-force winds. We do not think that any other roofing system (nonmetal) uses such an outstanding piece of closure metal flashing.

Inside corners are another good place to use flashing. Most wall finish systems would benefit from the addition of an inside-corner flashing. Wall finish systems such as stucco, brick, block, wood siding, or sheathing or any other non-transparent system will likely perform better in high-wind-driven rain if metal corner flashings are used. These flashings would be integrated with all other roof and wall flashings to act as a conveyance system that also protects the softer, more flexible products that may be inside of them, such as felts, AIBs, or MRBs that should not be exposed to the sun.

Figure 4-97
Photo, flashing up the rake.

Figure 4-98

Rake flashing section.

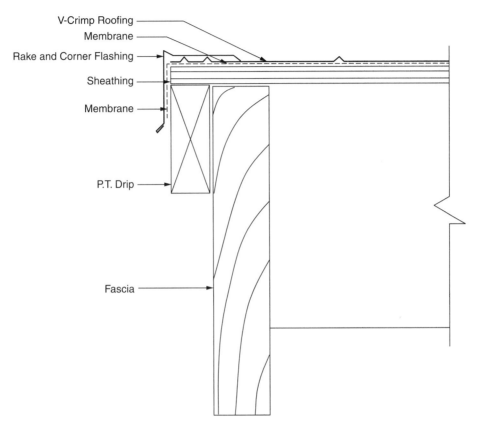

Low-slope roof systems also rely on flashings for their success. Designers have a variety of shapes and sizes of metal products at their disposal. The most important of them all, copings and receivers, help to keep rain water from getting behind the roofing plies. Most low-slope roofs are designed with parapet walls to prevent observers from seeing the "stuff" on the roof, as well as to protect them from falling rainwater. Interior roof drains are used commonly to conduct the rain that falls on a low-slope roof to the underground rain leader or storm piping.

Metal copings are used to protect the roof edges (see isometric sketch, Fig. 4-99). These copings serve two very important purposes: (1) to keep water from getting behind the wall membranes and (2) to prevent water from getting behind the vertical roof membranes. Parapet walls vary in height and width. Sometimes you might wish to block the view of roof-mounted mechanical equipment and the like. If the vertical face of the parapet extends more than 12 inches (0.3 meter) or at most a few feet (0.6 meter) above the roof surface, some manufacturers will not warrant their materials. We would like to have the warranty extended to the outside face of the parapet if we could so that the owners are protected to the fullest extent possible.

Figure 4-99

Coping isometric.

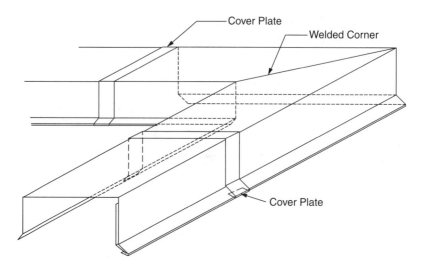

Metal copings can be done in a variety of ways. Depending on the process of construction and coordination of trades involved, the details may vary. The principle is the same. Use metal to protect the top of the wall and to keep water out of both roof and wall systems. Since the roofer may not be on the job site until months after the exterior walls are started, many walls get built before the roofer is on the job. There are occasions when the building needs to be weather resistant or dried in before the copings have been fabricated. In these instances, the walls need to have a temporary (or permanent) membrane installed over the top of the wall. It laps over the wall and possibly roof wall membranes on parapets, preventing rainwater from getting behind them. Once the metal copings are available, they can be installed over the dry-in membrane in some systems. Saddle flashings can be supplied by the roofer for the wall installer to place behind the wall membranes after the top-of-wall membrane placement and before the top-of-wall coping. This prevents reliance on sealants in the future, and the metal protects the membranes from the sun's harmful rays. It also resists the force of wind-driven rain, birds pecking, etc. Metal is good.

Copings are not normally provided in lengths exceeding 20 feet (6 meters). The laps or joints often are placed aesthetically but need to be installed to permit movement as the metals expand and contract. Since we like welded metal corners on our copings, not riveted (see Photo of riveted corner, Fig. 4-100), we plan for our joints to be located no closer to the corners than 4 feet (1.2 meters) (see Fig. 4-101).

Provide details for the joint covers as you would like them built. Some designers like underplate and coverplates with the void between lengths of coping materials about $1/4$ inch apart. The cover plates extend about 2 to 4 inches (1.5 centimeters) in both directions from the joint (see Section A, Fig. 4-102).

Figure 4-100
Photo, riveted coping.

We most often choose to fix one side of the cover plate and permit the other side to slide. We prefer to have no penetrations through the horizontal surfaces of flashings or cover plates. We place slotted screw fasteners, or rivets on vertical faces, since they are less prone to have standing water (see Section B, Fig. 4-103). A slight over-break (also referred to as a hem edge) in the coverplate reduces wind-driven rain intrusion past the cover plate. Double rows of sealant improve the performance of this detail. The under plate stops whatever defeats the cover plate, preventing it from getting behind the membranes.

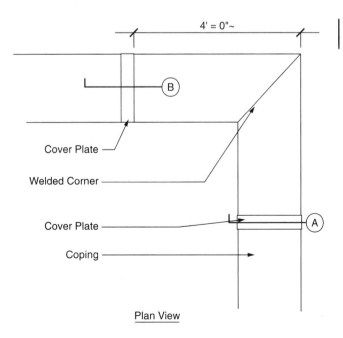

Figure 4-101
Plan View.

4' = 0"~

B

Cover Plate

Welded Corner

Cover Plate

A

Coping

Plan View

Figure 4-102

Section A.

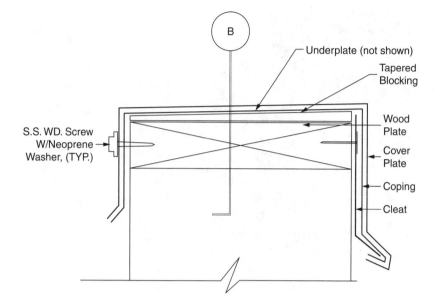

Depending upon site conditions and building orientation, you might not wish for others to see sidewall roofing membranes on the roof side of the parapet. Vertical metal panels and stucco are two common materials used on the backsides of parapet walls. Whatever the choice, there needs to be a transition between vertical roofing membrane and vertical finish material. You need to terminate the roof plies so that they stay in place, prevent water from getting behind them, and allow for repair and replacement over time. This is where we often rely on termination bars and receiver flashings (see Fig. 4-104). Termination bars take many shapes, but are used to evenly distribute forces from fasteners to sheet membranes in order to keep water from getting behind them as water may flow down vertical surfaces above.

Figure 4-103

Joint lap coverplate, section B.

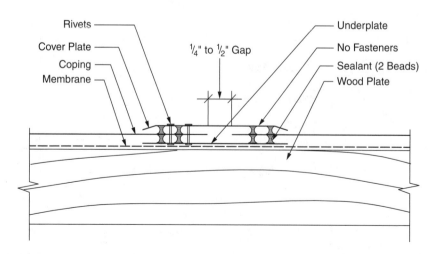

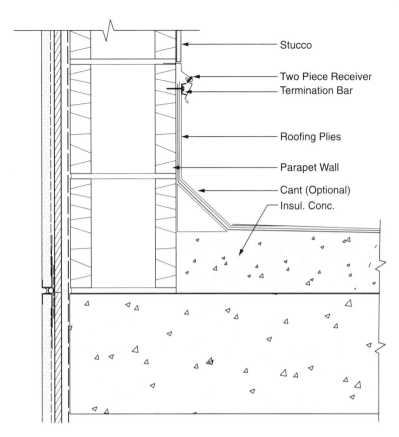

Figure 4-104
Receiver metal and termination bar.

Stucco

Two Piece Receiver
Termination Bar

Roofing Plies

Parapet Wall

Cant (Optional)
Insul. Conc.

There are several acceptable means for terminating roof membranes, and each has pros and cons. The National Roofing Contractors Association (NRCA) has published a wide range of details covering a majority of roof-related conditions. While they do provide a variety of time-tested means that most roofing installers can follow easily and that can be warranted, you will find they offer a range of performance options. Some approved details that are adequate for a warehouse may not be suitable for a condominium. You may find ways they can be improved for your project's specific needs.

Figure 4-105 shows a standard NRCA roof edge detail that relies upon sealant at the top. We do not recommend that for every type of project, depending upon the occupancy, maintenance, and other factors. Figure 4-104 goes against the first two of our three rules. It breaks gravity and geometry (rules number 1 and 2).

That detail (once sealant fails) makes a funnel on top so that any rain water falling down from above has a bigger target. Then it allows any water that hits the funnel to get behind the roofing membrane, where gravity and vapor drive will make sure that it finds an occupied space or cavity to get wet. The third thing it does wrong is to rely on sealant. By now, you should know that this is not a good practice for long-lasting protection. We inherited the detail shown in Fig. 4-104 on a

Figure 4-105

Roof edge flashing detail, similar to standard NRCA.

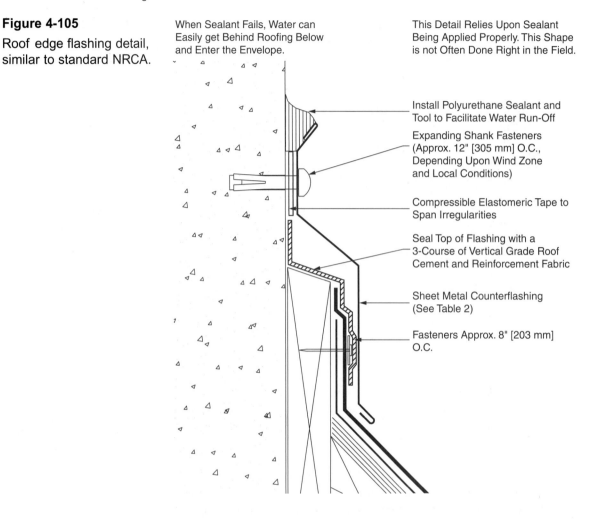

When Sealant Fails, Water can Easily get Behind Roofing Below and Enter the Envelope.

This Detail Relies Upon Sealant Being Applied Properly. This Shape is not Often Done Right in the Field.

Install Polyurethane Sealant and Tool to Facilitate Water Run-Off

Expanding Shank Fasteners (Approx. 12" [305 mm] O.C., Depending Upon Wind Zone and Local Conditions)

Compressible Elastomeric Tape to Span Irregularities

Seal Top of Flashing with a 3-Course of Vertical Grade Roof Cement and Reinforcement Fabric

Sheet Metal Counterflashing (See Table 2)

Fasteners Approx. 8" [203 mm] O.C.

recent project as it was shown on approved shop drawings (reviewed by others). We met with the installer in a pre-construction meeting. We expressed our concerns. When pressed for an improved detail, we were told, "We can install another funnel above the one we have and caulk it too!" While we admitted that redundancy did reduce the weathering on the lower sealant, thereby increasing its lifespan, we did not jump at the chance to rely on two funnels.

Rather than embrace two funnels as a means for reducing water intrusion over time, we went out on a limb. "Isn't there a better way," we asked? "One that cuts the top edge of the flashing into the surface of the tilt concrete wall, thereby avoiding the funnel top altogether?" This was at a preconstruction meeting with the construction manager, owner's project manager, two representatives from the roofing installation subcontractor, and several other tradesmen. We began to draw a quick sketch on the back of our notebook. As soon as we had finished a few lines, the roofing superintendent acknowledged that he had done something like it once before. We agreed that it was far better than the initial submittal indicated and got the owner to agree. Then the construction manager chimed in with his support. Of course, he was making a commitment the general superintendent had to live with and complained about later, but we all knew it was being done for the right reason. For most commercial, government and similar projects we recommend something like Figure 4-106.

After the meeting, we had the contractor send in a revised detail as part of the revised roofing submittal. Since it was part of a concrete tilt wall project, we began to take it a step further. We drew up how it affected the panel joints and both inside and outside corners.

This was about the time the clients decided that they could no longer afford to maintain painted stucco walls located more than 8 feet above the finish grade (where they could pressure wash them). We changed from stucco on lath over sheathing to a metal panel system. This caused us to rethink how we were doing our intersections between parapet walls and vertical wall surfaces. Figure 4-107 shows a photo taken a few weeks later, after the metal panels had been installed and before the coping went on. We drew up a saddle flashing detail (see one of

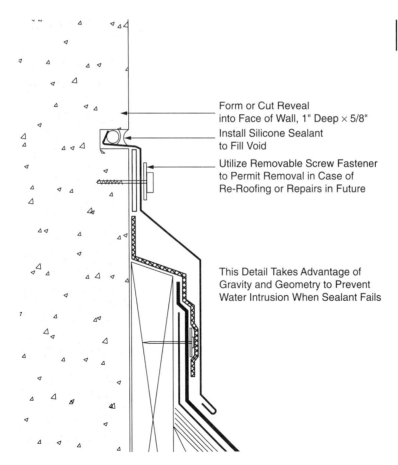

Form or Cut Reveal
into Face of Wall, 1" Deep × 5/8"
Install Silicone Sealant
to Fill Void

Utilize Removable Screw Fastener
to Permit Removal in Case of
Re-Roofing or Repairs in Future

This Detail Takes Advantage of
Gravity and Geometry to Prevent
Water Intrusion When Sealant Fails

Figure 4-106
Reglet detail, from WLW.

Figure 4-107

CMU parapet wall intersecting metal wall system.

the sections, Fig. 4-108) that was later installed, after selective removal of a portion of the metal panels. In this way, the saddle went back under the wall membrane as it should be, (see Fig. 4.109). This ensures that any water that might later defeat the sealants at the coping to wall joint, will be conveyed outside a protected wall system and not get behind the membranes.

Figure 4-108

Saddle flashing detail.

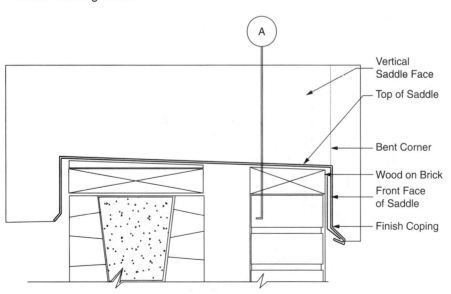

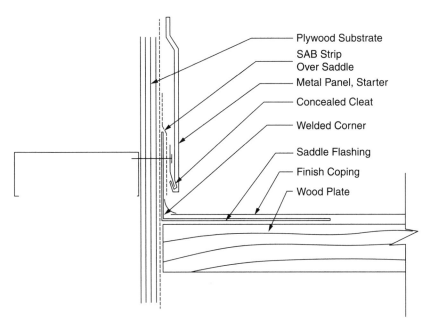

Figure 4-109
Section at wall.

Plywood Substrate
SAB Strip
Over Saddle
Metal Panel, Starter
Concealed Cleat
Welded Corner
Saddle Flashing
Finish Coping
Wood Plate

4.6.8   Insulation

Thermal insulation does a lot more than keep us from getting too hot or too cold. It affects how much it costs us to heat or cool our buildings and plays a significant role in preventing condensation. Insulating materials retard the movement of heat energy though a wall, roof, or any other part of the building envelope. The higher the insulation R value, the slower is the transfer of heat energy through the system. Refer to Table 4-5 for approximate R values for common insulating materials. There are several effective means for calculating

Table 4-5

Insulating values of materials

Number	Product	Thickness	R Value
1	Gypsum board	$1/2$"	0.45
2	Impreg. Sht'g	$1/2$"	2
3	Felt building paper	15 lb.	0.06
4	Fiberglass (unfaced)	3.5 inch.	11
5	Expanded Polyurethane	1 inch.	5.5
6	Extruded Polystyrene	1 inch.	4
7	Stucco	$3/4$"	0.15
8	Brick	4" Nom.	0.7
9	Concrete Block	8" Nom.	1.1
10	Stone	4" Nom.	0.32
11	Cement Plaster interior, w/gypsum	$3/4$"	0.4
12	Asphalt Shingles	240 lb.	0.44
13	Built-up roof	3 ply	0.3
14	Wood Siding	$1^5/8$"	2

the required minimum amount of insulation for anticipated conditions, but you must start out with good information. Historical data for average monthly temperatures can be used to see what the climate was in the past; however, we should be building to last more than 100 years. What if global climatic changes do occur? How will R10 walls perform in temperatures that exceed 20°F beyond historical data?

Many HVAC engineers only design mechanical equipment that maintains our set points when ambient temperatures are about 90 or 95 percent of the average high and low temperatures from historical data anyway. Even if it never gets much hotter, what happens if it doesn't cool off at night? The total average insulation required by most minimal codes will not keep occupants comfortable if the world sees wholesale changes. What we are recommending is designing and building future buildings with a greater average R value. Run scenarios with 10 percent higher and lower values. If your envelope performs well, then you will have reached a good minimum R value. Use a 30-year payback when calculating the marginal return on insulation, and use a realistic, conservative inflation rate of 6 to 10 percent per year for energy costs.

Having said this, we would add that most engineers don't design envelopes; architects do. Computer software is available, but it can be as simple as drawing lines on graph paper. We created our own spreadsheets using standard software. We began by placing a list of materials in the wall section in rows, and adding R values for each. We list the inside and outside temperatures and calculate the difference. The ΔT equation is used to calculate each temperature as heat passes through the wall section. In an R20 wall, for example, a material with an R value of 5 would resist one-fourth the total resistance in the wall. If $\Delta T = 28°F$, that material would reduce the temperature one-fourth of that, or 7°F. We then draw a simple graph in Excel and add that same information to a computer-aided design (CAD) line drawing (see Fig. 4-110).

4.6.8.1   Insulation design to prevent condensation

It is no longer enough to have a wall or roof system with minimal insulation for creature comfort. As designers, we should do more than look at a map of the region with a blanket recommendation for average R values. We should consider and calculate insulation in order to control temperature relative to dew point in the building envelope. By now, we should have designed air and moisture barriers that will work together to limit the amount of moisture in the cavity. This will reduce the amount of water formed by condensation. By reducing the volume of water, we minimize the potential growth of mold spores.

It is not difficult to calculate temperature gradients through roof and wall sections. The most difficult part is determining which values to use for indoor and outdoor temperatures. There are several means for finding average and record-high and -low ambient outside temperatures. The question is what values to use. You are never going to know what inside temperatures to design for. Be conservative. We look at both winter and summer temperatures, since one wall

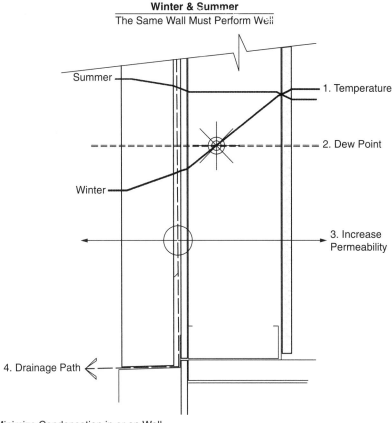

Figure 4-110
Temperatures in wall section.

Winter & Summer
The Same Wall Must Perform Well

Summer

1. Temperature

2. Dew Point

Winter

3. Increase Permeability

4. Drainage Path

Minimize Condensation in or on Wall

1. Keep Temperatures Above Dew Point
2. Keep Moisture Levels (RH or Grains) Below Dew Point
3. Increase Permeability of Materials from Moisture Barrier Both Ways
4. Provide Drainage Pathway for Condensation that may Form

has to perform well in both extremes. In summer, vapors move from the outside (warm side) toward the inside as represented in the dashed lines in Figure 4-111. In the winter, vapors move from in to out. We can calculate dew points in walls (also floors and roofs) based upon temperature and relative humidity. This example uses a straight line for humidity, such as if there were no vapor reduction in the walls. The point where temperature intersects dew point is marked with a big circle and other lines to signify the importance of this value. We need to keep the temperature above dew point to prevent condensation.

Recent lawsuits against an architect have come as a result of occupants not being able to afford to use the building heating system in cold winter weeks in Florida. The interior spaces got down below 45°F (7°C). During the day, the

Figure 4-111

Calculating Temperatures in Wall.

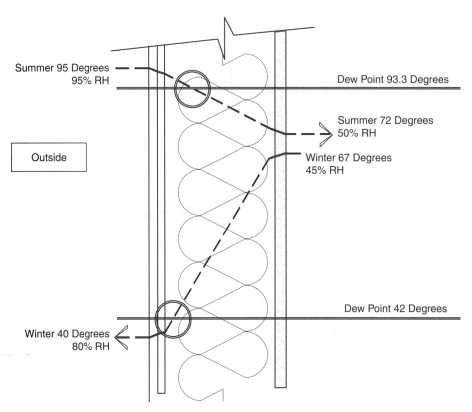

outside temperature climbed into the low 70°F range (25°C). The resulting condensation on the inside face of the gypsum sheathing led to claims against the designer. In this case, the moisture was finding its way in through substituted windows and poor detailing, but it was condensing on the inside face of the drywall. It appeared to form on the metal studs because they were the coldest impermeable surface in the path of temperature-driven moisture. You could see where each stud was located through the wet stains on the wall.

Considering the recent number of record-high and -low temperatures we have seen and unknown consequences of global environmental changes, we recommend that you use very conservative temperatures for determining the amount of insulation in your designs. The incremental cost for added insulation thickness is very low. To be conservative, we would design for 5 percent below the record low and 10 percent above the record high. We prefer not to use the monthly average figures, using instead the daily minimum and maximum for winter and summer. This establishes the values for outdoor temperatures. From there, you must determine the inside temperatures. We know people are comfortable in the summer within 5 to 10°F of 70°F (25°C). But people are not always home, and people are different, and some people can't afford air conditioning or heating in the peak-load times. What values should you use?

To protect yourself from litigation, use extreme values. Do not settle for low R values because there was only a small space for insulation in the void created by furring strips. Change the wall section to accommodate whatever insulation is required to do the job well. Figure 4-112 shows a typical wall section with a table of values that we use to illustrate the process of predicting thermal performance for a frame wall. We list all the materials and airspaces in the first column and the R values next to that. In the third column we indicate the resulting temperature that will occur based on that R value. To get the ΔT, we first have to calculate the total temperature difference on both sides of the wall, in this example 23°F. We then sum the total R value for the composite wall, in this case 15.41. We then divide the total R by the R value for that line to get the effect of that material on the temperature and multiply that value times the ΔT. The R value for the interior still air film is 0.68. When we multiply 0.68 times 23°F, the product is about 1.3°F. We continue the same process until we have calculated the temperature for every point in the wall. Computer spreadsheets make this and subsequent comparisons very easy to do.

There are several ways to approach the dew point calculation. You may choose to use a straight line based on wall permeability. This is not very accurate. The best way is to calculate absolute humidity in grains of water per unit volume of air at a certain pressure. As you move through the wall section, you can calculate the grains of water that pass through each successive material based on perm rating. By calculating a moisture gradient, you can show the dew point values for each portion of the wall. Then we change values for operating and/or ambient, run the calculations again, and draw the charts again (see Fig. 4-113). By doing many variations, you can model likely dew point scenarios. Then you change insulation values and locations within the wall. The goal is to prevent condensation from forming inside the vapor or MRB in any temperature likely to occur.

There are several ways to calculate dew points. The old way was to use a psychometric chart. There are several Web-site calculators that do the math for you. Type in "dew point calculators," and use the one you choose. Once we establish the predicted temperatures and grains of moisture, we can find dew points. We then look to see where in the wall that value is reached and place our target (circle with cross hairs) at that point on the temperature-gradient line, (see Fig. 4-114). You will note that there is not enough insulation in this wall section to prevent condensation for the sample temperatures, resulting in condensation taking place in the wall. This location is inside the CMU and likely would be creating the right environment for the growth of mold spores. If the target were to occur outside the MRB, you would succeed in preventing water from forming in the wall. There are additives for block that reduce potential bacterial growth in CMU, but the best prevention is prevention of condensation from forming in the block.

Figure 4-112

Data and graphed
temperature in wall.

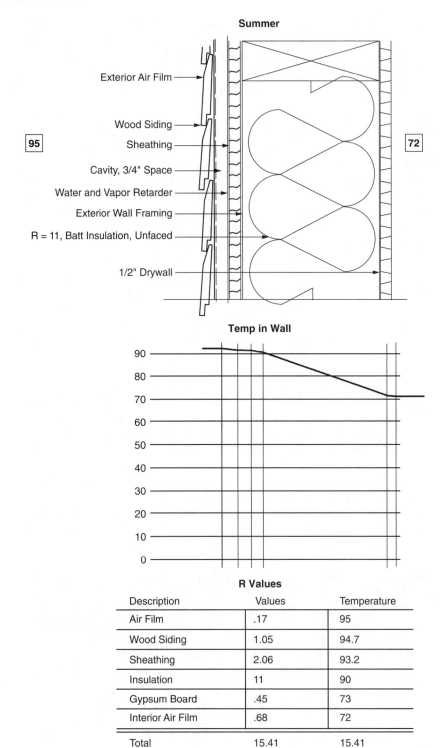

Summer

Exterior Air Film

Wood Siding

Sheathing

95

72

Cavity, 3/4" Space

Water and Vapor Retarder

Exterior Wall Framing

R = 11, Batt Insulation, Unfaced

1/2" Drywall

Temp in Wall

R Values

Description	Values	Temperature
Air Film	.17	95
Wood Siding	1.05	94.7
Sheathing	2.06	93.2
Insulation	11	90
Gypsum Board	.45	73
Interior Air Film	.68	72
Total	15.41	15.41

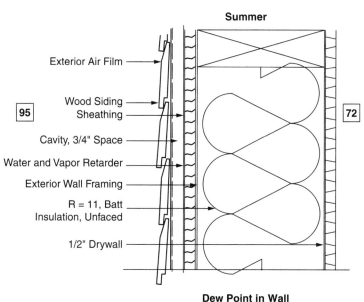

Summer

Exterior Air Film

95

Wood Siding
Sheathing

72

Cavity, 3/4" Space

Water and Vapor Retarder

Exterior Wall Framing

R = 11, Batt
Insulation, Unfaced

1/2" Drywall

Figure 4-113
Temperature and dew points.

Dew Point in Wall

90
85
80
75
70
65
60
55
50
45

Perm Rating, Wet

Description	Temp.	RH		Dew Pt.	Perm Rating
Indoor Air	72	50		-	NA
Latex Paint	72	52		.85	3
Gypsum Wall BD	68.8	55		.2	40
Insulation	66.7	56		.01	28
Ext. Sheathing	73.7	58		.03	3
Membrane	93.2	70		11	.1
Siding	93.2	85		.9	10
Stain	94.7	88		.25	8
Outside Air	95	90		.25	NA
Total	12.5	12.5		12.5	12.5

Figure 4-114

Temperature gradients in CMU walls.

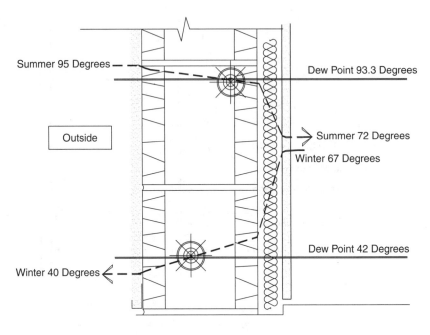

Summer 95 Degrees

Dew Point 93.3 Degrees

Outside

Summer 72 Degrees

Winter 67 Degrees

Dew Point 42 Degrees

Winter 40 Degrees

In the next example we have used a far better insulated wall system, batt insulated metal frame walls with exterior rigid insulation and finish system. We also varied the grains of water in the wall to illustrate how that impacts dew point. Since this wall has a vapor barrier outside the insulation, it is not likely that the moisture level would ever reach more than about 25% in the wall. It would take major leaks in the air or moisture barrier to introduce enough moisture for condensation to reach more than 40 percent in the wall. The three humidities shown are 40, 60 and 80 percent relative humidity, (see Fig. 4-115). The predicted temperatures are 79 degrees dew point for 60% and 67 degrees for 40% RH. With an R24 wall as shown, and with a vapor barrier it would take a major introduction of moisture from the interior, such as 60 percent humidity or greater to permit conditions in the wall to reach dew point. The designer then should look at the performance of the same wall in winter conditions expected for the location.

You can see in Fig. 4-115 that the same wall would have condensation when temperatures reached in the wall are only a few degrees F lower than outside temperatures (around 8°F). If condensation in the insulation is to be prevented, we need to reduce moisture and dew point by placing the vapor barrier outboard of the insulation. This wall also performs well in winter conditions, with the wall sheathing reducing moisture from the conditioned (interior) side of the wall as it moves toward the cooler exterior face. By calculating temperature and dew points in the wall in both summer and winter conditions, we can prevent condensation year round. While it may sound like a lot of work, after you have set up the spreadsheets the first time, it is fast and easy to change one value and see the results. Whatever the method you use, the results should be pretty much

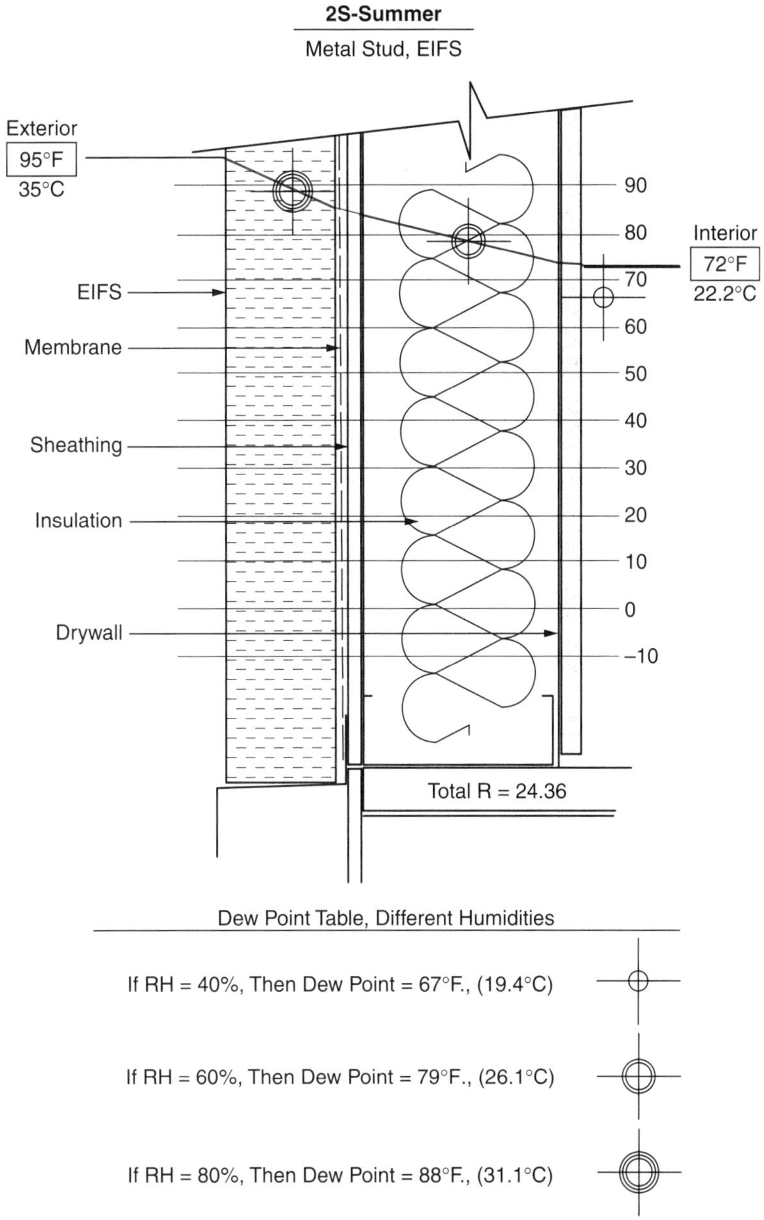

Figure 4-115
Temperature and dew point.

2S-Summer

Metal Stud, EIFS

Exterior
95°F
35°C

Interior
72°F
22.2°C

90
80
70
60
50
40
30
20
10
0
−10

EIFS

Membrane

Sheathing

Insulation

Drywall

Total R = 24.36

Dew Point Table, Different Humidities

If RH = 40%, Then Dew Point = 67°F., (19.4°C)

If RH = 60%, Then Dew Point = 79°F., (26.1°C)

If RH = 80%, Then Dew Point = 88°F., (31.1°C)

the same. What is important is performance over time. Insulation is cheap insurance against condensation-related moisture problems, that is, moisture on piping and ducts, as well as within the building envelope. You must keep in mind thermal bridging such as metal framing provides and voids in insulation, as may exist in wood frame construction. Both affect localized temperatures. The preceding and following discussions assume uniform values.

Masonry walls are not necessarily good for all climates either. While there are advantages to increased thermal mass in dry climates, and moderately cool climates, they can be problematic in hot, humid and cold wet climates, unless properly designed with insulation and vapor retarders in the right locations and with the right values. In a cool, dry climate, in the winter time, the wall section indicated in the following example might be adequate, (see Fig. 4-116). In the summer, however condensation will always take place interior of the vapor retarder. In the example provided, exterior latex paint is the vapor retarder. It is located on the exterior face of the CMU. Regardless of the humidity, dew points are reached inside the vapor retarder. Depending on the perm rating of the paint, it may sufficiently reduce grains of moisture when new to maintain dew point below temperatures reached in the wall. What happens when the wall gets old is that it may crack, and paint may begin to loose some of its ability to prevent moisture transmission. That is when localized and/or global condensation may occur. This is why barrier walls need frequent maintenance checks. Paints and sealants must be reapplied when degraded. There is no secondary line of defense on a barrier wall.

Figure 4-116

Temperature gradients, CMU wall.

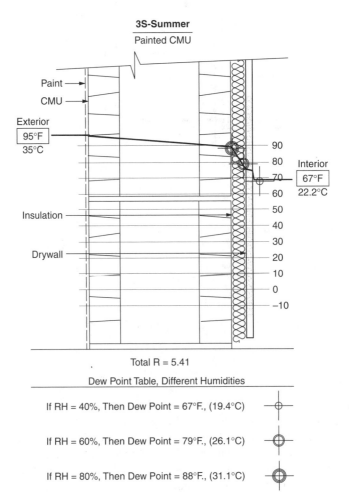

4.6.8.2 Types of insulation

There are many different materials that have insulating properties. Many of them also have structural properties, such as concrete and wood. For the sake of clarity, this section considers only materials that you can count on primarily for their thermal properties. These include loose-fill materials, sheet products, expanding or sprayed foams, and roll goods. Each has a different insulation value per unit thickness, as well as different permeabilities, etc. We use insulation below floors, in walls, and in roof or ceiling systems. Since glass has a different functional role than just thermal, we will not include it in this discussion, other than to say that every component that contributes to the building envelope, contributes to the average R value, and therefore affects air and water movement in and around the skin. Similarly, we will not address air films, wind velocities, and such because they are not really a part of the envelope.

Generally speaking, the more dense a material, the lower is its R value because it is the airspace or voids in the cells that act to reduce the transmission of heat energy. The most dense of all insulating materials is insulating concrete. It differs from normal-weight concrete owing to the addition of other, light materials such as perlite or vermiculite (like kitty litter). It is placed on horizontal bases, most often metal deck or normal-weight concrete. Some lightweight concrete is placed by pumping long reaches using a boom and hopper system. Workers slope it to or from the drain sump areas as they place it. Once the concrete is fully cured, the first layer of roofing membrane can be installed over it. The cure time reduces the amount of trapped water under the membrane.

When we speak of rigid or semi-rigid insulation, we are commonly talking about rectangular sheets of a chemical derivative of the petroleum industry. Among the many names you might recognize, are isocyaneurate, urethane, and styrene. Semi-rigid boards are adhered or mechanically fastened using impalement pins, typically on vertical surfaces. Rigid boards are used in nearly every application imaginable. On the roof, you have a multitude of possible uses, including tapered insulation systems or constant-thickness boards on sloped decking. Roofing products are installed over the foam. Foam boards are also used under floors and in walls and foundation systems. Foam boards have many benefits, including resistance to water transmission. R values for foam insulation range from 1 to more than 7R, but they average about 3.5 per inch (2.5 centimeters).

Batt insulation is typically fiberglass or polyolefin that comes rolled up in different lengths and widths, with choices in backing. Kraft paper, "smart membranes," and aluminum foil are common backings; plastic is not quite so common. Cellulose-based fill and spun glass fiber can be applied loosely by blowing it from a hopper through a long, large hose.

Spray-applied foam products gained popularity during the energy crisis of the 1980s and early 1990s. It is typically polyurethane foam with R values in the

4 to 6 per inch range. As it cures, it tends to skin over, which gives it more dimensional stability and allows it to be used as an air and moisture barrier as well. It is closed-cell foam, meaning that the cells do not absorb water easily. These properties help to increase the use of sprayed-on polyurethane foam (SPF) in attics, basements, and crawlspaces. It is also fast and easy to install, making it a low-cost solution.

4.7 ROOF DESIGN

There are many different ways to insulate a roof, just as there are ways to design a roof system. You can group roof insulation into three main approaches. You can insulate above the roof decking, right below the roof surface, or on the ceiling plane (see Fig. 4-117). The proper choice depends on the form and materials used, the climate, and the method of ventilation. You can classify roof pitch or slope into four main categories: flat, low slope, intermediate slope, and steep. Flat roofing can be as low as $1/2$ inch per foot (1 percent, or 0.5 degrees) and up

Figure 4-117

Ways to insulate the roof system.

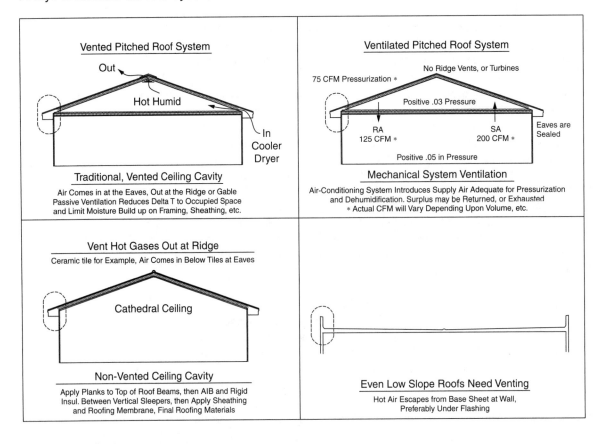

Figure 4-118
Dew point avoided in roof.

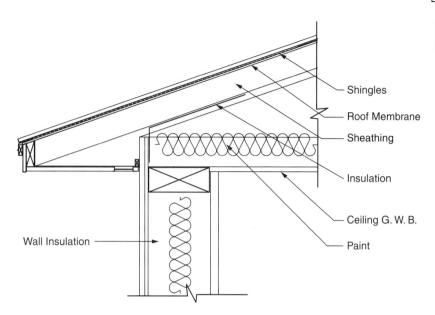

Shingles

Roof Membrane

Sheathing

Insulation

Ceiling G. W. B.

Paint

Wall Insulation

R Values

Description	Values	Temperature
Air Film	.17	0
Shingles	.4	0.5
Sheathing	2.06	1.7
Insulation	20	68.6
Gypsum Board	.45	69.9
Interior Air Film	.68	72
Total	23.76	

to about $1/2$ inch per foot (2 degrees). Low-slope roof systems start there and increase up to about 3 inches per foot (12.5 degrees). Intermediate-slope roofing goes up to about 6 inches per foot (22.5 degrees). Steep roof pitches are in excess of 6 inches per foot. Different materials are used in the different sloped systems. It is just as important to prevent condensation being formed in the roof system as it is in the walls, (see Fig. 4-118). We can calculate insulation and temperature gradients in the roof like we did in the earlier wall examples. Using perm ratings of materials, we can also calculate dew point and by careful application of our basic principles minimize moisture formed and therefore reduce mold and mildew.

4.7.1   Flat roof design

Flat roof systems are the kind you find on large commercial or industrial projects. Depending on live and dead loads, the flat roof structure may vary. Most commonly, you see economical bar joists on about 5-foot intervals with metal decking or purlins. Single- or multiple-ply roofing systems such as EPDM or modified bitumen are installed on top of insulation. If ratings and loads dictate, the metal deck may have lightweight concrete topping. When possible, perforated G-90 galvanized metal deck is used in combination with lightweight concrete. The top chord of the bar joists and decking may be installed level or sloped to drains. If the deck is level, the concrete may vary in thickness to attain the desired slope or be installed at a uniform thickness. If the concrete is level, then tapered foam insulation is installed over the lightweight concrete. The average R value for the composite whole needs to equal or exceed the value used in the energy calculations. Insulation R values vary with the thickness of the tapered insulation. The minimum thickness typically occurs at roof drains, with maximum thickness at the ridge or crickets. The best condensation protection is provided by using the minimal insulation value instead of the average value that was used in dew point analysis.

Another common roof system is constructed of concrete. If it is being used on other floors, a post-tensioned (PT) concrete roof system could be used. Depending on the spans and loads, the PT concrete might be in the range of about 7 to 9 inches thick. Most PT slabs are formed level, but mono-pitched PT can be done by many crews. It is usually easier to set the bottom elevation form level and, if needed, taper the thickness to achieve the slope. This may save concrete and weight. We typically see lightweight concrete applied to the top to slope to roof drains. In the cold climates, we would like to place insulation above the roof membrane. One way to achieve this would be to apply a bi-level drain system. Install one set of drains at the PT slab elevation, and apply a semi-permeable vapor retarder at that level (say, about 0.8 perm). Then apply the lightweight concrete and tapered foam insulation to get the R values required and $^1/_4$-inch slope to drain (see Fig. 4-119). The rooftop membrane would be applied above the tapered foam, with a perm rating of about 0.03. This would be in keeping with our paradigm of increasing by a factor of 4 from the lowest permeability membrane to the next. Membranes can be screwed down, mopped down, torched, ballasted, or some combination. Four- or three-ply hot-mopped modified bitumen roofing is the standard for areas with high annual rainfall. The advantages of multiple-ply roof membranes are in their strength and redundancy. The first ply is often the dry-in layer on which other subcontractors work. It often gets damaged. Subsequent layers get lapped on each other to reinforce the corners as well as to resist abuse. Cap sheets are what really stand up to UV light. Modified bitumen roofing product lines are expanding to meet special demands. These products are now available in several finishes and colors, including white and aluminum finishes. Single ply thermoplastic roof membrane systems are increasing in use because of their excellent heat rejection properties and low initial cost. Other single-ply roof membranes are available, such as EPDM. Each has pros and cons, and should be selected first and most importantly upon the flame spread rating required. Some products are available to withstand more than 125 mph winds, and exceed FM600 rating.

The difference between class A and B roofing is the difference in flame spread ratings. One component used to achieve the better, Class A rating is in the reinforcing fabric, but there are other differences as well, such as underlayments,

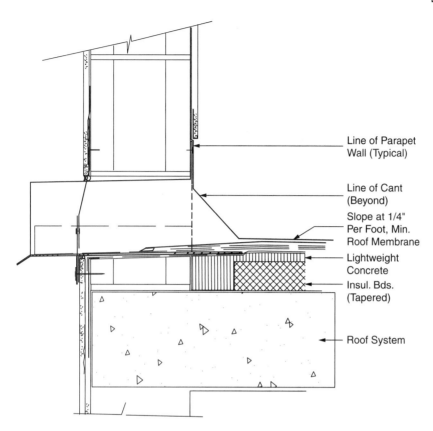

Figure 4-119
Roof section at overflow
scupper.

Line of Parapet
Wall (Typical)

Line of Cant
(Beyond)

Slope at 1/4"
Per Foot, Min.
Roof Membrane

Lightweight
Concrete

Insul. Bds.
(Tapered)

Roof System

decking, and fastening methodologies. Class A system membranes using woven polyester may be tougher but may be difficult to get to lay flat than a more pliable Class B or C system if there are a lot of bends and corners, especially at drains. Class B is easier to bend and can be applied over sumps at drains with less likelihood of fish mouths. Fish-mouths are opening caused by puckering material when everything is not flat and planar. They can permit water intrusion and should be avoided. Single- and two-ply roofing is specified where initial cost is more of an issue than long-term performance. Both put a premium on protection of installed roofing membranes. If the design is such that other trades are kept to a minimum after the base sheet is applied, or if the construction manager (CM) can protect the membrane successfully, these lower-cost systems can be acceptable. Most roofing systems can be warranted for more than 10 years.

Many building codes still permit coal tar roofing to be installed at $1/8$ inch per foot. We believe that the reason most codes do not still allow $1/8$ inch per foot for any other membrane is that ponding water is more likely to occur if the design value is $1/2$ inch. When plies get lapped, such as at roof drains, the additional plies make the roof membrane thicker. This extra thickness can result in a relative high point in the flow path of water, effectively trapping water. The best

Figure 4-120

Roof drain section.

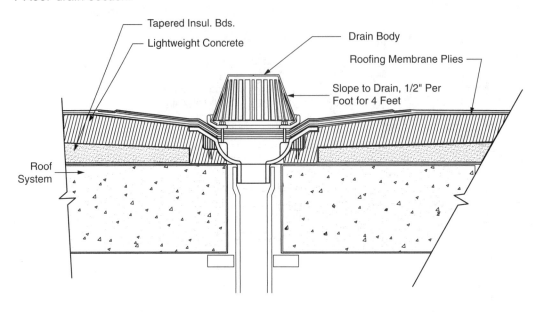

Tapered Insul. Bds.

Lightweight Concrete

Drain Body

Roofing Membrane Plies

Slope to Drain, 1/2" Per
Foot for 4 Feet

Roof
System

way to prevent water intrusion from a roof is to get the water off the roof as fast as you can—all of it. The higher the pitch, the faster is the flow, and the fewer dams will occur. When designing a roof, we try to show $1/2$ inch per foot in the area surrounding roof drains for 4 feet in every direction (see Fig. 4-120). In this way, lapped plies usually result in the desired $1/4$ inch per foot taper.

4.7.2   Low-slope roofing

Low-slope roofing often will be done in many of the same materials as flat roofing. Roll goods often are mopped or torched down on sheathing as a membrane to stop moisture and with another material for protection against the sun. Starting at about $1^1/2$ inches per foot, metal roofing is a common product line. Metal roof systems can be installed over sheathing but typically get clipped onto purlins. These roofing products include standing-seam metal products with varying profiles depending on spans and loads. These products are available in a variety of colors, materials, and coatings. The lowest-cost applications are painted steel. Upgrades include galvanized steel, aluminum, stainless steel, and copper. Insulation most commonly is rolled out on top of the purlins in long rolls before the metal goes on. Standing-seam metal roofing is popular because the fasteners are concealed, and it goes on quickly. Each successive panel gets crimped over the preceding one with a special tool that captures the clips between two pieces of bent metal. The clips need to be spaced close enough to prevent rippling, as well as to resist uplift. The clips get fastened to the purlins.

Roll insulation comes with plastic inside facing referred to as *scrim*. The scrim can be painted (see Fig. 4-121) or left unpainted. It can be ordered with a reinforcing mesh that acts as safety netting for installers working far above the ground. The mesh-reinforced scrim also reduces deflection of the insulation between the purlins over time. We have used metal roofing products over exposed metal decking and plywood sheathing to give a nice finished aesthetic to the underside in a fast, cost-effective manner. Metal roofing companies provide a series of closure pieces for ridge and exterior wall conditions, as well as fascia and soffit systems, louvers, integral windows, skylights, etc. One additional advantage to this is sole-source responsibility for all these installations. Another is compatibility of colors, finishes, etc.

Different shapes of metal roof products are available. Some replicate barrel tile, others, slate. One of our personal favorites is the rustic look and long-lasting performance of galvanized V-crimp metal. This is applied in a variety of ways depending on the space below. we like to use it above battens on 90-pound granulated roll roofing that has been hot-mopped to $^{15}/_{32}$-inch four-ply exterior plywood. An alternative is to dry it in with 30-pound fiberglass membrane and add SAM strips under the battens. One by four battens are installed over the SAM at 10 to 14 inches on center with wood screws through the plywood right into joists or trusses. These battens will have drainage channels or notches cut into them before installation. The metal is finally screwed into the sheathing and through the battens into the joists at 12-inch on-center (OC) spacing horizontally. Batten and fastener sizes and spacing must be designed for wind loads, which is especially critical on corners and at end zones. These fasteners face the greatest loads in resistance to hurricane-force winds. Accessory pieces close off the sides to prevent wind from getting behind or under the panels at

Figure 4-121
Painted scrim-faced insulation.

the drip edge and along the ridge. We typically specify stainless steel wood screws with neoprene-gasketed washers to better seal against the weather. In hot climates, the insulation is below the sheathing. In cold climates, you might use rigid foam above the membrane with the battens on top of the insulation. Longer fasteners (approximately 4 inches) would be required to fasten the metal through the battens and, say, 2 inches of foam and sheathing into the joists. In some jurisdictions, the V-crimp can be fastened directly over the granulated roof membrane and does not require stripping.

4.7.3 Intermediate-slope roofing

Starting at about 3-in-12 pitch, you start to see shingle roofing and lapped membranes. This is the minimal slope recommended for most shingle applications. For best performance, SAMs are used for shingle underlayment with their self-sealing aspect again as one of its best features. Each shingle is to receive at least six nails per tab, which could mean several square inches of opening per 100 square feet of roof (referred to as *squares*). A simple home may have 20 squares of roof shingles. Since the membrane is functioning as the air and vapor barrier in most cases, you need it to be as sealed as possible. In using the SAM, you lose the ability for moisture to dry by passing through the membrane, as it could through traditional roofing felts. This moisture needs to be dealt with in another way.

There are three common ways to construct the intermediate-slope roof system. Each needs to meet (or exceed) the building codes for insulation and ventilation. The traditional way is to have eave and ridge vents with a ventilated attic. Variations on this theme include turbine ventilators, gable vents, etc. In each, ambient outside air is brought into the attic in an attempt to keep the sheathing and framing from moisture buildup and rot. Insulation typically is placed above the ceiling (see Fig. 4-122). In cold climates in the winter, vapor drive could cause condensation on the warm side of the ceiling if insulating values and perm ratings of materials weren't selected correctly and/or the materials weren't installed correctly. This situation is affected by operating temperatures in the space and ambient conditions, as well as the volume of outside air admitted per minute. In hot, humid climates, condensation risk is in the attic.

An alternative means of design is the sealed-off, actively ventilated attic. In this solution, the soffit, fascia, and exterior walls are not open to the attic. Conditioned supply air is introduced into the attic. Depending on envelope tightness and mechanical design, this supply air may positively pressurize the attic space relative to the outside (see Fig. 4-123). You would like it to be slightly negative to the occupied spaces. In most designs, return air is ducted back to the air handler. If this space is fed by a dedicated air-conditioning unit, you may be able to use temperature and humidity sensors to control when the system introduces conditioned air. In humid climates, it may be sufficient to have a dehumidifier run 24/7 and just use a temperature sensor to control an operable damper to supply the attic only if temperatures become problematic relative to the dew point. Insulation is placed more effectively at the roof rafters than at the ceiling, but

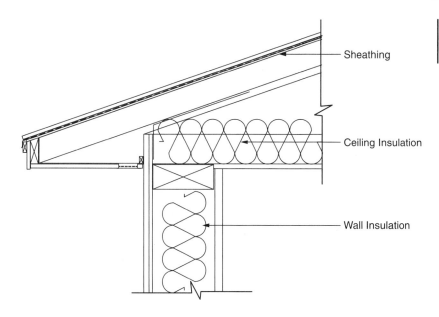

Figure 4-122
Insulation above the ceiling.

Sheathing

Ceiling Insulation

Wall Insulation

calculations for both summer and winter may reveal that insulating both ceiling and roof planes would avoid condensation in all seasons, even at record-high and low temperatures.

The third scenario is where foam insulation is sprayed to the underside of the roof sheathing. This foam skins over and acts like a vapor retarder and air barrier. We have heard that some manufacturers are not warranting their asphalt-based roofing products if used in these applications. Always confirm that manufacturers will warrant the application around which you design. Temperatures can build up at the roof in excess of the operating limits for some roofing products. We

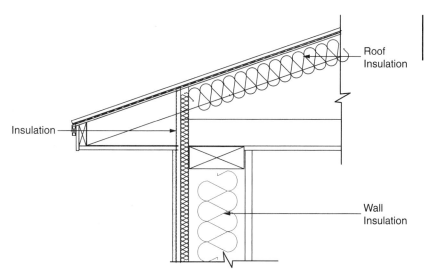

Figure 4-123
Ventilated pitched roof system.

Roof Insulation

Insulation

Wall Insulation

would imagine that there should be no problem with a high-temperature-tolerant membrane and ceramic, concrete, or metal roofing products. However, we could imaging temperatures of metal flashings, copings, and valley metal reaching in excess of 175°F. Whenever specifying materials, be sure to read the manufacturer's warranty exclusions and recommendations for operating conditions. This may apply to high-salt or high-chemical content in rainfall resulting in a voided warranty as well.

4.7.4 Steep-pitched roofing

The differences between intermediate- and steep-pitched roofs are many. It is much easier to work on a roof that is less than 6 inches per foot (6-in-12, or 22.5 degrees). Safety precautions increase and productivity decreases as you get steeper. The good news is that snow and rain don't stay on a steep roof very easily. The steeper you get, the more surface area is exposed to the elements. Therefore, air-barrier leaks get multiplied times a greater surface area to calculate infiltration or exfiltration. The same three kinds of insulation schemes explained earlier are permitted in most jurisdictions. If none of these fit your architectural aesthetic, there are always other ways to solve the problem. A cathedral ceiling with large exposed beams and plank ceilings can be designed to meet any climatic constraints. In the section provided in Fig. 4-124, you will find a solution that was used in Florida's hot, humid climate. In this example, 6- by 16-inch glulam beams were used at 80 inches OC. Then 2- by 6-inch tongue-and-groove no. 3 southern yellow pine (SYP) planks were nailed to the top using 20d spikes.

Thirty-pound fiberglass roofing membrane was installed next. Rigid extruded polystyrene (EPS) foam insulation 3 inches thick and $22^{1}/_{2}$ inches wide was installed at 24 inches OC on top of the dried-in planking with 2- by 4-inch nailers ($3^{1}/_{2}$ inches in vertical axis) at 24 inches OC. That $^{1}/_{2}$-inch airspace between the top of the foam and the bottom of the plywood was used as the ventilating airspace. Air was introduced at the bottom under the fascia and expelled at the top under the cap flashing. Next, sheets of $^{5}/_{8}$-inch CDX plywood was nailed to the 2 by 4s on end. Ninety-pound hot-mopped roll roofing was applied next. This served as the air and vapor barrier. Strips of rolled roofing were applied next, where the purlins were going to be at about 10 inches OC. This dimension is critical and should be matched to the width of the pans and cap tiles. Next, $1^{1}/_{4}$- by 3-inch purlins were toe-nailed through the roofing into the plywood. The strips were used to help seal the nail holes. Finally, the pans were set in place by using a compatible adhesive where the tile sat on the roof. Caps were nailed and mortared into place, trim tiles installed, etc. This resulted in a well-insulated, long-lasting roof system that looked good on top and bottom.

4.7.5 Roof penetrations and roof-to-wall conditions

If it were as simple as installing membranes on a rectangular, fully completed substrate, roofing would be easy. If it were as simple as unrolling a SAM from bottom to top and walking away, anybody could do it. In the real world, roofing

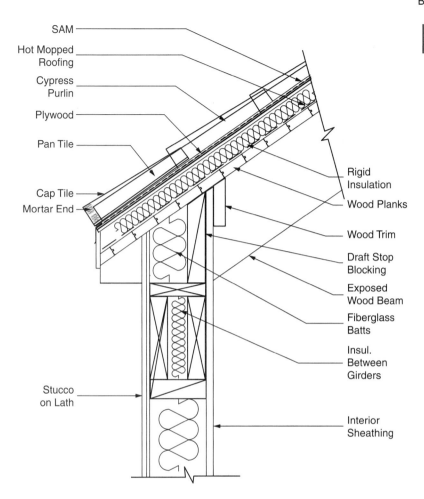

SAM

Hot Mopped Roofing

Cypress Purlin

Plywood

Pan Tile

Cap Tile

Mortar End

Stucco on Lath

Rigid Insulation

Wood Planks

Wood Trim

Draft Stop Blocking

Exposed Wood Beam

Fiberglass Batts

Insul. Between Girders

Interior Sheathing

Figure 4-124
Steep roof section.

is never this easy. Even the simplest shed roof has edges that need drip metal. However, most roofing jobs are not simple. Roof-to-wall conditions, parapets, roof drains, plumbing vent stacks, and a number of other things above the roof make it challenging to complete a roof installation. Rooftop mechanical equipment, exhaust ducts, chimneys, skylights, lightning protection, expansion joints, and other objects penetrate roof sheathings, decks, and membranes. The manner in which roof penetrations are protected has a lot to do with the pitch and products being used, as well as the wind speed anticipated. It is safe to say that most roof leaks happen at penetrations and vertical projections meeting the roof.

Steep- and intermediate-pitch roof systems typically do not have membranes that are sealed at their seams. Proper lapping of the membranes works with gravity to keep most of wind-driven rain from going uphill far enough to get behind the membrane. This is all that prevents rain from wetting the sheathing. Vertical surfaces such as fireplace chimneys on a sloped roof are installed with crickets that divert the water to the sides instead of letting the force of water flowing down the roof, striking the base flashing of the chimney at the level of the roof plane.

Crickets are used wherever the vertical face of an intersection surface extends more than 8 inches past the ridge of the cricket. This leaves room for the vertical leg of flashing to extend up the wall behind the wall membrane.

Plumbing vent stacks are sealed by applying bent flashing (referred to as a *boot*) over the top of the pipe (see Fig. 4-125) and under the shingles at the high side. At the low side of the boot, the shingles are installed under the boot. Low-slope roof penetrations are dealt with in a similar fashion. As long as membranes are lapped from the bottom up and flashings are applied to keep water from getting behind joints, penetrations can be sealed with few problems. Parapet walls should be avoided on all but flat roof systems.

Flat roof penetrations are potentially easier to seal than on sloped roof systems. Flat roof systems typically are sealed at the seams and laps to act as a single sheet of membrane material. Penetrations need to be sealed to the roof membrane. This is accomplished in one of two common ways. The preferred method has been with membrane; the other is with liquid-applied sealing products such as asphalt or tar. Most roofing manufacturers offer a wide range of products, some of which are designed for sidewall applications. These can be applied in the same manner

Figure 4-125

Plumbing vent stack.

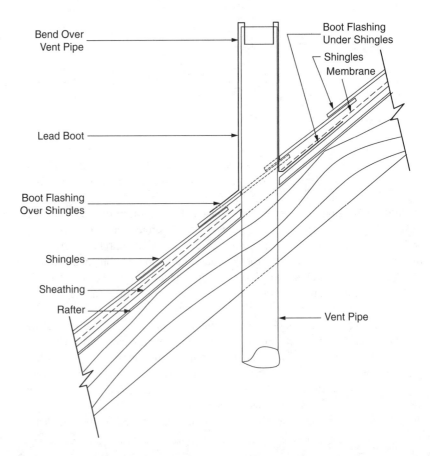

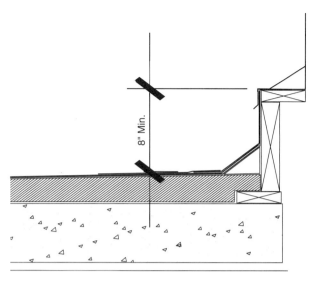

Figure 4-126
Minimum 8" height.

8" Min.

as the base and cap sheets. We recommend mop-down and torch-down membranes. For skylights and roof access hatches, the minimum sidewall height above the roof is 8 to 12 inches (see Fig. 4-126). In every case, the top of the sidewall membrane should be higher than the overflow scuppers by at least 4 inches.

Flat roofing also can serve as activity areas, pool decks, or patios. These kinds of applications require different roof coatings and membranes for their protection. For patios, you often see liquid-seal coatings applied directly to the concrete structural slabs. Hot-liquid-applied asphalts and modified bitumens make good water-protective coatings but aren't attractive or particularly nice to walk on with bare feet. There are special topping products for pedestrian use that can be warranted for up to 20 years. They also serve to seal the floor-to-wall condition (see Fig. 4-127). Other areas may need a concrete paver system

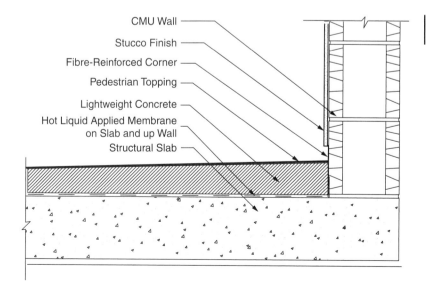

CMU Wall
Stucco Finish
Fibre-Reinforced Corner
Pedestrian Topping
Lightweight Concrete
Hot Liquid Applied Membrane
on Slab and up Wall
Structural Slab

Figure 4-127
Pedestrian topping.

Figure 4-128

Pavers on sand fill.

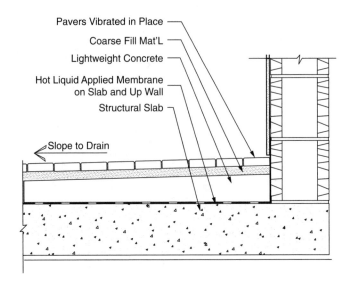

Pavers Vibrated in Place

Coarse Fill Mat'L

Lightweight Concrete

Hot Liquid Applied Membrane on Slab and Up Wall

Structural Slab

Slope to Drain

for poolside lounging. Pavers typically are installed on pedestals or on sand beds. In both instances, the structural deck may require waterproof coatings to prevent incidental water from causing problems with slab-reinforcing steel or damage to spaces below. Liquid or sheet membranes typically will be installed on the structural slab, followed by tapered lightweight concrete sloped to drains. Then a coarse sand or soil cement bed and pavers with sand or screenings as fillers between the brick or cement pavers (see Fig. 4-128) is applied. Similar details are provided for amenity deck planter beds to prevent stains or water damage from soil and rainfall adjacent to million-dollar condominium units (see Fig. 4-129).

Figure 4-129

Planter detail at exterior wall.

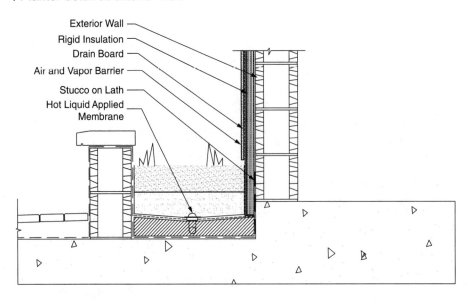

Exterior Wall

Rigid Insulation

Drain Board

Air and Vapor Barrier

Stucco on Lath

Hot Liquid Applied Membrane

4.8 MECHANICAL SYSTEMS

As we mentioned earlier, gravity, as well as temperature, humidity, and pressure differential, affects water vapor. This is referred to as *vapor drive,* with the driving forces being the physical laws and chemical properties. We have discussed the desire to control moisture in the built environment by the use of membranes, barriers, flashings, and coatings, coupled with good design principles and practices. This section addresses the role played by powered mechanical systems, including HVAC equipment. These mechanical systems work with the envelope materials to keep people comfortable, healthy, and happy. We have found that the way to do this is to provide some local control of an effective building HVAC system. This contributes to the happy part—individuals like to have the ability to adjust settings. This is especially true in government and commercial buildings, where a large number of people spend the majority of their waking hours with a lot of other people around.

Creature comfort is often as much psychological as physical. However, this can be a double-edged sword because you can't give people too much control. If you do, they will make other people miserable. It just happens. We have seen placebo controls work well in some settings, whereas they increase complaints at other times or in other places. The building HVAC system is only as good as the sum of its parts. This means that all major components must be capable of functioning at an acceptable level of performance at all times. The sensing and controls systems must be communicating properly with the control valves, variable-speed drives, dampers, heaters, and other parts. The fans have to be able to move enough air, ductwork must resist the pressure and convey the air, and the louvers have to allow outside air into the duct. Compressors, pumps, and piping must be able to meet the demand, and coils must have sufficient gas and liquid levels and pressures. The electrical power must be available. All these pieces need to be ready to work when needed.

Temperature and humidity control are the two primary functions of a building HVAC system. In order to minimize condensation in the envelope, you also must control pressure. You may remember Charles' and Boyle's laws from chemistry class, $P_1V_1/t_1 = P_2V_2/t_2$. This expresses the mathematical relationship of pressure and temperature in a fixed volume such as a building. Since the volumes are the same, they cancel out. What you are trying to do is maintain positive pressure on the building skin to minimize outdoor air and possible contaminants from coming in at the perimeter. Such air infiltration is bad; it can introduce hot, humid air in the summer or cold, damp air in the winter that can lead to localized condensation and other unwanted effects. You want your building envelope to be tight and slightly positive (relative to outside air). The tighter the envelope, the less pressurization air is required to maintain positive pressure. This equates to less energy consumption. It also means a better opportunity for a potentially healthy indoor environment for your people.

It is always a good idea to look at your overall building balance before you begin to look closely at any one space or area in the building. This can be as simple as a sum of ins compared to out. It lists values (in cubic feet per minute) of outside air coming into the building minus the total being exhausted, which leaves the amount for pressurization. This is a quick and important step in assessing any building HVAC design, which every architect should check before the building plans go out to bid. Make sure that you have pressurization air. If the exhaust is greater than the outside air intake, you have a negative-pressure building. This can cause problems. Do not let it happen.

Pressurization air can be as little as 0.03 to 0.07 inches of water column static pressure. This can be measured with a manometer and two small plastic hoses. Your mechanical engineer can calculate it for you and should indicate the value in a table on the plans (or specifications). Too much pressure can result in exterior doors staying open; too little can result in normal wind velocities causing infiltration on the windward side of the building envelope. An easy way to test it is to tear off a small strip of paper from a notebook and hold it in front of a set of double doors. If the strip blows out straight, the pressure is probably too much. If the paper curves less than 45 degrees, it is about right. Your test and balance report should list test values or at least calculate the value for you.

The main advantage of pressurization with outside air after it passes through the HVAC system is that it contains less moisture. This is especially true in the summer months. Figure 4-130 shows a section for a four-story representative building with positive pressure. Outside air is collected at the facade and ducted through a filter section and passed through an enthalpy wheel. An enthalpy wheel is made of a good heat-transfer medium such as honey combed

Figuire 4-130

Outside air mixed with return.

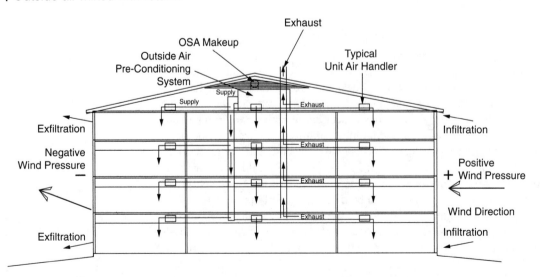

plastic. Outside air passes through the wheel, where it is preconditioned. In this example, building exhaust air passes through the opposite side of the outside air intake. In the summer, the exhaust is at around 75°F, whereas the outside air may be at 95°F or higher. The cool, dry air being exhausted lowers the temperature of that section of the wheel in the path of the air, and as the wheel turns slowly, it moves in front of the outside intake airstream.

One of the big challenges in bringing in large amounts of outside air is keeping rainwater intrusion to a minimum. On the building diagram provided in Figure 4.130, the intake for outside air is at the high point in a gable end condition. This is where wind pressures can be greatest. If it is raining, and you're introducing outside air to the outside air unit, you need to be able to remove as much rain as you can before it enters the mechanical equipment coil or fan sections. This can be achieved through the introduction of a water-trap, such as the one provided in section view (see Fig. 4.131).

This kind of water separator is low tech and low maintenance if built right. It uses gravity and geometry to remove moisture from the air stream. The intake area is large, with water separator louver blades. Behind that is a drain sump and weirs that cause the air to speed up as it rises, and then slow down as it

Figiure 4-131
Water trap at outside air intake.

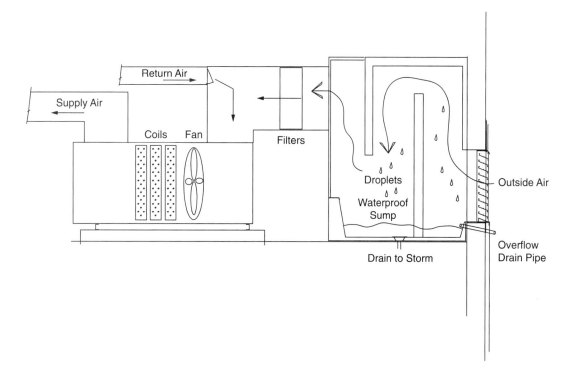

falls so that droplets collect and gravity pulls them down into the sump. Dryer air is then pulled up once more where it can be filtered prior to the outside air enthalpy wheel.

For flexibility, you may choose to have a variable-velocity exhaust fan, along with a variable-speed outside air makeup fan section. Interconnected with building differential pressure sensors and room occupancy and/or CO_2 sensors, you can tune the performance for maximum savings while exceeding ASHRAE and mechanical code standards for ventilation. Many outside air units have heating and cooling coils incorporated into their design for optimal discharge air regardless of outside air conditions. We have seen as much as a 15°F drop in outside air temperature, along with a 15 to 20 percent drop in relative humidity, through an enthalpy wheel. The savings in energy calculates out to about a 4- to 6-year payback.

The pressurization air now has been preconditioned at the outside air unit (OSA) and is ready for distribution to the air-conditioning units. Because the volume of outside air is only a small portion of the total volume of air (typically measured in cubic feet of air per minute, also referred to as *building cfm*) being moved by all the unit air conditioners combined, this OSA ducting is not as large as the unit air-conditioning system supply air duct. A diagram for a representative unit air-conditioning system is provided (see Fig. 4-132). You can see the OSA makeup duct, supply air (SA) ducting and return air duct indicated. For cost-effective operation, the program that operates the unit and building components all have night setback and non-occupied modes programmed in, as well as normal occupied modes. Regardless of the mode, the program should minimize infiltration through positive pressurization.

Figure 4-132

Pressurization controlled at unit air handlers.

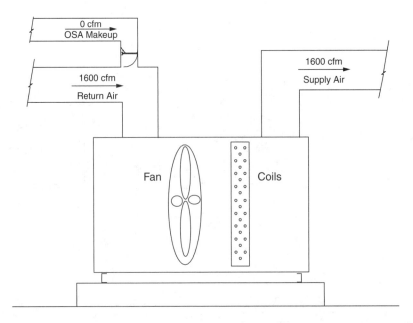

4.8.1 Ventilation

Air conditioning and heating systems rely on three principles for creature comfort—ventilation (moving air), temperature, and humidity control. This chapter will not go into radiant heating or trombe walls for building envelope considerations. This book is intended to focus more on mainstream building design and construction. Most building types rely on moving conditioned air to regulate occupants' temperatures. For heat rejection, the more air you move over a person's skin, the better is the potential exchange rate. You can either move more air over the person or lower the temperature of the air to increase heat rejection. There is a balance point in air velocity where the air is moving so slowly that it is not noticeable. Some of the air cools the surroundings, which is why you often direct air-conditioning supply grilles at exterior windows and walls.

As the conditioned air moves through the interior space, it moves from supply to return, creating patterns of flow and eddies. This air mixes with the air already there, diluting odors and providing fresh air. This mixing air also carries away moisture from walls, floors, ceilings, people, plants, and animals. This air is returned to the air handler, where it is remixed with outside air, dehumidified, cooled, and resupplied. This cycle continues.

4.8.2 Exhausting

Moisture is moving from the wall to the space as the wall dries, and at the same time, you may be introducing moisture to locations within the building. This localized moisture can cause problems if it is allowed to move freely. This is why we recommend collecting high concentrations of moist air at the source and exhausting it (see Fig. 4-133). Several common sources for concentrated moisture are showers, laundry, and cooking, but there are others too. Hot tubs, clothes dryers and washers, laundry sinks, and indoor clothes lines in the laundry

Figure 4-133
Ducted exhausts from sources of moisture, plan view.

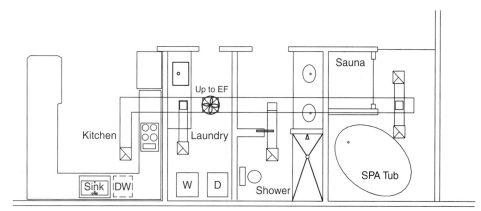

room are just a few. What is important is local collection and exhaust. In buildings with a lot of business machines, it is prudent to locate exhaust grille inlets above them to remove concentration of harmful or undesirable fumes.

This is why many condominium design teams stipulate interfacing lights in laundry and bath areas with exhaust fans. These used to be specified only in toilet rooms with no exterior walls, but their use has expanded to include most sources of moisture. We recommend against the use of ductless exhaust fans over stoves in kitchens. These essentially remove (by filtration) some cooking odors and blows the moisture from boiling water or cooking foods right back into the space. You want to get that moisture out of the envelope.

4.8.3 Dehumidification

The obvious advantage of HVAC systems is cool or warm air. It is not so obvious but equally important to consider the role of moisture reduction—dehumidification. Have you ever had an air-conditioning system in the attic of a house or apartment in which you lived? When did you realize that the attic was where it was located? Not when it was working perfectly. Probably when the condensate drain pan overflowed. That big ugly stain in the ceiling won't go away, not even after you unclog the drain line. Well, that drain pan probably leaked at the peak of the cooling season, didn't it? This is when the air is hottest, so it holds the moist moisture. Did you know that air at 95°F can hold more moisture than air at 72°F? Well, it can and often does. The condensate drain pan, even when partly clogged, could keep up with the normal rate of condensation in the early summer. But those cooling coils work overtime in the middle of the summer, and the air holds a lot more moisture. So it generates more water as it drips from the cooling coils. The drips overwhelm the 1-inch lip on the drain pan, and look, a brown spot that won't go away!

You want your indoor air to be relatively dry in the summer. A good rule of thumb is less than 50 percent RH. If you can stand it, afford it, and your system is able, you may wish to keep it below 40 percent. This goes for the unoccupied mode too. By keeping the air that low, you maintain a relatively low moisture level in the walls and continue to draw moisture out of the walls, where it can be removed by the building HVAC system. Dehumidifiers can be installed in buildings as well. We are seeing them in attics, basements, laundry rooms, wine cellars, and mechanical closets (even in residential units). By locating one in the mechanical closet, you can do two things. You can dry the returning air (in an unducted return plenum condition), and you can minimize potential condensation on the unit and walls of the closet. If the air-conditioning unit is cycling with the fan on and not the compressor, the supply air (SA) will be dryer because the return air is dryer. Of course, the air-conditioner and dehumidifier condensate pans need piping to drains. Check with your local codes for the possibility of using condensate water for irrigation or other nonpotable uses. Consider at least one air handler and dehumidifier be powered by emergency generator or stand-by power.

4.8.4 Sensing and controls

For a modest home or even a small hotel room, the building mechanical system can consist of a single window unit or through-wall air conditioner. It has a compressor, condenser, fan, and cooling coils, along with the condensate drain pan, in one compact package. All you need is a power source, and you can get cooling. Even this basic system typically has a couple of different fan speed settings for cooling and heating modes, along with a temperature sensor to regulate output. This device is called a *thermostat.* A thermostat is a "smart" switch. Historically, these were made by combining a bimetallic coil with a mercury switch. As it gets cooler, the coil changes length because one of the two metals contracts faster than the other. This changes the position of the mercury switch. Since mercury conducts electricity, the two electrodes are connected when the mercury is level in the glass tube, actuating the relay that powers up the air conditioner. This is the basis of antiquated sensing. It is not very accurate, but it is reliable. It requires no maintenance, repair, or replacement unless the glass tube breaks or one wire comes off. Owing to the poisonous potential of mercury in our environment (in landfills and such), this technology is being replaced by digital sensing devices.

Digital sensors are simple electronic devices that measure temperature by comparing it to a known value; they sense and "think." Their output is typically 24 volts direct current (DC) ranging between 4 and 20 milliamperes. The device receiving the signal converts the signal to a response in the air-conditioning system output. Taking this technology a step farther, digital sensors can be connected to programmable controllers. These controllers have logic built in that can be programmed to make decisions based on preset information. A series of "if-then" scenarios is placed in memory. When the sensor gets information, it decides what to do with it. These devices can be programmed to conserve energy, turn off lights, calculate the number of people in a building and adjust outside air input, and so much more.

A networked system of digital sensors and programmable controllers can be set up to operate building security, heat up the hot tub, answer the phone, and much more. Here, however, we want to focus on building envelope sensing and actions. Beyond the capability of a programmable controller, there are now building automation systems that are computer-based. These have exponentially more decision-making capabilities and interface opportunities. They have sensors that can detect motion, fingerprints, thermoclines, smells, gases, and more important, pressure differential and humidity. Differential pressure is referred to in the controls jargon as *DP.* You use DP sensors in water and air systems, as well as compressed gases in large chillers. You can use DP sensors in the exterior walls to regulate building pressurization and minimize infiltration.

Taking this a step further, you can use moisture sensors, or *humidistats,* to sense moisture in the exterior wall and roof cavities. Rather than rely on room air sensors to regulate moisture in a wall, you can measure moisture in the wall. Rather than keep room air at 45 percent RH in an attempt to minimize condensation in the wall, you can use dew point sensors in key locations in the wall. For buildings where you are conditioning ceiling cavities, attics, or basements, you can measure conditions accurately and limit the amount of conditioned (precious) air being introduced for pressurization. This will result in efficient use of two of our most valued resources—energy and money.

There are two common means presently being employed for providing ventilation air for occupied buildings. There is the old method of providing around 15 cfm per person that has been the standard basis for gross ventilation calculations for decades. This number varies depending on the person and his or her activity level but was accepted for years as an acceptable basis for calculating outside air in sizing building air-conditioning systems. Some less conservative designers conclude that the 15 cfm per person does not have to be all outside air. In their designs, a portion of the room air being supplied into the space is air that has not come from the air handler directly. Instead, air that has been in the space is not exhausted or returned to the air handling unit and it is mixed with a lower percentage of air from the unit (see Fig. 4-134). This recycles indoor air and

Figure 4-134

Sample unit supply and return ducting.

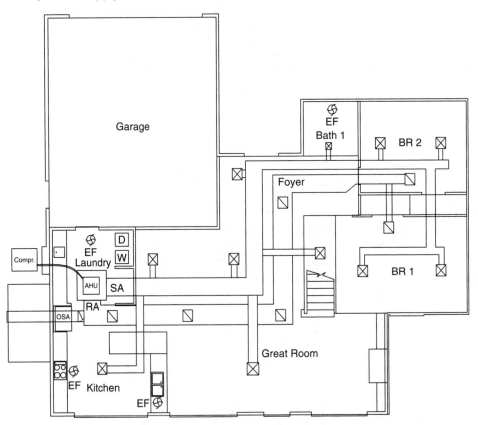

results in lower cost per square foot of energy. It also results in a potentially higher CO_2 level and a higher concentration of other indoor smells. It means more off-gassing from building materials and machines in the occupied portions of the building will be staying in the air the occupants breathe.

The second scenario being used in some buildings today relies on CO_2 sensors to control the ventilation air. This can result in the lowest volume of outside air being introduced into the building air-conditioning system. In theory, this results in lower operational cost for the client or building owner without allowing the air to dip below acceptable levels for CO_2 in the airstream. This system should be combined with a system for capturing less desirable air, such as previously mentioned capturing of exhaust air from large copiers or other equipment, at the source for removal from the building. The choice as to which methodology to use as the basis of design should be made in the programming stage so that the associated costs are figured in from the beginning stages and so that when the project is finished it meets or exceeds the client's expectations. It is important for clients to weigh the pros and cons of the two ventilation schemes. More outside air generally means healthier inside air, unless, of course, the air outside isn't very healthy.

Fortunately, with variable-velocity fans and adjustable dampers on ducts, programs can be changed to increase or decrease outside air and tune performance. Unfortunately, building automation systems also make it easy for operators to totally change the way a system runs. They can close off outside air with the push of a button. They can disable heat components and ignore sensors if they choose. As responsible designers, we do not want those decisions made by the local mechanic who may not be trained in or care about occupant health and safety. He or she may be trying to save operating cost or not know how to replace and calibrate a 4-milliampere output from a humidistat. This is why we must consider the operational and maintenance aspects of the building in the future before we design a system for a project. It may be that the low-tech thermostat is the only thing that the client's maintenance crew is able to keep working.

This is why we recommend that you specify building materials that can handle the small amount of occasional water that can result from condensation if all your precautions are not enough during extreme conditions. Furthermore, this is why we have discussed the importance of providing a drainage pathway for moisture that is formed at the vapor or moisture barrier.

There are many ways to design a building, and each results in a different level of performance, as well as a different initial and operating costs. By starting out with clear intentions and keeping focused on what is important, you can develop a good foundation for a good envelope. By careful consideration of operating and ambient conditions, you can look at ways to prevent condensation from forming in walls, roof systems, or interior surfaces. If you provide great illustrations and communicate your details well, you can improve the weather tightness of the skin. You know that there are excellent products for controlling air and moisture intrusion, and you can use them in concert regardless of the weather conditions. Roof, wall, floor, and site design decisions that are made with regard to gravity, geometry, and technology should result in a composite whole that prevents water intrusion and mold and mildew growth in buildings.

5

Bidding and Preconstruction

5.1 CLEARLY DEFINED SCOPE

One good way to make certain to continue with the execution of the building envelope the way it was intended is to have defined it well from the early stages of design. If the project was well defined, there should be less *scope creep* that can result from bidders learning about things that were not represented in the earlier cost estimates.

Scope creep can result from two root causes, and either can be problematic. Owner scope creep results from the owner continuing adding elements or, worse, square footage and perhaps even upgrading finishes. The longer the design stage stretches out, and the less control there is in the owner's organization, the more scope keeps getting added to the project. "We wanted to have retractable glass walls around the pool area; didn't we tell you?" Or worse, "You're going to be putting in that state-of-the-art audio visual system, like we saw in Las Vegas, aren't you?" This kind of continuing change can add up in a hurry, taxes a budget, and can strain a relationship.

5.2 AVOIDING SCOPE CREEP

Bid scope creep may be worse. There are many ways to estimate a project from early-bid documents; one of the most common is the *area-takeoff method,* also known as the old *square-foot-cost method.* This is usually done based on gross takeoffs of plan and elevation views of the building using systems cost data. It can be done quite accurately. One of the good things about this method is that not everything has to be shown in order to be included in the number. By this, we mean the fasteners, membranes, and paint do not all have to be called out in the details. The estimator doesn't have to measure the linear feet of flashing. Those kinds of things are included in the gross systems cost information. As long as the design doesn't increase the floor-to-floor heights or stretch the building length or something, the estimate should prove quite close.

If, on the other hand, the early pricing checks are not including things that may not yet be shown on the details or specifically called out in notes on plans and elevations, the early estimates may not include them. This can be the result of poor assumptions on the part of the estimator or using material and labor component pricing or subcontractor bids at the early stages before the drawings are complete. Another thing that can result in later cost exceeding early estimates is if the architect and/or engineer keeps adding improvements as the plans are developed. This can be as innocent as showing accessories or trim tiles in rest rooms as the large-scale interior elevations are developed. Or it could be the addition of roof drains, walls, doors, and sealants that were changed because the designer thought they might work better or look better.

There are hundreds of potential issues that may arise as the process of completing drawings is carried out. Scope creep can result in rising costs, and that can be problematic. If there is insufficient communication among the designers, owners, estimators, and contractors throughout this process, the problems can cause bigger problems. The best way to prevent this from happening is continuous and full communication among all parties involved. If the client has experience at building, he or she typically will know how much contingency to have in reserve for completion of bid documents. Some owners call this *design contingency*. This should be in addition to the contingency budget for escalation and for owner-requested changes.

Scope creep should be managed so that it does not cause a reduction in project quality. Some of the reactions that project management teams have had in the past have led to reductions in the quality of the roof (change from three-ply modified bitumen to single-ply EPDM), lower-cost (and lower-quality) windows and doors, less capacity in the HVAC system, reduced-performance paints and sealants, omission of the air barrier, cancel commissioning, cut back on the roofing inspections, reduction of roof overhangs, reduction of insulation thicknesses, and so on. We would hope that you can see the resulting reduction in building envelope performance likely coming from these changes. This is what we call *cost cutting,* and it is certainly not value engineering and will not result in an equally performing building.

5.3 BID ENVIRONMENT

Another dynamic variable is the bidding environment. Throughout the late 1990s, we saw some very good bidding environments and steady and low inflation rates. In the period from 2002 to 2004, it was difficult to get anybody to hold his or her price on anything. Price escalation hit historic highs. Prices in copper, concrete, cement, drywall, and several building products skyrocketed.

Labor prices went up because the work force was unable to keep up with demand. Bidders were able to build great profits into their bids because their competition also was doing so. Nobody was hungry in our region. We had to get bids on roofing from thousands of miles away. Hurricanes, terrorism, and social pressures can make prices jump up one month and seldom do prices go down. Changes in the bid environment are hard to predict very far into the future because they can be dramatically affected by current events. For these reasons, experienced project leaders budget for just such occasions. Two common terms for this are *owner's contingency funds* and *project reserve.* In many scenarios, the early estimates from contractors carry escalation figures based on how far in the future the project is scheduled, other work on the books, and advance prognostication from experts. While these practices can result in higher initial cost estimates, they also can be very useful in planning worst-case project cost estimates for marketing plans and to prevent projects from coming in over budget later.

5.4   VALUE ENGINEERING

You may hear this term used in a multitude of ways. Decades ago, we never heard this term at all. If a project bid came in too high, we would reduce scope (such as make the building smaller) or hammer on the subcontractors to lower their number for the designed scope (such as promise them that they can make a good profit on the next job). In certain bid environments and with certain relationships, this still can be observed in many regions today, although perhaps to a lesser extent. This is not value engineering but *scope reduction* or *cost-cutting.* True, value engineering could be described as coming up with a better way to get the same (or an acceptable and nearly equal) thing. This is the best for all concerned. The bidders do not have to reduce their unit costs or profit, the designer doesn't have to accept a poor substitute, and the owner is able to afford the resulting solution.

All too often, "value engineering" does not result in all three parties coming out with this kind of win-win-win position. For value engineering to work properly, the persons making the decisions need to have all the information pertinent to the choices. Overly simplified assessments of cost comparisons can leave out important considerations in an attempt to make the numbers work out. An example of this would be to take credits for a stick-built frame wall with stucco and insulation, cavity airspace, fiberglass sheathing, air barrier, waterproof membrane, R = 19 insulation, and paint and replacing it with a tilt concrete wall system. In the first place, this is not an equivalently performing system from a water intrusion and condensation point of view. To make things worse, the cost comparison didn't take into account the textured coating for the outside surface and other cost considerations, such as casting beds, crane mobilization, etc. We could list hundreds of decisions made in the heat of a cost-cutting meeting that did not weigh all the cost increases compared with taking all the savings.

There are many examples of good value engineering, some wherein the results performed better than the original design and cost less. This can result from a system or systems that were initially either over designed or perhaps not the best fit for the needs. What we are trying to prevent is ending up with a solution that cannot perform well, requires too much maintenance, and can lead to water intrusion in the building for any reason. In the building envelope, there are few lower-cost systems that perform as well as higher-cost systems—you generally get what you pay for. But there are opportunities in every component of the building to look for good performance at lower cost. Rather than start off by eliminating the paint or waterproof membrane, let's look at a few other areas first.

We like to look first at the foundation system because this is where we have had great success in the past. There are typically many decisions made in designing a foundation system without feedback and directions from the owner or contractor. There are always ways to look at the implications of an alternate way of doing the same thing. As an example, the schematic design is often done prior to receipt of a soils report. We don't know why, but most owners don't know the subsoil conditions or water table until after the design is well underway. They should consider paying for site soil and water table tests before the offer to purchase is tendered. But most do not. So the foundation may be designed based on a false assumption; it happens all the time. Then, months later, the report comes in, and designers now learn what is beneath the soil surface. The bearing capacity could be far worse than the assumptions and is almost never better.

Let us assume that the soils report reveals seven borings in a line that have no bearing capacity for more than 65 feet in depth (20 meters). The conclusion is drawn that there are voids or subsurface caverns such as exist in the Floridan aquifer. The civil engineer (CE) may respond by recommending driven piles throughout the building footprint. For a medium-sized building footprint, say, 100,000 square feet (33 meters), the resulting pile and cap costs can exceed $1.5 million depending on loads and depths. This indeed did happen on a 16-story mixed use project, and would have eaten up the owner's contingency fund before we completed the design. This was not good. To make a long story short, we redesigned the slab on grade to use a hybrid anger-cast pile mat with adequate reinforcing steel to span a calculated sinkhole diameter with a factor of 2. The resulting increased cost was only around $450,000, or one-third the contingency budget. This is value-engineering thinking applied during the design process. The hybrid mat was as good as the piles for a lot less money.

We could list numerous examples of value-engineering successes and failures from past projects. Among them, it is more important to learn from the mistakes. Mistakes in value-engineering include changes that result in lesser-performing systems than the original, or *cost-cutting*. When that lesser performance results in future problems such as moisture intrusion, condensation, and mold, the resulting corrective measures cost far more than the savings that were returned for the change in systems.

Let us share a success story from a recent project going through value engineering. We were in the role of design/build architects after a design criteria firm had completed the design development (DD) documents. We had to shave about 15 percent from the DD estimated cost of $16.6 million without reducing square footage or changing the look. We looked in every division of the specifications for requirements that did not yield equivalent returns for the initial cost. We looked at the details and the bids for areas where we could reduce costs.

We found several areas for savings. One was in the glass. The Design Criteria Architect had specified a very expensive glass in the project, and the facade was to be half glass. By increasing the emittance slightly, we opened up the bidding to include several competitors, thereby lowering material and labor costs. By reducing the size of the board chambers slightly (about 3 percent), we reduced occupant load to below the threshold level and were able to reduce the importance factor from 1.15 to 1.0. This resulted in the structural beam sizes, light-gauge framing spacing, and curtain wall system thickness all being reduced. We refused to look at reducing air or moisture barrier components. We reduced the size of the emergency generator to a lower-cost size after confirming that it was more than adequate for the planned loads.

We found some savings in the roof insulation as well. As a result of the geometry of the roof area, one portion of the roof had extensive cricket length to build up slope to drain at $1/4$ inch per foot. The cricket was nearly 60 feet in length, which would have resulted in about 17 inches of tapered insulation at the ridge. Roof insulation has become expensive. We were able to build the bar joists with most of the taper in them, requiring little additional steel cost, and were able to save thousands in roof insulation.

The last thing we did was to modify the HVAC equipment to omit CO_2 monitoring and fan-powered boxes. Our mechanical designer used variable-air-volume (VAV) mixing boxes instead of fan-powered boxes. This resulted in lower duct and equipment costs, as well as lower operation and maintenance costs. Our mechanical designer prefers the reliability of VAV boxes regardless of the comparative cost. He believes that the VAV boxes provide better dehumidification and creature comfort. The CO_2 monitoring issue can be debated in terms of the resulting indoor air quality, but we believed that omission of CO_2 monitoring results in dryer supply air in the spaces, as well as healthier air with more outside air and less CO_2 in the rooms. These kinds of cost saving measures were seen as reducing cost substantially without a negligible reduction in building envelope performance or occupant health. These changes resulted in significant electrical bill reduction too.

5.5 BIDDING

There are many ways to approach the transition period between design and construction because each project delivery system, permitting and review authority, and designer/contractor relationship can be different. Once the plans and specifications hit the street, the process of bidding begins. Typical bidding periods can range from 2 weeks to 2 months. Bidders may ask questions before the contract documents are complete, as well as after. Changes in the documents during bidding usually are referred to as *addenda* (plural of addendum). Often the bid questions come in the form of prebid *requests for information* (RFIs) and may have an impact on the resulting bid values. Therefore, prebid RFIs should be distributed to all bidders.

At some point in this process, plans and specifications are signed and sealed by registered professionals, and multiple copies are submitted to the permitting review agency or agencies. Several agencies may be involved, and the process may be linear, where one agency must approve them before they move to the next agency. If the project is not linear, you may be able to submit to multiple agencies at the same time. Frequently, each agency will issue a list of questions for the designers to answer. These are usually code-compliance issues and may contain administrative questions or requests for additional information. Under the best conditions, permitting can be quick and easy. The longer and better the relationship between permitting agencies and submitting firms, the better the process can go for all concerned. This process can take more than 6 months. Any changes to the drawings for permitting need to be signed and sealed, usually clouded (encircled with segmented arcs that resemble clouds) and accompanied by a written narrative of changes, and resubmitted. Additional permit fees can be charged for reviewing the modified permit drawings and specifications.

6 Construction

6.1 PROCESS

Once the contracts are awarded, questions are asked by successful bidders, usually during construction. Depending on the project particulars, the process can take on many paths from this point. Based on recommendations of the American Institute of Architects (AIA), *requests for information* (RFIs) are but one of many documents for processing changes to the contract documents. RFIs are most often initiated by contractor or subcontractors needing more information. They can also be asked by the owner's team, or offered by design team members, depending on the client, contractor, and project dynamics (schedule). Other documents that one might use would include *architect's supplemental instructions* (ASIs), *requests for proposal* (RFPs), *directives,* and *change orders* (COs). Over the years, these basic documents have been expanded.

ASIs were intended to be clarifications to scope previously shown in the documents and initially (at least in theory) had zero cost and time implications. They simply were to be clarifications. For example, the ASI could instruct the contractor as to which color paint to use where or to supply a dimension to assist in layout. RFPs initially were supplemental drawings issued by the design team for the contractor to price. These often were for added scope but could be as simple as evaluating optional carpet pricing for glue-down carpet squares in lieu of roll goods. After the owners received the proposed price for the change, they could make a decision as to whether or not to proceed with the change.

There are at least three variations of directives. If something comes up during the course of construction that requires immediate action, a directive may be issued. We have seen the architect, contractor, and owner all use directives in one project. The architect might issue an *architect's field directive* (AFD) such as the addition of water stops in a concrete pour that may be underway. A contractor may issue a *directive* to proceed with work that was not shown rather than hold up the progress of the job. An owner may direct a contractor or construction manager (CM) to proceed on a cost-plus basis, on a not-to-exceed basis, or even on a pricing directive. Only one client in all our experience used directives like his or her favorite credit card or checkbook. When a contractor received a directive, he or she felt confident they would be receiving additional payment for the work. This was on a resort project where time was money. As it relates to the envelope, a directive might be a good way to add a detail or get an additional membrane put on the wall before the next materials goes on.

6.2   PRECONSTRUCTION

Preconstruction meetings can be very beneficial to all parties. It is an opportunity for the designers, owners, and contractors to discuss upcoming issues with the subcontractors. It is a good time to express how important the building envelope is to the success of the project and to begin to get buy-in for the hierarchy (relative importance) list developed earlier. As the meeting relates to the site, site sections, water tables, soils, drainage, bearing capacities, and the upcoming season can be discussed. If it is going to be raining during piping and foundation excavation, this is a good time to make plans of action. Most important, it may be the first time the subcontractors meet the project manager for the owner or the design team. Familiarity can lead to open communication throughout the next year or two.

Continuing with the preconstruction meeting theme, roofing, waterproofing, and wall installation subcontractors also should be present at the meeting. Great success can result from spreading out the plans on the meeting table and going through the details one by one. Perhaps the subcontractors will have a good idea as to how to improve a flashing detail, or you can talk about substitutions for materials that may not be readily available owing to global pressures or new materials on the market that might work better than what is shown in the plans. This should not be seen as a chance to substitute lesser-cost solutions for what was required by the contract documents. This is also a good time to discuss those seldom read documents—the specifications. Of particular interest, you should review warranty, mockup, shop drawing, and testing requirements. Try to build camaraderie through your mood and actions.

6.3   SUBMITTALS

Properly processed submittals modify the contract documents. They usually provide more accurate and detailed information than the design documents. The initiator is usually a subcontractor who specializes in this scope, perhaps an installation-only subcontractor or perhaps a material supplier. Designers and construction engineers need to take their time reviewing shop drawings and every other form of submittal for compliance with contract documents and for coordination with every submittal that has come before. Of particular importance to me are submittals that define points of interface between systems. Dimensions are only the first thing to verify. Check the thicknesses of materials and their composition, and read manufacturers' recommendations. We recently learned of delaminating metal-clad wood windows used in an ocean-front home in West Palm Beach, wherein the manufacturer specifically stated that these windows should not be used on or near the coast.

Most window and door submittals stop at the edge of the product being provided. This can disguise important flashing, membrane, fastener, and sealant considerations that will affect the envelope's performance against the elements. Check to ensure that the particular extrusion shapes provided work with the intended geometry of the sections. All these steps should be undertaken first in the general contractor (GC) or construction manager (CM) office by their field engineer or person of similar responsibility before forwarding them to the designer for review. In the ideal world, all specification requirements are met by the product being submitted. If something needs special attention, the contractor should put a green cloud around it, and note it for the architect or engineer to look at with their marks then made in red. The same process just described should be performed by the design team after receipt. If either the GC or designer is too busy, too lazy, or perhaps unaware of the importance of full review of submittals, problems that could have been avoided will have a higher probability of happening.

6.4   SCHEDULING

Most construction contracts contain language requiring detailed schedules for activities shortly after award of the contract. These schedules are comprehensive task lists with sequencing and durations for all major components of the building. Such schedules frequently list submittal dates and allow reviewers time for the process of approval. Three important activities as they relate to the building envelope are the roof and wall systems, windows skylights and mock-ups. The initial schedule will serve as a planning tool for sequencing all construction activities for the duration of the job. It is usually updated constantly as things change in the dynamics of a construction project in the real world.

The reason we list roof, wall, and mockups is that we want to make certain that these submittals come in sufficiently early to permit adequate time for review, as well as time for revised, returned submittals. The issue of mockups gets overlooked all too often or delayed until they are less useful. We urge everyone to have mockups built early in the schedule. These often solve details for the most complex conditions on the envelope and let everyone know the sequence of trades required to build these details. Often, in the rush to get buildings done on time, trades can get shuffled around, submittals get sent in late, and (as an example) the stucco crew can get ahead of the flashing or roofing counter-flashing crews. These out-of-sequence installations can help the schedule but can lead to pathways for water intrusion and compromise the performance of the building envelope.

Well-crafted schedules link activities that need to follow each other to prevent such out-of-sequence installations from happening. The initial schedule should also show critical path activities, calling attention to key tasks that must be completed by a specific time if the target completion date is to be met. One more important aspect of the schedule is float (or fluff). *Float* is time in excess of what may be required, extra time if you will, so that if something takes longer than anticipated, it does not affect the next task in sequence. An achievable schedule will have float in many areas when it is first developed. A good team will manage float, even adding to the float whenever possible early in the job.

Finally, with regard to the schedule, make certain that sufficient time is allowed for dry-in to be achieved prior to starting inside finishes. Look to see the relationship between the start of roofing activities, wall sheathing, glazing, and door installations as it relates to stocking the job with interior sheathing, insulation, etc. Make certain that there is float in the roofing schedule to permit installation to slip a few rain days (or weeks) without causing delays. See where heating, ventilation, and air-conditioning (HVAC) equipment startup is relative to finishing drywall, installing any wood products, etc. Then look at substantial completion and the preceding activities. Make certain that there is adequate time for punch-list inspections and corrective work. The worst schedules can lead to installations out of sequence, installing roofing when the lightweight concrete is still wet and paint or sealant application before substrates are sufficiently dry, clean, or cured, etc. Don't let the schedule cause future problems. If a conflict arises, get the construction team together with the design team to figure out a way to work around the situation. There are ways to overcome most challenges; they just may not be obvious at first glance, easy, or free.

As an example, we would like to share with you a detail that was developed for a project where the roofing contractor was 2 months behind schedule. The metal stud and drywall crews were ready to install sheathing and begin stucco activities. Unfortunately, all flashings were in the roofer's contract. The detail as designed required the flat-seam metal roofing installation to be complete before stucco could begin (see Fig. 6-1). The CM needed the stucco subcontractor to start immediately. As the on-site architect's representative, we were able to develop a revised detail (see Fig. 6-2) that revised the design to enable stucco work to begin in advance of roofing. The simple work-around enabled work to proceed without compromising the performance of the envelope. Do not allow the schedule to be an excuse for creating future problems.

6.5 LONG-LEAD ITEMS

As soon as the contract is awarded, scheduled tasks should include purchase of *long-lead items*. For those unfamiliar with the term, it applies to items that

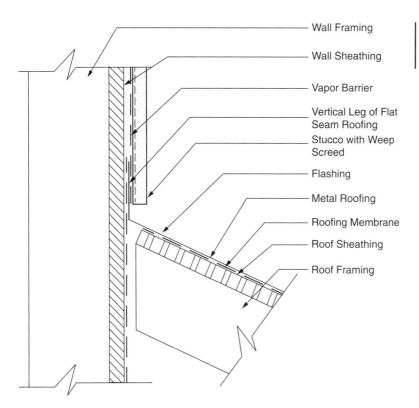

Wall Framing

Wall Sheathing

Vapor Barrier

Vertical Leg of Flat Seam Roofing

Stucco with Weep Screed

Flashing

Metal Roofing

Roofing Membrane

Roof Sheathing

Roof Framing

Figure 6-1
Roof-to-wall detail, as designed.

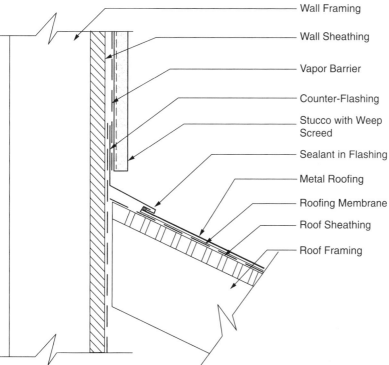

Wall Framing

Wall Sheathing

Vapor Barrier

Counter-Flashing

Stucco with Weep Screed

Sealant in Flashing

Metal Roofing

Roofing Membrane

Roof Sheathing

Roof Framing

Figure 6-2
Roof-to-wall detail, as built.

require a long time between initial intent to purchase and delivery of completed items. This frequently may include fabricated steel parts such as bar joists and custom structural members or curtain wall systems. The reason these are important to recognize is their potential impact on closing in the building. Successful projects manage to coordinate installations of roof and wall components so as not to affect the proper sequence and duration of trades. Failure to acquire long-lead items on schedule can lead to an interruption to the optimal rate of application, curing times, hydration, or other deviations to the trades that follow.

6.6 EARLY-BID PACKAGES

There are several ways that construction schedules can be shortened. One way is to put more people on each installation crew. Another is to work three shifts. While there may be projects where this is the only way to achieve the owner's objectives, it is certainly not the normal way buildings are built. It is not unusual for projects to work 10-hour days or 6 and 7 days a week, but this is usually reserved for a short burst and not for several months. One method for delivering buildings earlier is to get an earlier start. Since we can't usually get under contract sooner or speed up the permit review process, we have to look elsewhere. One other place to look is in shortening the design process, but designing a custom building takes time, and the process is iterative. It is completed in stages, with solutions being developed through a process of calculation, analysis, and synthesis. It often requires an accumulation of information from outside sources such as surveyors, soils-testing labs, and other people. All these take time. Often, it takes longer to get questions answered by the client group than it does to design the building.

Rather than take a chance on shortening the process of architecture, structure, mechanical, electrical, furniture, landscape, acoustics, and all other design disciplines, it has become common to break out early-bid and construction packages. This can work in concert with long-lead items, as touched on earlier. On one of our current projects, we were able to submit an early foundation package and get it fabricated and the foundations built while the building permit was being completed and accepted. The result was a 4-month reduction in total project duration. When inflation rates approach 10 percent per year and you are able to purchase materials soon after contract award, the time saved could lead to more than 4 percent savings in project cost. A lot of material, such as concrete, steel, piping, mechanical and electrical systems, gear, and fixtures, can be bought sooner as a result of good planning and an early-bid package.

One thing that I've learned is that the sooner you get the building finished, the sooner the owner quits making changes. Changes can kill a project's momentum and lead to lower cost-effectiveness and less profitability for all involved.

6.7 STORAGE AND PROTECTION

Manufacturing companies such as General Motors are expert in ordering materials from suppliers and stipulating delivery just in time for installation. Builders have moved in the same direction but have not achieved the same control over their suppliers. Often we will accept a delivery more than 6 months before we need something. There are several reasons why this can occur, and if it is part of the purchasing plan, then provisions must be made to protect early-delivered materials. Some suppliers can store materials until needed, whereas others must deliver them to make room in their yards. Some purchasers store materials in air-conditioned storage areas. This protects them from the elements and theft.

The worst thing that can happen to stored materials is exposure to water. Materials stored on site need to be well covered and stored in an area that will not flood or even be wetted by wind or rain. The other important consideration is preventing wind-borne mold spores from settling on the materials. Both water and mold spores must be prevented from contact with materials, especially porous materials with organic content such as wood and paper products. Most construction specifications will address protecting materials and work in progress. Exterior walls constructed out of concrete masonry units (CMUs) or brick should be covered with a waterproof membrane after each day's work or before rain events during working hours. These coverings should be maintained in a manner as to not be displaced by wind or by other trades. Failure to do so may lead to water getting in the wall where it is not supposed to be. This can lead to mold growth that may go unnoticed for months or years until a trigger event in the future leads to occupant complaints and potential remedial work. Once spores begin to spread their tendrils, the best means for correction is removing the materials. Another problem caused by masonry exterior walls getting wet is excessive efflorescence. This is the result of moisture causing reactions with lime, calcium or other chemicals in the wall. Efflorescence is very difficult to stop once it begins. If possible, protect masonry, brick, stone, and block until the exterior finish is applied, whether it is paint, stucco, or a clear protective coating such as silane. Install roofing, flashings, gutters, and drains as soon as proper sequencing will allow.

Interior materials are even more important to protect against water and mold spores prior to installation, especially organic and hygroscopic materials that may contain paper or wood. Any material that gets installed inside the vapor barrier has a greater potential to affect future occupants than those outside the membrane. Paper-backed gypsum wall board, typically referred to as *drywall,* is the first interior finish material to be installed in many projects. Depending on the type of exterior wall system and the number of floors and wings, drywall installation may begin before the building is totally dried in and the air-conditioning system is on. As soon as the subcontractor hangs the first interior walls near an exterior wall, get your umbrella out because it is going to rain. With 3 inches of rain on the floor in areas, drywall will be getting wet. We recommend against installing any interior products that contain paper or wood until the envelope is complete or temporary closure is in place. Ideally, the temperature and humidity should be less than 90°F and 50 percent, respectively.

Often electrical equipment rooms need to be constructed before the envelope is dried in so that temporary power can be distributed. One way is to construct them out of metal studs and fiber-reinforced gypsum products that are made without paper. This permits panels to be set, doors and hardware to be installed, and wires to be connected with an acceptable level of safety and control.

6.8   COORDINATING THE TRADES

Depending on the project team, coordination can be easy or nearly impossible. The best general superintendents make it possible for all trades to work together in noise and harmony. There is no such thing on a job site (at least not in our experience) as total peace and harmony. There is always grumbling. You can't make everybody happy all the time. But a good superintendent has the ability to get cooperation. A good superintendent will have planned the job and managed the schedule so that subcontractors can get in and get done with the least interference or interruption by others. More important than harmony is cooperation, and it starts with attitude. Hiring a good bunch of subcontractors and giving them enough time and money is a great starting point. Giving them space to do their work and getting those before them to finish is the real trick. Due to the complexity of many building envelopes, you may have more than 12 subcontractors whose efforts have to be managed for one detail to work. A simple wall section may require the organization of 15 different trades. If one of them, for example, the metal framing subcontractor, installs his or her work wrong or doesn't finish, it affects everyone who follows. Project schedules are usually updated weekly as a result of status checks and available work force. A material shortage can throw trades out of sequence if corrections are not made in the schedule as the problems are made known.

One of the beauties of a big project is that there are usually other areas of the project where a group of workers can be assigned in response to change in another area. This keeps the overall building schedule on track. Work that must be done off scaffolding creates its own challenges. The subcontractor paying rental for the scaffolding may not wish to leave it up in one section after his or her scope is done, and it is uncommon to have two different trades working off the same scaffolding at the same time unless it is provided by the GC or CM. When it comes to constructing multiple wythe walls and/or complicated details requiring close coordination between framers, sheathing installers, flashings, and finish material installers, it is a good idea to limit the number of subcontractors. Try to award the flashing to the subcontractor installing the sheathing, membrane, and finish material. You may find that subcontractors often coordinate better among themselves because they work for the same boss than if the roofer is to install the flashings and another subcontractor has the membrane in his or her contract. Coordination of trades can begin with a careful award of subcontractor bids.

Figure 6-3
Resolve details before you
get on the scaffolding.

This is another benefit from building a mockup before work starts on the building. The subcontractors will learn who needs to go first, who goes next, and how best to work out the interface before they get up on scaffolding (see Fig. 6-3). Let the subcontractors work it out on the ground before anybody has expended much material and labor on the project. This can lead to a better understanding of the intent of the drawings and give everyone involved more time to look at alternatives or to review the mockups and explain their expectations for quality workmanship.

6.9 ATTENTION TO DETAIL

It doesn't take much of an opening or a void in the exterior wall system to allow air and water intrusion. The old attitude of doing your job as fast as you can and letting the next guy worry about fixing problems you cause cannot be tolerated. Such a mentality can be pervasive and end up carrying through from beginning to end. A good project starts out right. Beginning with the design team, attention to detail often separates good envelopes from problem projects. When that attention is carried through the construction personnel as well, it will result in better fit of parts, better scheduling for delivery of materials that work, and less air and water intrusion.

Each successive trade needs to be on the same page, starting with utilities and site work. If the utilities go in wrong, say, the storm drainage piping is run too flat, it can lead to roof drain failure or burst piping and fittings in walls. If the finish grades are not correct, surface water can be carried up to the exterior walls. The slabs must be cast properly, laid out right, and placed properly. When the foundation or floor gets installed with a problem, this can trickle through all the following subcontractors' work. Corrections should be made as soon as possible (see Fig. 6-4). This outside corner condition for a resort was left uncorrected despite being reported to the general superintendent. We were told for weeks that the subcontractor would get around to fixing it. On the following Monday morning, the framing crews had already framed up the exterior wall, and exterior sheathing was installed before 8:00 A.M. The contractor allowed the condition to remain untreated long enough for it to become too much trouble to correct it. The resulting void was large enough to put a golf ball in. It was on the punch list at project closeout and received some cementitious patch material from the outside, after paint was on and landscaping was in. Slab-edge dimensions and form-stability issues can be the most problematic in closing off the floor to foundation and wall-sill condition. No project ever goes without some problems, but successful projects deal with these challenges as they come up—preventing them from becoming problematic.

Attention to detail is more of an overall theme than it is a practice applied to any one issue. It means paying careful attention to the general conditions and specifications. Do not just scan the table of contents and decide to read only the portions on payment applications and start date. While some general conditions may be standard, off-the-shelf "boiler plate" specifications, you may find some

Figure 6-4
Outside corner void in slab.

of them useful in understanding what is important to the client. The sections on verification of existing conditions may be important in remodeling, as might sections on responsibility for code research and compliance. For building warranties and testing criteria, you need to look at the front end as well as the particular division you are bidding. Specifications often list acceptable manufacturers, materials, fasteners, and requirements for testing and approval agencies such as Underwriter's Laboratories (UL), American Standards for Testing and Materials (ASTM), etc.

As they relate to air and vapor membranes, specifications often list thicknesses, perm ratings (dry cup and wet cup), tack ratings, facings, reinforcing, contents, volatile organic compound (VOC) limits, application techniques, and more. Pay attention to the specifications; ask questions if you don't understand something. Do your own research. Ask people you trust, even sales representatives or your peers. Sometimes it helps just to hear yourself talk about something. It doesn't happen often, but specifiers can make mistakes too. Review the plan and section details with a keen interest toward where the vapor barrier is in the wall system and roof sequence. Look to see how this fits with your planned sequence of installation. Look at flashings, windows, doors, and louvers and compare the details with what you have built in the past in the same climate and building type. Pay attention to compatibility issues. These can occur in metals, particularly where two different metals come in contact with one another. Metals with different valences (this has to do with their available electrons for chemical reactions) will react with one another. You should isolate dissimilar metals, such as steel, lead, copper, iron, and aluminum. Stainless steel doesn't react (much) when it comes in contact with any of these, so it is commonly specified for use— especially where exposed to weather or view.

Paying attention also applies to observing construction in progress. Look at what is going up as to how it may affect your scope. If something just doesn't look right, there is a chance it isn't right. It is amazing how when you walk the job site on a daily basis you will observe some activity that attracts your attention. On closer examination, you may learn something that is done well or see something that is not. Of special interest are voids in materials, large gaps between systems, penetrations that were not planned, and finishes going on before preparation is complete. Some of these items can be loose-fitting or unsecured components, dirty substrates, lack of or wrong fasteners, or worse— things that were left out.

Blocking and nailers can be a lot of work to install properly before sheathing begins. It takes a special kind of trained eye to look at framing and determine the places where sheathing needs end nailing or coping needs screws. If left out, these pieces can result in materials coming loose in heavy winds, and this allows rain in the envelope and water damage or flooding. After Hurricane Charley, we could see which builders had installed nailers and fasteners in corner conditions just by seeing what came loose and what stayed in place. This was especially evident in shingle roofing and vinyl siding.

We have observed roofing going on before surrounding work was framed in and wall finishes being applied before roof flashings were installed. We have seen installers try to hide rips in membranes by covering them up before too many people arrive at the job site in the morning. By carefully observing the details and specifications, and by watching it all go together, most future problems can be avoided—by fixing them before they can become problems.

6.10 DIMENSIONAL TOLERANCES

We touched on this previously but feel that it is important enough to make into a separate topic. With computers doing a lot of our dimensioning in design, we can get dimensions on plans down to the thousandths of an inch—but it doesn't help us very often. Construction dimensions seldom should be listed in increments smaller than $1/8$ inch. Unless a part or component is being fabricated by a computer, about all humans can lay out consistently is eighths. There needs to be some room for the width of a line or sawblade to permit a construction worker the opportunity to make hundreds of cuts each day and the building still fit together adequately. Designers should never dimension walls, floors, beams, columns, decking, or anything else construction workers are to fabricate and install to $1/64$ inch. You should plan for some flexibility. This is especially useful when different materials are being joined, such as windows being installed in concrete block and stucco walls. Concrete blocks aren't always the same size, the joints vary in width, and the jamb may not be perfectly plumb, but in the end, they have to work together. Skilled and experienced carpenters can plan their cuts so that when wall sheathings and vapor barriers are installed, there is a consistent $1/2$-inch gap between the prepared rough opening and the aluminum or wood window, but when they come back in the morning, the wood may have moved or warped. We must construct buildings so that they have room to move without causing leaks.

Design dimensions are important to maintain within acceptable deviations. Overall out-to-out dimensions are usually adhered to closely, but the angle of wall intersections is harder to check. In tilt and precast concrete construction, there are many opportunities for layout errors to be made that may result in future difficulties. Every panel point and window or door opening gets formed and poured long before it is used and sometimes before the floors are built. Prior to concrete placement, the forms should be checked and rechecked for conformance with intended dimensions and for "square." The length of one diagonal should equal the other diagonal measurement (see Fig. 6-5). If not, the angles or side lengths are off, which could result in panels going up out of plumb or level. Resulting voids between panels could vary in width, making it difficult to seal them properly, and this can be noticeably offensive (see Fig. 6-6). Once dimensions are not followed or things get out of plumb or level, it can become difficult to make subsequent materials fit and seal properly.

More problematic than a void that may be too big is one that gets too small. When window openings are completed, membranes and sill pans are installed,

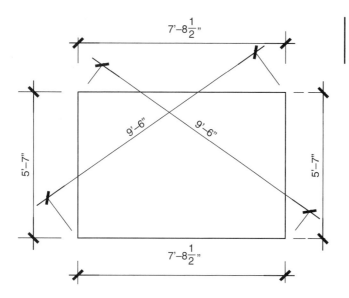

Figure 6-5
Check for square using diagonal measures.

Figure 6-6
Out-of-square drip edge.

and the windows don't fit, this is another challenge. The cause is not as important as the cure. Maybe the wrong style windows arrived, or maybe the dimensions weren't checked closely in shop drawing review. Perhaps the rough openings did not account for the thickness of the sill pans and two layers of self-adhesive membrane (SAM) and folded air infiltration barrier (AIB). This is what we have tried to prevent and where things can go bad. This is where the right corrective decision is critical. It gets back to time and money. The project may have been waiting for these windows for months and needs them installed to get the next draw from the bank. Maybe the brick or stone is already on the building. What happens next? Cram them in place and caulk over the gaps real fast so that nobody sees it? Cut off the fins so that the windows aren't so wide? Cut back the jamb returns a half inch on each side? After all, who will notice?

Any of these three proposed solutions can result in potential leaks at the windows. Forcing the window into an undersized opening can lead to bending of the jambs or sills. This can result in bound operation or warps, and it would not leave room for expansion and contraction. Do not ever caulk over a movement joint—that job is for sealants, and without proper joint geometry and bond breaker, sealant joint performance will be compromised. A project that is designed and specified for fin-type windows should not have non-fin windows installed without redesigning the opening protectives. This can lead to massive water intrusion and lawsuits the builder probably will lose. If the jambs are cut back, there is a good chance that the membrane may be exposed or cut. There are two obvious options that come to mind; however, avoiding this situation is the best solution. Having the windows premeasured and built to fit the openings before they are delivered would have prevented this from happening. Of the two options available, modifying the windows is probably the least problematic solution if the waterproofing is complete and the finishes are on. Have the installer measure the openings and take the windows apart, recut them, and reglaze them prior to returning them to the job site. This may prove prohibitive in terms of both cost and schedule. The other option is to back up and remove the finishes, peel back the membranes, and correct the openings.

We recommend that similar types of actions be taken when the envelope gets penetrated by louvers, conduit, or pipe after the finish is installed. We offer the example of the 4-inch pipe the plumber has to install after the exterior wall has been complete and painted (see Fig. 6-7). In this illustration, we had the stucco carefully removed for an area about 12 inches past the pipe penetration in all dissections. Wire lath was cut, screws were removed, and the lath was peeled back. The hole then was cut through the exterior sheathing, oversized by about $1/2$ inch (see Fig. 6-8).

A new square of SAM was installed, primed to the sheathing, and behind the original SAM by a few inches. The new SAM was primed and sealed to the old SAM. A new piece of envelope AIB was cut and installed on top of the SAM. We then had the AIB (in this case Tyvek Commercial wrap) sealed to the pipe with Tyvek tape after cleaning the pipe and taped to the surrounding AIB (see Fig. 6.9). This

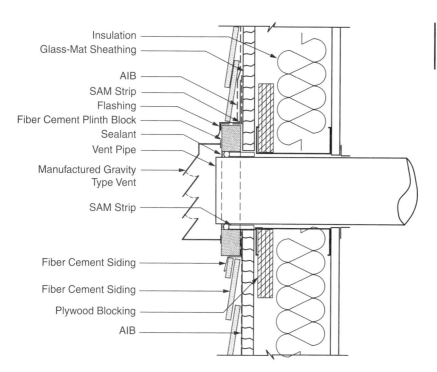

Insulation
Glass-Mat Sheathing
AIB
SAM Strip
Flashing
Fiber Cement Plinth Block
Sealant
Vent Pipe
Manufactured Gravity Type Vent
SAM Strip
Fiber Cement Siding
Fiber Cement Siding
Plywood Blocking
AIB

Figure 6-7
Detail for vent pipe penetration of wall.

Figure 6-8
Photo of vent pipe installation, part 1.

Figure 6-9

Photo of vent pipe
installation, part 2.

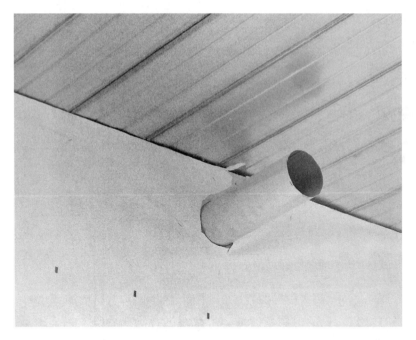

was stucco exterior finish, with cement board trim, so we installed an 8 inch square of cement board to trim the penetration. We then had j-bead installed around the edges, leaving a small void for sealant (see Fig. 6.10). The lath around the hole was repositioned and wired to strengthen the cut mesh, and new three-coat stucco was applied. This is the least common path of correction but would

Figure 6-10

Photo of vent pipe
installation, part 3.

result in the responsible parties learning from their mistake. Sealing patched air and vapor barriers is not difficult.

6.11   ASKING QUESTIONS

With so many advances being made in chemistry and material sciences, new products are being introduced to building industry each year. No one person or firm could possibly know everything about any of them. With information so readily available on the Internet, it has become the first source of information for many designers and builders alike. There are articles on products, means, and methods for most products, but you have to be a little careful. Much of what you may read can contain biased information, such as from a manufacturer's sales representative. Sales representatives tend to recommend their own products and list problems with their competitor's. Manufacturers' data sheets, catalogs of products, and manufacturers' recommendations for use generally are the most reliable sources of technical data. Check the permeability ratings for yourself. Look at Material Safety and Data Sheets (MSDSs) to see recommendations for worker's safety, off-gassing information, and possible solvents used. See how long the materials can be exposed to ultraviolet (UV) radiation before voiding the warranty. Find out how long the materials take to cure and how soon after application they can be covered up. Call the factory technical department and talk to them about your location and planned use. Ask the tech people for tips and tricks.

Another excellent source of good information is the installing subcontractor. This source should be familiar with materials used in the region and may have first-hand knowledge about success stories or failures associated with the system. Of course, installers can be the most biased, and their information should not be the only data used in making decisions. An installer might tell you that you don't need to use fasteners in window fins because the caulk will hold them in or that you don't need to use an AIB because the sheathing is good enough. Local building code officials also can be a good source of information on the performance of systems, as well as on the right way to install them. Other sources can include associations involved in similar work, such as trade unions, or local chapters of Association of Building Contractors (ABC).

One of the best quality-control measures we have used is walking the job site as work is progressing and looking around. See if you can figure out things for yourself. If you see something you don't understand, ask someone on the crew (preferably the foreman or superintendent). If you see that someone is installing out of sequence, ask yourself, is it going to work right? Perhaps the worker is doing the right thing, but it is inconsistent with the design documents. What do you do then?

Ask the architect! The one group that should know the most about the way a designed system of parts should go together is the design firm. RFIs are the right

Figure 6-11

A clearly marked RFI with circles and arrows.

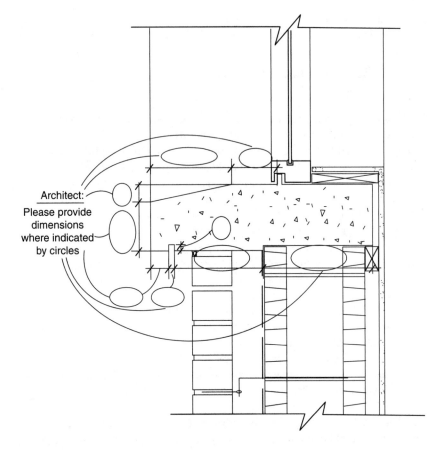

Architect:

Please provide dimensions where indicated by circles

way to document the question. An RFI should be generated to ask the designer for additional guidance or feedback. The best RFIs are complete, well written, and list reference drawings. Many RFIs should contain a copy of the section of the reference drawings that is in question, with circles or arrows clarifying the desired information. It can be as simple as asking for more dimensions to lay out a wall. If this is the case, draw a line with arrows or tick marks, and put a circle where you want the dimensions (see Fig. 6-11). RFIs that are poorly worded, confusing, and/or not accompanied by a sketch often take longer to answer and may in fact produce an answer to a different question than was intended. RFI answers should be posted to the contract drawings in both the design and construction offices. Any RFI that affects life safety or structural integrity typically will get signed and sealed and provided to the permitting agency.

6.12 MANAGING CHANGE

Managing the changes that may occur in more than 3 years of design and construction can be a task in itself. Controlling the process is important as far as keeping the project on schedule and under budget and maintaining the integrity of the building envelope are concerned. Over this 3-year period, thousands of decisions must be made by a variety of team members with different backgrounds and interests. From the earliest concept drawings and schematic estimates, each successive stage requires further development of the concept and further refinement of the design. After bidding and award, changes are made during buyout of subcontractor contracts, in development of submittals or shop drawings, and every day on the job site. Two-way communication is the best defense against changes that can come back to cause trouble. It is important to document change by written notes, issuing memos and minutes from meetings, copying sketches, and correspondence, to all team members affected and by changing the plans and specifications.

Keeping track of changes made in the plans can be accomplished in many ways. Different firms have chosen a variety of means for documenting changes. The set of plans that are approved for construction by permit review authorities typically get a stamp of approval by that agency. Those plans should be updated as any substantive change occurs. One way is by marking on them the date and reference RFI that changed them. Another is to copy and paste the RFI answer on the plans, perhaps on the back of the preceding page so that you can see it when the plans are open.

It is the responsibility of the three project management team leaders to make certain the changes do not result in unexpected or unacceptable envelope performance. The owner, builder, and designer all have a stake in the final performance of the completed project. The liability for future problems can reside in any or all of the firms involved. Most important to watch out for are potential reductions in performance of roof, wall, floor, foundation, windows, membranes, flashings, insulation, sealants, and HVAC systems. If the team successfully manages change affecting these critical components throughout design and construction, then the envelope should have the best chance for great performance over time.

We have touched on the ASI and RFI processes, directives, RFPs, and many tracking mechanisms for change. This is an appropriate place to elaborate on *change orders* (COs). Some large projects may have 2,000 or 3,000 thousand RFIs. Some of these have a potential impact on time and money. Contractors and especially subcontractors need to be paid extra for approved items without waiting until the end of the job. *Change order requests* (CORs) or *requests for change orders* (RCOs) can be used by the GC and CM teams to provide item-by-item tracking of several separate items. These can act as shopping lists for the owner to pick and choose from. Those that get approved can be combined into one monthly change order. Once change orders get approval signatures from the three parties (i.e., owner, architect, and builder), the approved values can be added to the contract sum. Contractors submitting monthly *payment requests* (referred to as *pay reqs*) then can include the approved scope items in their invoices. By keeping up with project costs in this manner, managers can avoid surprises when the project approaches closeout. Managing total project costs by adjusting contract sums on a monthly basis can prevent having to cut scope during the end of a project when there isn't much work remaining.

6.13 QUALITY CONTROL AND ASSURANCE

The theory of design and building are one thing. Once people get involved in the real world, nothing is quite as clear and simple as it was in the office. All the good intentions and great program and design ideas now need to be built. The dynamics of the workplace make it much more difficult to build buildings in the real world than in a laboratory environment. Starting with the first construction-related activities, each person who performs work can affect the next person's success. The layout crew needs to convey locations and elevations of building corners to the site-work people. Excavation, fill, and compaction all can have an impact on future structural systems performance. Application of subgrade membranes is the first critical component installation that must be observed closely. Depending on foundation design and the selected membrane, installation can be as easy as stretching out a sheet of plastic. On the other hand, membrane installation can be quite challenging. Maintaining a complete and uninterrupted protective membrane can mean sealing hard-to-reach penetrations as well as coordination with forms and shoring. Take and study photographs of the process, and forward them to the manufacturer's representative or waterproofing consultant if you have any concerns regarding work that is proceeding.

Protection of the membrane, once placed, can be even more challenging. If allowed, we recommend using concrete bricks to space structural steel above sheet membranes in lieu of metal chairs. Chairs create concentrated loads into sharp metal corners. You might not see any damage on inspecting the reinforcing steel. If you do, it can be patched up. Most damage is done by workers walking on the steel during concrete placement. Only once have we seen a crew stop placing concrete in an area where the membrane was punctured long enough to fix the tear.

It is always a good idea to check a slab-edge form for level and square before placing the concrete. Check for square the day before, and check for level right before the concrete goes in. Edge forms can change elevation from people or machines imparting loads on them. If there are underfloor membranes that need to lap vertical-face membranes, make sure that the laps are in the right direction. You would not want water coming down a wall membrane to get behind a slab membrane. If you are using a bentonite-type product, we have been told that the lap direction doesn't matter. Just in case, lap bentonite products to avoid backwater laps. Make certain that adequate fastener spacing is used to hold the bentonite mat strips in place until backfill is complete. Watch the backfill process to make certain the mats are not damaged by equipment operation. Compaction of fill should be done in lifts to ensure that the fill is tightly pressing the bentonite side to the concrete. Make sure that sealed laps in rubber or plastic sheet membranes are clean and sealed properly. Avoid backwater laps in sheet membranes in case the seal is not 100 percent watertight. Laps below the water table typically go in the opposite direction than above the water table because water will be rising up toward grade.

If strip footings are used with CMU stem walls and floating slabs, this should not be below seasonal water table elevations. Floating slab edge conditions typically get expansion joint material treatment that is not acceptable for use with hydrostatic pressure. Watch as materials get delivered to the project site to make sure that the materials are in good condition when they arrive, are not damaged during unloading procedures, and are protected from the elements during and after receipt. Require concrete and brick products to be delivered on pallets, with plastic protective wrap. Do not allow unprotected block cubes to be placed on the ground, where some CMU get in contact with contaminants that can fuel future mold growth. This goes for interior building materials, as well as exterior wall components. Air-conditioning equipment and ductwork are very important, along with paper-backed or wood-based sheathings.

Look closely at the details for subtle things at the intersections of exterior walls with ground floor and grade. If slab-edge recesses are shown, the starting and stopping points for the pockets need to be coordinated with doors. If there is a detail calling for flashings or a water stop, make certain that they are carried out. Review the drawings for coordination between finish floor and finish grade elevations. Make sure that exterior wall sections provide a means for stopping water intrusion between floor and wall (see Fig. 6-12). Look at where water will go if and when it encounters the vapor barrier.

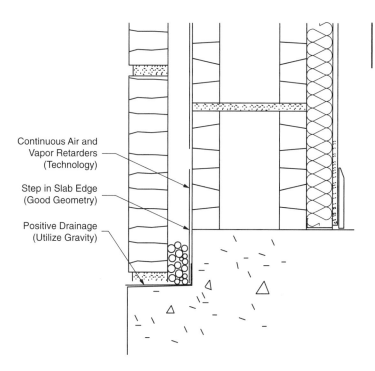

Continuous Air and
Vapor Retarders
(Technology)

Step in Slab Edge
(Good Geometry)

Positive Drainage
(Utilize Gravity)

Figure 6-12
Wall designed to stop water penetration.

Depending on the structural and skin systems selected, work may proceed in many different sequences. Assuming that we are building a load-bearing exterior wall system, we can watch alignment of exterior wall materials with the edge of the slab to avoid cantilevered framing, which can provide easy pathways for water (see Fig. 6-13). Before air or vapor barriers are installed, look to see that all electrical, mechanical, and plumbing penetrations have been either installed or planned in order to avoid future penetrations of the completed barriers. If air barriers are used, make certain that laps are proper. Since the air barrier needs to be a complete, uninterrupted system, make certain that the air barrier is sealed to the edges, sides, bottom, and top. Plan for future airtight seals for any portions of the work that may not be complete, such as soffits and fascia. Look for things that don't make sense, such as wall membranes that might not have been shown where needed. It is often much easier to see something left out as the building goes up than it was from the computer workstation.

If a vapor barrier is used, make sure that the materials to which it will be applied is ready to receive it. For sheet membranes, make sure that primers are applied to nonporous materials and at laps. Make certain that window wraps are installed the right way, sill pans are placed in sequence, and everything fits.

Figure 6-13

Avoid poor alignment of finishes.

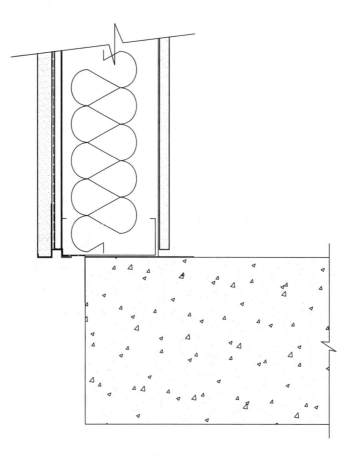

Make certain that gaps left for sealant are uniform and of the right size and shape. Make sure that fasteners are installed so as to limit undesirable movement when subjected to wind loads and other dynamic forces. If liquid membranes are to be applied to masonry units, make sure that the block was struck smooth and not tooled. Look for defects in the block or cracks in the mortar that may reveal structural problems and could cause problems in the future. If CMUs have been knocked loose or their mortar didn't bond to both sides of the joints, have that fixed before the membrane goes on. If a sheet membrane is used above grade, look to make sure that the installation is fully adhered to the substrate. Watch the workers as they roll the SAMs with the special tool. Make certain that membranes drip over flashings below, not behind them.

This kind of attention to detail does not come without effort. You must make time to walk the project site and look at plans and shop drawings. Do research about products you aren't familiar with. Avoid substitutions. If substitutions are made, take extra time to study the way that change could affect future trades. Do not accept fin-type windows if the details call for something else unless and until you have looked at what the change does to the performance of the systems. Require the design team to redraw the details affected, and issue revised details to the field for construction. Do not accept verbal acceptance and expect that to close the issue. Do not think that this kind of change can be covered in as-builts at the end of the job.

Wall flashings must be installed in the right sequence for water to cascade down harmlessly. If flashings are not installed properly, water can get in behind wall membranes. Think about wall flashings as a way to get water from behind one material to in front of the next. If a wall finishes subcontractor is ahead of the flashing subcontractor (often the roofer), then changes may have to be made in the original detail (see Fig. 6-1). In this example, the stucco crew wanted to go before the flat-seam metal roofing was installed. The detail was drawn initially with the stucco J-bead being installed after the roofing was on and flashed to the wall. The detail was redesigned to allow installation of a counterflashing the roofer could tie into later (see Fig. 6-2). This permitted the wall moisture reduction barrier (MRB) and stucco J-bead to be installed before the roofing installation, even though this is not what was intended. This kind of work-around allows trades to keep moving even if others are finished ahead of them, as was intended in the design documents. Even more important is the fact it did not result in a detail with poor performance.

Look for sill pan installations to make sure that the fit is right and that lapping of materials and placement of shims, backer rod, sealant, and fasteners are as intended. In Fig. 6-14, the sill pans had been delivered a little late. The subcontractors had cut up the wall membrane and cut important components off the sill pan to try and make it fit the opening.

Figure 6-14

Workers field modified sill pan to the point of ruin.

Check the fasteners to see that they are the same material, size, and configuration. If 300 series stainless steel fasteners are specified, put a magnet up against them as a field test. The magnet should not be attracted to the fastener because 302, 304 and 316 stainless have such low iron content. Check to see that fasteners are spaced as required, that they are fastened into the desired material, and that they are not causing deflection in the fastened material, etc.

Look for things above the roof that do not look right. It might be a good idea to look for things you reported earlier that were reported to have been fixed. You may find something interesting, such as a plumbing vent stack that is too low to the roof (see Fig. 6-15). On a flat roof, a new boot can be applied and sealed easily around the perimeter. Our favorite detail calls for stripped-in membrane to be hot mopped up the face of the stack boot with a termination clamping ring. A one-piece flashing ring welded to the boot flashing is a long-lasting solution (see Fig. 6-16). Other things to look for are voids in the membrane or areas that might have been filled with liquid asphalt roofing cement rather than covered with a membrane product. Figure 6-17 shows the void caused by shrinkage of a 3-inch-deep asphalt fillet that was so large that we could put a pocket knife in the crack. This kind of crack allows a lot of water in somewhere, and it would be difficult to find from below.

Look for copings that should have had saddle flashings (see Fig. 6-18). You may remember the saddle flashing discussion and detail from chapter 4. The saddle was to have been installed behind the wall membrane, and behind the

Figure 6-15
Plumbing vent stack, photo.

Figure 6-16
Plumbing vent stack detail.

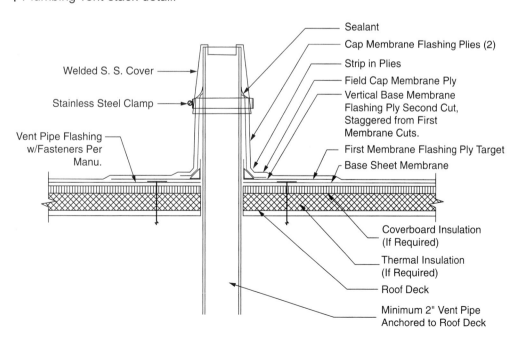

Sealant

Cap Membrane Flashing Plies (2)

Strip in Plies

Field Cap Membrane Ply

Vertical Base Membrane
Flashing Ply Second Cut,
Staggered from First
Membrane Cuts.

First Membrane Flashing Ply Target

Base Sheet Membrane

Welded S. S. Cover

Stainless Steel Clamp

Vent Pipe Flashing
w/Fasteners Per
Manu.

Coverboard Insulation
(If Required)

Thermal Insulation
(If Required)

Roof Deck

Minimum 2" Vent Pipe
Anchored to Roof Deck

Figure 6-17
Void in asphalt.

Figure 6-18
Coping photo with no
saddle.

metal siding (not surface applied and sealant applied). On a recent roof walk at substantial completion, we discovered an air intake louver whose sill was within 4 inches of the roof surface (see Fig. 6-19). We had mentioned this, months earlier and had been assured that every effort would be made to remedy it. Even more troubling are big, obvious concerns, such as a chunk of tilt wall that had broken off the panel when being erected (see Fig. 6-20). The contractor had 5 months to patch that panel before paint and roof-edge metal went on. This is unacceptable and is evidence (in our minds) that the superintendent didn't walk around enough. We would rather believe that than think that he knew it was still there and his subcontractors hadn't fixed it, and he let it go.

Taking frequent walks around the job site also has an overall quality-assurance effect that is immeasurable. When workers see you walking around looking at their progress, and you express a genuine interest and concern in what they're doing, it can have a profound impact on their attitude. When you walk around trying to help coordinate things, perhaps asking questions, trying to learn, and not pointing fingers, most workers will take a little more care in what they do. This attitude can spread through all levels of workers on the job and have a unifying effect. This kind of team attitude can lead to better two-way communication. If one worker comes up to you with a question that might not have been asked, it could result in the avoidance of a future problem.

Figure 6-19
Louver installed too close to roof.

Figure 6-20

Corner of wall missing.

6.14 PUNCH LISTS

At some point, typically near substantial completion, a punch list is generated that is intended to contain each and every item that is not compliant with the contract documents. Some punch lists go beyond this to include personal preferences and "wish list" items. If the team is proactive, the punch list is short because issues that have come up all have been addressed by this time. We have seen 125-page spreadsheets generated from punch-list walks. This usually indicates that the contractor is not complete and may be using the punch list for something other than it is intended. A punch-list walk should be scheduled after the contractor has done his or her own list and the subcontractors have completed the vast majority of listed items. An exception might be a task that requires several steps, such as three-coat stucco and paint to repair something damaged by equipment.

A punch-list walk should begin at one level, such as the roof, and work its way down to the ground. Life safety, structural, and building envelope observations are the most important to identify. You should look at roof membrane installations after it has been flooded or after a rain shower. Many of us like to look less than 24 hours after a rain event. Any water that is still standing on the roof long after the rain stops can be problematic and must be reported and remedied. Look for properly sealed laps in membranes (see Fig. 6-21), roof drain installations, and any obvious voids. Measure the heights of louvers, vents, flashings, and other accessories above the level of the roof membrane. Of course, these should have been reported earlier and fixed by now, but you never know. Access hatches and skylights, inside and outside corners, and overflow scuppers should be inspected for tears, fishmouths, or other visible defects. There should not be any standing water or puddles anywhere on the roof—certainly none deeper than a quarter of an inch. If you can put a coin (preferably a penny, dime, or quarter) on any surface ponding, it should not cover the quarter. Look at flashings and copings. Look for ways that water can get behind or under roof products. It is always a good idea to review the plans and submittals before starting the punch-list walk and to take the plans with you.

After the roof is complete, perform a comprehensive evaluation of wall, window, and door areas. Look for workmanship, adhesion, flashings, and proper laps, fasteners, etc. Some things will be obvious, while others may not be readily seen. Look for closeness of fit and finish between all component parts that make up the building envelope. Even in a cavity wall system, look for voids that can be easy pathways for wind driven rain (see Fig. 6-22). Again, most of the potential water-intrusion problems should have been seen during the

Figure 6-21
Standing water on roof.

Figure 6-22
Voids in envelope.

installation of materials and fixed by now. Most will not be visible at the time of the punch-list walk. You can see sealants and flashings, weeps, vents, control and expansion joints, and other exposed pieces of the puzzle. Review water test results, and if possible observe the test in progress.

6.15 TEST AND BALANCE

Mechanical systems should have been running for some months by now. Hopefully, precautionary measures were taken to prevent dirt and contaminants from coming into ducting, cooling coils, and grilles during construction. A thorough *test and balance* (T&B) report will list every fan, pump, valve, and grille in the completed systems. They should have compared actual with design values and made adjustments as required to meet design criteria. This may require replacing sheaves on fans to get sufficient volumes and pressures of moving air. Similarly, pump outputs and water temperature (if applicable) should be very close to design values. If a T&B report does indicate that nearly every diffuser has exactly the value it was designed to have, ask to see a representative few retested, selected at random. If the numbers are too close, they might not have achieved real test values. If they can't get close to design values (within about 5 percent), the system needs to be remedied. The designers and installing subcontractors need to figure out the problem and fix it.

It can be difficult for a T&B firm to create loads with which to test system performance. Buildings that are tested in the spring or fall will not have the ambient air temperatures to challenge the capacity of chillers. Values such as chilled water supply temperature won't be as far removed from returning temperature as they would with a 95°F outside air temperature. Building control systems can be thoroughly tested, though. They should be run through every operational scenario anticipated, and operation of each heating and cooling element should be confirmed. You may choose to recommend a retest of the system after 3 or 6 months when loads are at peak values.

6.16   ONE-YEAR-WARRANTY WALK

It is usually a good idea to schedule the warranty walk with the owner, builder, and designer all present. This can be a good way to continue the relationship you worked so hard to build for 2 or 3 years. It can be a very cordial walk, with no problems to report. This can be a nice culmination to the effort put forward by all. Conversely, you may find components or systems that show signs of impending failure. Maybe the roof membrane is tearing at the inside corner by the stairs, or maybe the sealant is coming loose from the window jambs. This is a good opportunity to show the owner that you are on his or her side, looking out for his or her best interests. Maybe you can list a few deficiencies and have the subcontractors come back to fix them at no cost to the owner. This can be a great way to strengthen the relationship and will improve your chances for repeat business. Beyond this, this is the best way to prevent future problems that may come back to haunt your firm.

Look for evidence of water intrusion, condensation, or discoloration. See what the owner has changed since the building was completed. Ask about occupant comfort; see if there were any complaints about office temperatures that couldn't be improved by control set-point modifications. Ask about any maintenance or repair issues that have come up. By learning what worked well and what didn't, you can create your own lessons-learned memo to share with your design and construction staff. This kind of feedback loop can reduce future problems and build the kind of reputation we are all striving to have and to keep.

Index